THE CODING BOOK

hinkler

Published by Hinkler Books Pty Ltd
45–55 Fairchild Street
Heatherton Victoria 3202 Australia
www.hinkler.com

hinkler

© Hinkler Books Pty Ltd 2018

Authors: Virginia King, Lee Ryall and Invent the World
Cover design: Paul Scott
Internal design: Lisa Howard, Julie Hally, Emma Pike,
Aimee Zumis and Trudi Webb
Editorial: Louise Coulthard
Illustration: Dmitrii Vlasov

Images © Hinkler Books Pty Ltd or Shutterstock.com

ISBN: 978 1 4889 1050 0

Printed and bound in China

THE CODING BOOK

Virginia King, Lee Ryall
and Invent the World

Contents

Guide for Parents

For kids, learning to code is a fun and creative activity. But it's more than that—it's also becoming an essential part of their educational journey. With *The Coding Book* you can help your child to gain invaluable skills while also learning some new skills yourself.

Below we provide you with 6 easy steps to support your child as they learn to code.

The Coding Book guides kids through a series of fun, achievable, playable, and show-off-able coding projects! It's designed to be a practical guide that will build their enthusiasm for this important subject and give kids experience with the tools and concepts that professional coders use every day.

I'm not a coder! How can I help?

1. Mistakes are part of coding

It's important that kids are aware that no coder gets everything right the first time. Reinforce with your child that bugs, errors, and logical missteps are a part of the coding process and learning to solve those problems in a systematic manner is far more useful than being a "natural"!

2. Don't skip the tests!

This is where coders will discover problems in their work. Testing can be a frustrating part of coding, so the temptation to skip it is strong!

The tests provided in the sections tell the coders how to test each piece of code they've written and what should happen. In early chapters, we provide example errors and fixes. Then, as they progress, we encourage kids to discover fixes on their own using the bug-hunting tips we provide.

We've tried to make this part of coding fun, and successful tests are always great, but we encourage parents (especially in the initial stages) to work through the tests with your coder. Celebrate failed tests as an opportunity to learn. There is an enormous amount of satisfaction in hunting down a pesky bug and fixing complex problems. Celebrate the successes too: they are hard won and take patience, dedication, and creativity.

3. Ask questions

Articulating complex problems is something that takes encouragement and practice for all of us. Children are introduced to this in chapter 3 with Agent Glitchbane's bug-hunting questions. You can help by asking these questions too:

- What is happening that shouldn't?
- What do you want to happen?
- When did it start or stop happening?
- What has changed since it worked last time?

4. Read the code aloud

Encourage your coder to read their code aloud. To help with this, we've provided **pseudocode** for a lot of the scripts.

Pseudocode is the plain-English translation of the code blocks. Some people find it makes the process easier to understand, while some people prefer the code itself. In *The Coding Book*, the pseudocode is colored and indented similarly to the blocks of code, so it can also be handy for checking variables and block ordering as well. Any text that kids need to type into their code is presented in bold and underlined.

When you're stuck, have the coder read their code aloud, and then read the code in the book aloud. 80% of problems are solved this way!

5. Help with the bug hunt

Following a long list of sequential instructions is a skill that kids will need help with. Until they get used to it, a lot of small errors will come from missed or misinterpreted instructions. When this happens, go back through the instructions and check each one with them, starting from the end of the last test. Children quickly get into the rhythm of doing this themselves, but they benefit from example, as we all do!

6. Play the game

Even if computer games aren't your thing, play the games that the kids make. Beat your best score. Enlist grandparents, siblings, neighbors, and friends to play the game. One of the joys of coding is making something that's useable, functional, beneficial, and entertaining. Coding is not a dry set of exercises that children learn in class. It's creative, complex, and useful. And, of course, it's fun!

Meet the Characters

Meet Pax and the supercoders of VALID: an intergalactic agency tasked with protecting Earth and the galaxy from the evil organization known as CORUPT!

Pax
Pax (or Potential Agent X) has been identified by VALID as possessing promising coding skills, and so has been recruited to train with the best supercoders in the galaxy.

ETAMI
A super-computer android designed by VALID supercoders, ETAMI (or Extra-Terrestrial Android Monitoring Intelligence) oversees VALID, directs the team, and introduces Pax to the **basics of coding**.

Natterninja
Natterninja is an alien whose telepathic mind-sending skills make him a specialist in **broadcasts** and **events**. He may talk a bit much, but he's one of VALID's top field agents.

Glitchbane
Glitchbane can tell if someone is telling the truth or lying, which is easy when you can read minds, and super-helpful when you're VALID's lead **bug-hunting** investigator and **conditionals** expert.

Finity
VALID's superspy, parkour-loving Finity trained as an Olympic gymnast. She can loop a **loop** and **co-ordinate** a co-ordinate faster than the next person can do a cartwheel, if the next person isn't Agent Finity. . .

EchoZero & EchoOne
VALID's coding twins, EchoZero and EchoOne run the science lab. Fascinated by **cloning** and **duplication**, they can clone anything and everything, and EchoOne probably would, if EchoZero would let her!

The Introspecter
The son of a notorious cyber-thief, the Introspecter uses his coding powers for good. As VALID's foremost security expert, there's nothing he doesn't know about **variables**.

Doubleshot
People assume Doubleshot is all brawn and no brain, but his photographic memory makes him an expert strategist whose skills with **functions** and **block-making** have saved the day more than once!

A mysterious force is gathering in the galaxy. Coders, both human and alien, are being taken by the minions of a vast, shadowy organization known only as **CORUPT** and are being forced to use their logic skills for evil.

In response, Earth's governments have set up **VALID**: a team of humans and aliens with special skills tasked with fighting CORUPT agents and protecting Earth. VALID's leader, an android super-computer named **ETAMI**, has been scanning for people with the coding skills to help save Earth . . . and the galaxy. ETAMI has found you.

Before you can join VALID's elite team of supercoders, you must prove you have what it takes. Today is your first day as a potential recruit for VALID. You've never met a walking computer before and you aren't even sure what coding is. Maybe it's time to find out.

MISSION DOSSIER

>> LEARN MORE ABOUT COMPUTERS AND CODING

Find out more about ETAMI, VALID, and the high-stakes world of coding.

LEVEL: 1
INSTRUCTOR: ETAMI

ETAMI

MISSION OBJECTIVE 1: WHO IS ETAMI?

Greetings, Potential Agent X. I am the Extra-Terrestrial Android Monitoring Intelligence. I am told my name is hard for humans to say, so you may call me ETAMI.

My name is . . .

PRIVACY BREACH

Never reveal your real identity to anyone!

OK

MISSION OBJECTIVE 2: CODER NAMES

But aren't you the good guys? Keeping the world safe?

Correct. You can help us, but only if you keep your real-world identity safe. VALID agents have coder names to use on missions. While you are in training, you will be known as Potential Agent X. Do you understand?

That's kind of long...

MISSION OBJECTIVE 3: WHAT IS A COMPUTER?

True. But it is VERY logical. You would appreciate it more if your brain was made of plastic and metal circuits.

Is that what your brain is made up of?

I do not have a brain. I have a central processing unit: a finely honed computing system designed and coded by a team of the most advanced supercoders in the galaxy—the VALID team.

Is that why computers are so smart? Because they have CPUs instead of brains?

Computers are not smarter than humans or aliens. We are very good at some things and we are MUCH less squishy, but computers are just machines that follow a set of instructions. Your brain can do all sorts of things without instructions, but my CPU cannot.

MISSION OBJECTIVE 4: WHAT IS CODING?

Coders write your instructions?

Correct. Every time I land a helicopter or eat a book, it is because a VALID supercoder wrote some instructions for me.

That doesn't sound hard. Wait, eat a book?

Must be a bug in my code. I meant read. Even supercoders make mistakes.

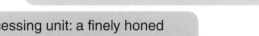

To get a computer to do anything, you must write VERY detailed instructions. For example, this door leads to the VALID coder-training dojo. Do you want to see my list of instructions for how to open it?

Sure.

> SCAN FOR DOOR HANDLE
> EXTEND RIGHT ARM APPENDAGE
> EXTEND FINGER APPENDAGE
> PRESS CODE BUTTON A
> MOVE FINGER APPENDAGE
> PRESS CODE BUTTON D
> MOVE FINGER APPENDAGE
> PRESS CODE BUTTON M
> MOVE FINGER APPENDAGE

> PRESS CODE BUTTON I
> MOVE FINGER APPENDAGE
> PRESS CODE BUTTON N
> SCAN FOR POTENTIAL THREATS
> IF THREAT DETECTED, INITIATE SELF-DESTRUCT SEQUENCE, ELSE RETRACT FINGER APPENDAGE
> RAISE ARM APPENDAGE
> PUSH DOOR . . .

Stop! You'll hurt the trees, printing that list of instructions. That's amazebeans.

Correct. Humans code computers to do all sorts of things. But it is important to remember that a computer is only as smart as its code. The VALID supercoders are the best. They created and programmed me to keep Earth safe.

Will I be able to write computer code? It looks hard to even open a door!

Every squish-brain can code, but it takes a special human to become a VALID agent.

Can machines code?

Yes, but only if we have instructions for it.

So, how can I help?

Some of our top coders have mysteriously disappeared. There have been raids on our databases, thefts, and odd smells appearing all over the world. The agents and I are worried, Potential Agent X. We need every coder we can get.

I want to help!

Are you ready for me to engage my door-opening subroutine and begin your training?

NEW MESSAGE ✕

Go with ETAMI and help save the galaxy from the mysterious and deadly threat?

Y/N

OK

MISSION DOSSIER

>> OCTODODGE TRAINING SIMULATION

Becoming a VALID agent takes training. As you move through your training, each VALID supercoder will teach you about their specialized skill.

ETAMI will show you how to make your first project. If you think you're up to it, let's begin. Your first mission is to code a training simulation to help you learn how to dodge CORUPT's agents.

LEVEL: 1

INSTRUCTOR: ETAMI

BACKGROUND: ETAMI is the supercomputer robot created by the supercoder agents of VALID to oversee the organization and fight evil. ETAMI is not a coder, but knows enough to show you the ropes: just make sure you stay on ETAMI's logical side!

MISSION OBJECTIVE 1: HOW DO I START?

1

Wowbeans!

A program called Snap! is our secret weapon for training VALID agents. You use the blocks in the code menu to write instructions for the computer in the script space. Clicking on different categories shows you different kinds of code blocks. The results of your coding show up in the white stage area.

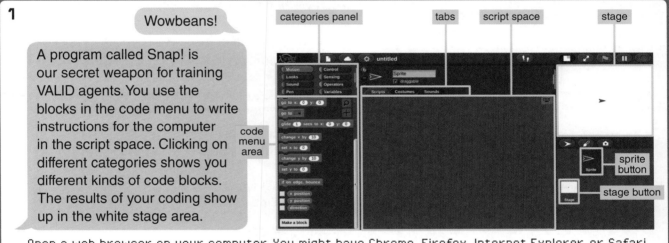

categories panel · tabs · script space · stage

code menu area

sprite button

stage button

Open a web browser on your computer. You might have Chrome, Firefox, Internet Explorer, or Safari installed. Type **snap.berkeley.edu/run** into your browser bar and hit enter.

2 Before you start, you must set up your VALID employee file on Snap!.

Click on 🌥 and the sign-up screen will appear. Create a username for yourself. Remember, VALID agents don't use their real names online.

3 Enter your username, birthdate, and email address. Get a grown-up to look at the Terms of Service. Click OK. You will get an email with your username and password!

THINGS YOU NEED TO SET UP YOUR PROFILE:

😃 An awesome username

😏 An email address

😐 A grown-up of some kind (preferably human)

4 Click on 🌥 and enter your super-secret login. You can choose the check box ☐ **stay signed in on this computer until logging out**

if you want to, or log in each time you start coding in Snap!.

HINT

This book instructs you to save your work in the cloud. If you don't want to make an account, you can export your project and save it on your computer instead of in the cloud. Just choose **Export project** each time you save and **Import** when you start Snap!.

OK

MISSION OBJECTIVE 2: GET YOUR SPRITE MOVING

1

To make this training simulation, we are going to use **sprites**. The term "sprite" describes the parts of your program that need to move, walk, talk, or explode. In your training simulation, this sprite will be a VALID agent. Your first mission is to name your sprite.

Click on the Sprite button.

Click in the sprite **name field** at the top of the screen and change it to "Agent X".

Agent X

2

Each colored code block on the left is a single instruction for a computer like me. As your agent training progresses, VALID's supercoders will show you what each code block does.

The code blocks snap together in the script space to form a set of instructions for the sprite. This is called a **script**. Your first script will get the Agent X sprite moving. For this training sim, I will show you what you need, and you will find the blocks and copy how I put them together.

go to x: 0 y: 0
go to ▾
glide 1 secs to x: 0 y: 0
change x by 10
set x to 0
change y by 10
set y to 0
if on edge, bounce
☐ x position
☐ y position
☐ direction

3

You can find different-colored blocks by clicking on the categories in the top left. Blocks to do with costumes are in the Looks category. Moving blocks are in the Motion category. It is VERY logical.

Motion | Control
Looks | Sensing
Sound | Operators
Pen | Variables

4

Find these six blocks to start. Two are the same.

Find these six blocks and drag them into the script space.

Click Control in the top left of your screen to find the three gold blocks.

Click Motion to find the three dark blue blocks.

when ▢ clicked
when ▢ clicked
forever
move 10 steps
go to x: 0 y: 0
point towards ▾

5

Why are some gold blocks curved on top?

You have a good eye for detail! The curved gold blocks tell a computer when a script begins, like a capital letter at the start of a sentence. Every script must start with a curved gold block or it will not work.

when ▢ clicked | when I am clicked ▾
when space ▾ key pressed
when ⬡ | when I receive ▾

6 Some code blocks contain extra parts that you need to change.

Click on the drop-down arrow in

`point towards ▼` .

Choose **mouse-pointer**.

`point towards  mouse-pointer`
`mouse-pointer`

The block should look like:

`point towards  mouse-pointer ▼`

7 The blocks snap together like puzzle pieces. A single block of code is very powerful, Potential Agent X. It can be the difference between HUGE SUCCESS and critical system error.

Drag the blocks together to form two scripts. Make sure they are in the same order as ETAMI's code.

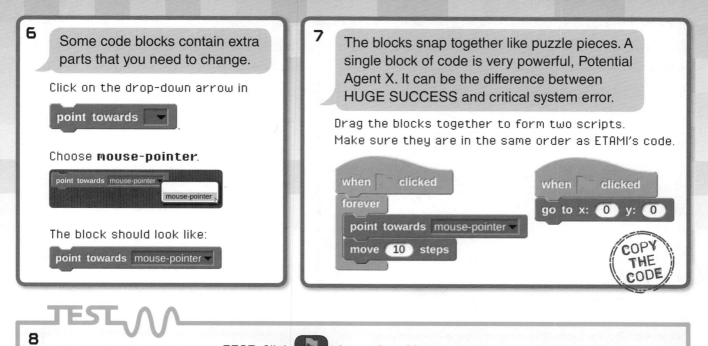

COPY THE CODE

TEST

8

How do I know if it worked?

Good question Potential Agent X! You must test your code before you move on. Humans, aliens, and computers make mistakes but a supercoder knows how to find errors and fix them. To test for errors, run your code and see if it works.

TEST: Click 🏁 above the white stage area to run your shiny new script and move your mouse-pointer around in the stage.
SUCCESS: The arrow follows your mouse pointer! WOO!
ERROR: The arrow stays in the middle looking confused.
FIX: Are your blocks in the right order?

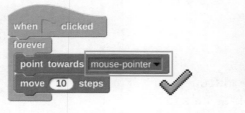

ERROR: It runs off the screen!
FIX: Make sure you've changed where it points towards.

STOP THE SCRIPT! After each test, click ⬭ above the white stage area to stop all the scripts running. Otherwise, things will get weiiird . . .

MISSION OBJECTIVE 3: KEEP YOUR WORK SAFE FROM EVIL

1

CAUTION! My sensors have detected enemy agents in cyberspace!

What? Are we OK?

Processing... It is a minor intrusion, but we must secure our data.

How?

We must save, Potential Agent X. Save FAST.

Coolbeans. How do we do that?

2

A VALID agent must always use **Save as**. Never just **Save**.

Click 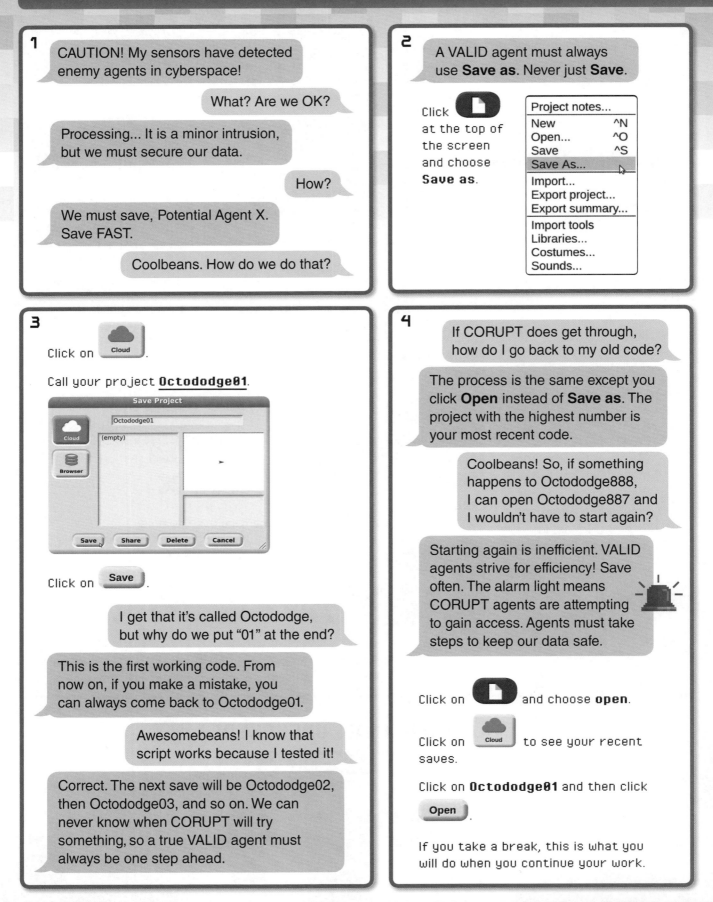 at the top of the screen and choose **Save as**.

Project notes...
New   ^N
Open...   ^O
Save   ^S
Save As...
Import...
Export project...
Export summary...
Import tools
Libraries...
Costumes...
Sounds...

3

Click on **Cloud**.

Call your project **Octododge01**.

Save Project

Octododge01

Cloud

(empty)

Browser

Save   Share   Delete   Cancel

Click on **Save**.

I get that it's called Octododge, but why do we put "01" at the end?

This is the first working code. From now on, if you make a mistake, you can always come back to Octododge01.

Awesomebeans! I know that script works because I tested it!

Correct. The next save will be Octododge02, then Octododge03, and so on. We can never know when CORUPT will try something, so a true VALID agent must always be one step ahead.

4

If CORUPT does get through, how do I go back to my old code?

The process is the same except you click **Open** instead of **Save as**. The project with the highest number is your most recent code.

Coolbeans! So, if something happens to Octododge888, I can open Octododge887 and I wouldn't have to start again?

Starting again is inefficient. VALID agents strive for efficiency! Save often. The alarm light means CORUPT agents are attempting to gain access. Agents must take steps to keep our data safe.

Click on and choose **open**.

Click on **Cloud** to see your recent saves.

Click on **Octododge01** and then click **Open**.

If you take a break, this is what you will do when you continue your work.

MISSION OBJECTIVE 4: CHANGING YOUR COSTUME

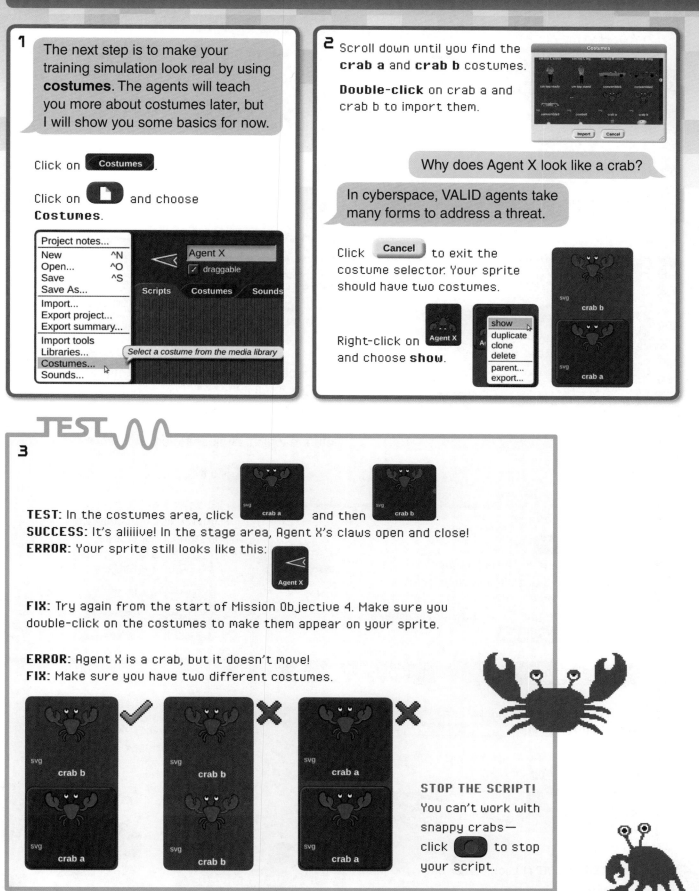

1

The next step is to make your training simulation look real by using **costumes**. The agents will teach you more about costumes later, but I will show you some basics for now.

Click on **Costumes**.

Click on [ ] and choose **Costumes**.

Project notes...
New   ^N
Open...   ^O
Save   ^S
Save As...
Import...
Export project...
Export summary...
Import tools
Libraries...
Costumes...
Sounds...

Select a costume from the media library

Agent X
✓ draggable

Scripts   Costumes   Sounds

2

Scroll down until you find the **crab a** and **crab b** costumes.

Double-click on crab a and crab b to import them.

Costumes

Import   Cancel

Why does Agent X look like a crab?

In cyberspace, VALID agents take many forms to address a threat.

Click **Cancel** to exit the costume selector. Your sprite should have two costumes.

Right-click on [Agent X] and choose **show**.

show
duplicate
clone
delete
parent...
export...

svg
crab b

svg
crab a

TEST

3

svg   crab a   svg   crab b

TEST: In the costumes area, click [crab a] and then [crab b].
SUCCESS: It's aliiiive! In the stage area, Agent X's claws open and close!
ERROR: Your sprite still looks like this:

[Agent X]

FIX: Try again from the start of Mission Objective 4. Make sure you double-click on the costumes to make them appear on your sprite.

ERROR: Agent X is a crab, but it doesn't move!
FIX: Make sure you have two different costumes.

svg crab b / svg crab a ✓

svg crab b / svg crab b ✗

svg crab a / svg crab a ✗

STOP THE SCRIPT!
You can't work with snappy crabs— click [ ] to stop your script.

4

The crab is so big. Can I make it smaller?

Yes. Find the correct block, Potential Agent X.

Do I change the size by clicking on the **Looks button** and using a purple block?

Excellent deduction.

Click on **Scripts**.

Click on **Looks**.

Find **set size to 100 %** and drag it into the **script space**.

5

This block is only useful if you change the number.

Like the **point towards block** earlier?

Exactly. Click on 100% and change it to 50%. That is a logical size for an agent.

Change the number to **50%**.

set size to 50 %

6

Where do I put it?

That is up to you, but you should know that any code inside a **forever block** will repeat over and over . . . forever!

So, if I put this inside the **forever block**, it will shrink over and over?

Correct. Let us avoid making a teeny tiny agent. This **set size block** must only happen once, at the very beginning of your script.

Hmm. This **go to block** only happens once because there are no **forever blocks**. I could put it there or I could put it by itself under a new green flag **starter block**.

Both are logical choices Potential Agent X.

I'll keep them all together for now.

Snap the new block into your existing script to match ETAMI's code.

when ⚑ clicked
set size to 50 %
go to x: 0 y: 0

COPY THE CODE

TEST

7

TEST: Click ⚑.
SUCCESS: Agent X is smaller now!
ERROR: Agent X is still ridiculously large. What is going on?!
FIX: Make sure you have the right numbers in the **set size block**.

set size to 50 % ✓   **set size to 100 %** ✗

FIX: Make sure your blocks are attached to a gold **starter block**.

when ⚑ clicked
set size to 50 %
go to x: 0 y: 0 ✓

set size to 50 %
go to x: 0 y: 0 ✗

STOP THE SCRIPT! Click ⬭ once you pass.

Intruder alert Potential Agent X! Remember your mission!

Save as **Octododge02**.

MISSION OBJECTIVE 5: AUTOMATE! AUTOMATE! AUTOMATE!

1

Can I write some code to make Agent X's costume change faster?

You are thinking like an agent. Coding is about making things easier.

Click on [Agent X]. Click **Scripts** to return to Agent X's script space.

2 Drag these four blocks into Agent X's **script space**.

That's three gold and one purple. Can do.

when [ ] clicked

wait 1 secs

next costume

forever

3 Match your code so it looks like ETAMI's.

when [ ] clicked
forever
  next costume
  wait 1 secs

COPY THE CODE

TEST

4

Agent X has stopped chasing the mouse-pointer.

You have three scripts. One moves Agent X towards the mouse-pointer and one places Agent X in the correct position at the start. The new script changes Agent X's costume.

But the old scripts worked before. I tested them!

Correct, but when you click on a script instead of the flag, you only run the code in that script. Just the costume script runs in this test.

Because I know the other scripts already work. Got it!

TEST: Right-click on [Agent X]. Choose **show**.

show
duplicate
clone
delete
parent...
export...

Click on your new script: it glows with mysterious coding power!

when [ ] clicked
forever
  next costume
  wait 1 secs

SUCCESS: The costume changes. . . slowly. . .
ERROR: Nothing changes. Ever.
FIX: Make sure your blocks are in the right order.

when [ ] clicked
forever
  next costume
  wait 1 secs
✓

when [ ] clicked
next costume
wait 1 secs
forever
✗

STOP THE SCRIPT!
Click [ ] .

EXPERIMENT

5

Agent X moves quickly but the claws move slowly. If I change it to `move 5 steps`, will he slow down? And if I change `wait 1 secs`, I can make the costumes change faster, so the claws seem to move faster.

Change the number in `wait 1 secs` so that the costumes change faster or slower. Lower numbers change them faster and higher numbers change them slower. ETAMI suggests a wait time of 0.2 for maximum efficiency. `wait 0.2 secs`

Check the **movement script** from Mission Objective 2.

Is it better if Agent X moves 5 steps instead of 10? `move 5 steps`

when [ ] clicked
forever
  point towards mouse-pointer
  move 10 steps

The data alarm is sounding!

ACHIEVEMENT UNLOCKED!
CODEMASTER

LEVEL 2

Save as **Octododge03**.

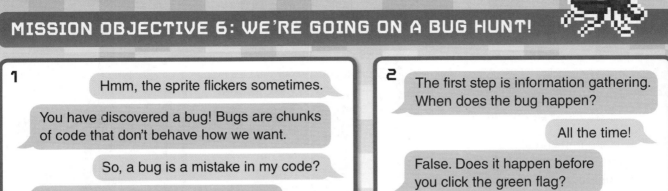

MISSION OBJECTIVE 6: WE'RE GOING ON A BUG HUNT!

1

Hmm, the sprite flickers sometimes.

You have discovered a bug! Bugs are chunks of code that don't behave how we want.

So, a bug is a mistake in my code?

Sometimes. Sometimes it's a mistake in your thinking. They are easy to fix if you know what causes them.

How do I know what's causing the bug?

You investigate! Agent Glitchbane is the expert, and will show you in more detail later. But I can show you how to find and fix this small bug.

Click [🚩] and let Agent X catch up with the mouse-pointer to see if you notice the bug.

STOP THE SCRIPT! Click [⬤].

2

The first step is information gathering. When does the bug happen?

All the time!

False. Does it happen before you click the green flag?

No, nothing happens before I click the green flag.

Does it happen when you click on only the costume script?

```
when   clicked
forever
    next costume
    wait  0.2  secs
```

Click on [___] to run the costume script by itself.

STOP THE SCRIPT! Click [⬤].

3

No.

What about when you click on the movement script?

```
when   clicked
forever
    point towards  mouse-pointer ▾
    move  5  steps
```

Click on [___] to run the movement script by itself. Make sure your mouse-pointer is on the white stage area.

4

Yes! It goes all flickery!

This means your bug is probably in this script. Does it happen whenever you run this script?

Move the mouse-pointer around to see when the bug starts and stops.

5

It only happens when Agent X touches the mouse-pointer!

Correct, Potential Agent X. Look at the script and figure out where it is going wrong.

Well, this **point towards block** tells Agent X to point towards the mouse-pointer, and the **move 5 steps block** moves it forwards. The **forever block** means that both those blocks happen over and over. It looks like a smooth movement, though, so it must happen very fast.

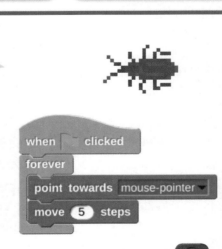

```
when   clicked
forever
    point towards  mouse-pointer ▾
    move  5  steps
```

STOP THE SCRIPT! Click [⬤].

6 True.

Agent X is flickering because when it touches the mouse-pointer, the code inside the **forever loop** is continually telling it to turn around and keep moving! It's like a dog chasing its tail. We need to tell it to stop when it gets close to the mouse-pointer.

Correct. When you code, you must always think about what **might** happen and you must give the computer instructions. This one is easy to fix. You require more blocks.

Find and drag these three blocks into the script space. Click **Operators** to find the green block.

Click **Sensing** to find the light blue block.

7 Match your code so it looks like ETAMI's.

distance ▾ to
                    mouse-pointer

if ⟨ distance ▾ to mouse-pointer ▾ ⟩ > 20

COPY THE CODE

8
when clicked
forever
point towards mouse-pointer ▾
move 5 steps

Add the new code into the old movement script.

if ⟨ distance ▾ to mouse-pointer ▾ ⟩ > 20

Click and drag the old blue code blocks inside the **if block**.

COPY THE CODE

9 Click and drag the **if block** inside the **forever loop**.

when clicked
forever

if ⟨ distance ▾ to mouse-pointer ▾ ⟩ > 20
point towards mouse-pointer ▾
move 5 steps

when clicked
forever
if ⟨ distance ▾ to mouse-pointer ▾ ⟩ > 20
point towards mouse-pointer ▾
move 5 steps

TEST

10

TEST: Click 🏳 and let Agent X catch up with the mouse-pointer.
SUCCESS: The sprite doesn't flicker!
ERROR: The sprite doesn't move anymore!
FIX: Make sure the **if block** is inside the **forever loop**.

ERROR: The sprite only moves when the mouse-pointer is close, and it flickers! OMG!
FIX: Check you used the correct green block and that (distance ▾ to mouse-pointer ▾) is on the correct side.

STOP THE SCRIPT! Click ⬤ .

when clicked
forever
if ⟨ distance ▾ to mouse-pointer ▾ ⟩ > 20
point towards mouse-pointer ▾
move 5 steps ✓

when clicked
if ⟨ distance ▾ to mouse-pointer ▾ ⟩ > 20
point towards mouse-pointer ▾
move 5 steps
forever ✗

⟨ distance ▾ to mouse-pointer ▾ ⟩ > 20 ✓

⟨ distance ▾ to mouse-pointer ▾ ⟩ < 20 ✗

20 > ⟨ distance ▾ to mouse-pointer ▾ ⟩ ✗

⭐ **ACHIEVEMENT UNLOCKED!** ⭐

BUG-HUNTER

LEVEL 1

Intruder alert! All agents are advised to be vigilant and save their work!

Save as **Octododge04**.

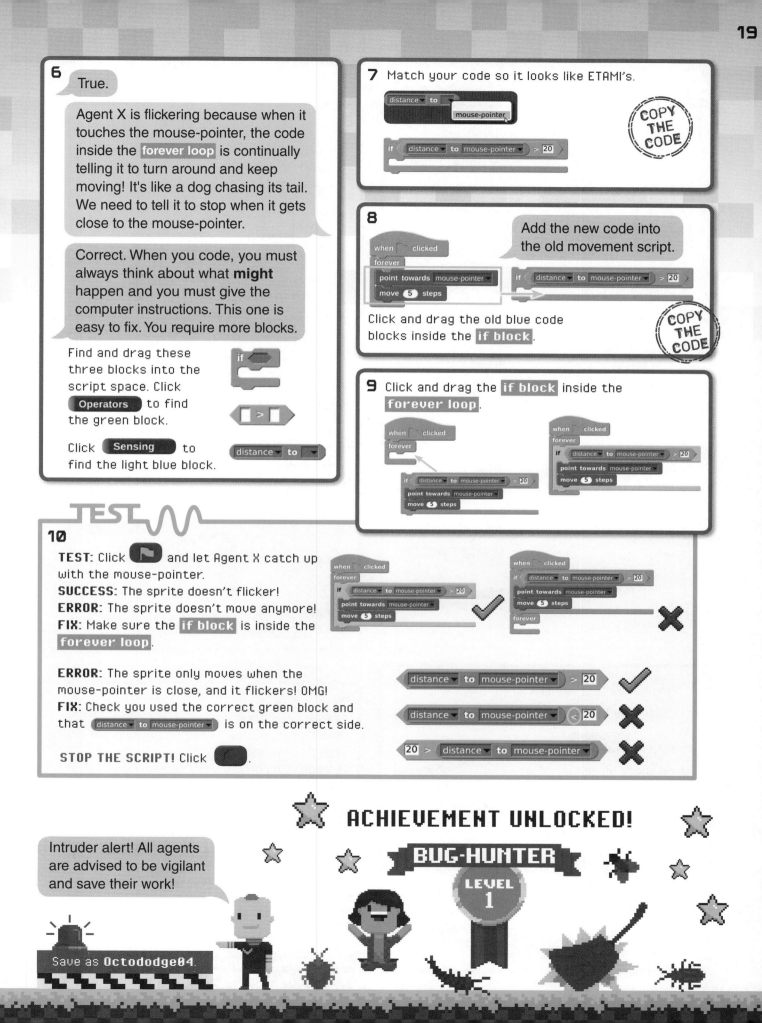

MISSION OBJECTIVE 7: BACKGROUND INFORMATION

1

Your training simulation must truly reflect a real-time field situation. We must enter the world of . . . **backgrounds**!

I thought that was going to be way worse.

Do not underestimate the humble background! An agent of VALID must be constantly aware of anything out of place in their environment.

2

The stage is plain white. This is not logical for a field agent. Distractions are everywhere, but an agent must learn to focus their mind like a laser.

Click Stage . Click Backgrounds .

Click the **paint button** to open the paint editor.

EXPERIMENT

3

Remember, the more distracting the background the better.

Experiment with the paint editor buttons and colors.

Create the most distracting environment you can by adding more and MORE distractions!

Change colors by clicking on the color bar. Use undo if you make a mistake.

Click OK to exit the paint screen.

HINT

If you can't see Backgrounds , make sure you've clicked Stage .

OK

4

Right-click on the background costume button.

Choose **rename**.

edit
rename
duplicate
delete
export

Rename your background **distractopia** and click OK .

distractopia

5

Do not forget to write instructions for the background.

Click on Scripts .

Find these blocks and drag them into the **script space**:

when clicked

switch to costume

Click the drop-down arrow and choose **distractopia**.

Do I drag them into the script space and join them up?

Correct.

Connect the `switch to costume block` underneath the `starter block`.

TEST

6

TEST: Click .
SUCCESS: Your background appears behind your sprite.
ERROR: Everything is still white! Why?!
FIX: Make sure you have the correct block and costume.

when clicked ✓
switch to costume distractopia

switch to costume ✗

STOP THE SCRIPT! Click .

You're the only one who can save us!

Save as **Octododge05**.

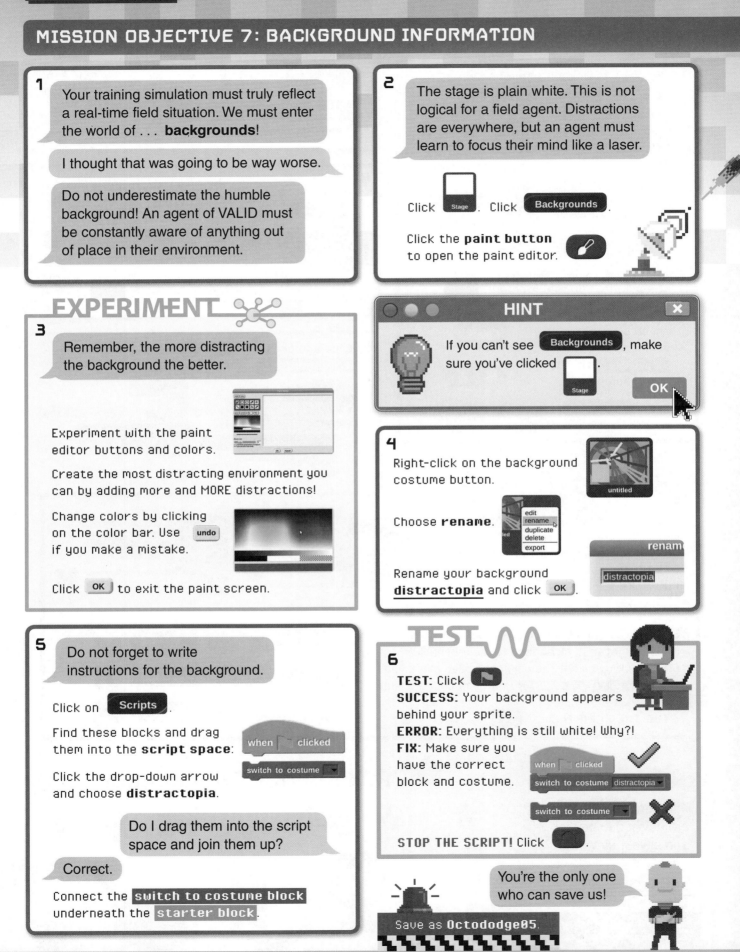

MISSION OBJECTIVE 8: AN ENEMY OF OUR OWN DEVISING

1

We never know what form the enemy might take in cyberspace, so we must train our agents to detect and avoid threats. Our goal is to create the first of the enemy sprites, but I can only take you so far. Later in your training, VALID's Echo Agents will teach you more about duplication.

Are we going to make a new sprite? And write code for it?

That is inefficient. Consider the things a VALID agent and an enemy agent have in common.

One is super evil!

True, Potential Agent X. But both move around, know about disguises, and have squishy brains. When two objects have things like this in common, we know their code will be mostly the same. Only one or two tiny things change.

Evil versus good is "tiny"?

In coding, good and evil are just variables. Later, the Introspecter will teach you more about variables.

So, we're going to copy the code from Agent X to use in our enemy sprite?

Correct. We will copy and then we will make changes.

To add the evil.

Correct. We must add the evil.

Right-click on **Agent X**.

Choose **duplicate**.

> show
> duplicate
> clone
> delete
> parent...
> export...

You should end up with two sprite buttons.

Agent X   Agent X(2)

2

When you duplicate a sprite, you also duplicate everything you created for that sprite.

So, Agent X(2) has the same code and the same costumes?

Correct. To make this new sprite into an effective enemy agent, you must change some things.

First off, the name, right? AgentX(2) is the second-most confusing name I've ever heard, after "Potential Agent X"...

Click on **Agent X(2)**.
Then click into the sprite **name field** at the top of the screen.

Zorg
✓ draggable

Change the name to **Zorg**.

The sprite buttons should look like this:

Agent X   Zorg

3

Easybeans! OK, I've got to change the costume too. It looks the same.

Click on [Zorg].

Go to [Costumes].

Right-click and delete the **crab a** and **crab b** costumes.

edit
rename
duplicate
delete
export

crab a
crab b
svg
svg

The Zorg sprite button should look like the default sprite.

Zorg

Click on [▶] at the top of your screen and choose **Costumes**.

Project notes...
New   ^N
Open...   ^O
Save   ^S
Save As...
Import...
Export project...
Export summary...
Import tools
Libraries...
Costumes...
Sounds...

4

But we don't know what the enemy looks like. How do I pick a costume?

Use the octopus, Potential Agent X.

Is that a gut feeling ETAMI?

Computers do not have gut feelings. Octopuses are very smart. They would make a worthy enemy agent.

Scroll down until you find the **octopus a** and **octopus b** costumes. Double-click to select them both and click [Cancel] to close the dialog box. Your costumes area should have two octopus costumes.

svg octopus a

svg octopus b

TEST 〰

5

TEST: Click [⚑] to test your new sprite.
SUCCESS: Zorg's tentacles move! Agent X and Zorg swim around together in peace and harmony.
ERROR: No peace and harmony! Zorg's tentacles don't move. He might be doing it on purpose.
FIX: Make sure you have two different costumes for Zorg.

STOP THE SCRIPT! Click [⬤].

svg octopus a ✓
svg octopus b

svg octopus a ✗
svg octopus a

Good work, Potential Agent X. You learn fast.

The enemy is attempting to breach the firewalls! Agents, save your work!

Save as **Octododge06**.

ACHIEVEMENT UNLOCKED!

CODEMASTER

LEVEL 3

MISSION OBJECTIVE 9: PLAN YOUR CODE!

OK, that's better. I can tell who's who.

Zorg may look different, but it is still the same under the costume. The outside appearance is not as important as the code underneath.

That's kind of the same for humans!

Correct. As you train, you will learn to plan and re-plan your code. Zorg doesn't act like a villainous agent, so what must you change in Zorg's code?

This simulation is about how to dodge enemy agents. It doesn't make sense that both sprites are always in the same position and move at the same speed.

Logical. What else?

Zorg should be chasing Agent X, not the mouse-pointer.

Logical.

And something should happen when Zorg catches Agent X. I mean, they'd fight or get captured or something in the real world.

I also suggest that you introduce a system of scoring performance. That way, I know to send only the most skilled agents into the field. Anything else?

Well... it seems too easy. Can I make more enemies?

The coder . . .

. . . makes the rules. I know!

REVISION LIST

1. CHANGE ZORG'S STARTING POSITION AND SPEED SO THAT AGENT X HAS A FIGHTING CHANCE.

2. CHANGE ZORG'S CODE SO THAT HE PURSUES AGENT X TO THE ENDS OF THE EARTH.

3. RATE THE TRAINEES. IT'S FOR THEIR OWN GOOD!

4. AGENT X CAN'T RUN FOREVER. DESIGN AN ENDGAME FOR THE SIMULATION.

5. CALL IN SOME DIABOLICAL REINFORCEMENTS FOR ZORG!

REVISION 1:
CHANGE ZORG'S STARTING POSITION AND SPEED SO THAT AGENT X HAS A FIGHTING CHANCE.

1

We change the position of sprites using their **x** and **y** coordinates. Agent Finity will go into more detail later in your training. For now, assume that Zorg starts in a mysterious location known only as x: -200 y: -140.

That's a weird name for a hideout!

Click on **Zorg** and go to the script space.

Find the `go to x y block` connected to the `starter block`. Change the text fields to match:

`go to x: -200 y: -140`

TEST

2

TEST: Click 🚩.

SUCCESS: Zorg starts in the bottom left corner. So sinister!

ERROR: Zorg is somewhere else, or is gone completely!
WHAT IS THIS MADNESS!?

FIX: Make sure your numbers have **minus symbols** in front of them!

`go to x: -200 y: -140` ✔   `go to x: 200 y: 140` ✘

FIX: Make sure your numbers are the right way around!

`go to x: -200 y: -140` ✔   `go to x: -140 y: -200` ✘

STOP THE SCRIPT! Click ⬛.

REVISION 2:
*** CHANGE ZORG'S CODE SO THAT HE PURSUES AGENT X TO THE ENDS OF THE EARTH. ***

TEST

1

The speed of a sprite is controlled by the number of steps it moves. More steps mean faster; fewer mean slower.

Change Zorg's **move block** from 5 to 1.

`move 1 steps`

2

TEST: Click 🚩 and race Zorg and Agent X.

SUCCESS: Agent X wins! Good triumphs over evil!

ERROR: Zorg and Agent X are evenly matched. Noooo!

FIX: Check that Zorg's movement script has `move 1 steps` and Agent X's movement script has `move 5 steps`

STOP THE SCRIPT! Click ⬛.

> Logical work, Potential Agent X! Your squish-brain serves you well.

3

OK, Agent X goes after the mouse-pointer because of the **point towards mouse-pointer block**. I wonder if I can change that for Zorg . . .

Change Zorg's movement script to match ETAMI's code.

COPY THE CODE

```
when 🚩 clicked
forever
  if distance to Agent X > 20
    point towards Agent X
    move 1 steps
```

> Data security alert! Agents, save your work!

ACHIEVEMENT UNLOCKED!
CODEMASTER

LEVEL 4

Save as **Octododge07**.

REVISION 3:
*** RATE THE TRAINEES. IT'S FOR THEIR OWN GOOD! ***

1 We have not discussed **variables** yet. Agent Introspecter is superior at explaining these but I will demonstrate for now. We are going to create a score to rate an agent's field readiness, so it is logical that to access that information, I would look at the Agent X sprite rather than the Zorg sprite.

It makes sense to keep all the Agent X info in one place.

Correct. A logical script is an efficient script, Potential Agent X.

Click on **Agent X**. Click on **Variables**.

2 The first step is to create the variable.

Click on **Make a variable**.

3 A logical name for this is "Dodge Test Simulation Score of Field Agent for Use in Active Duty Evaluations".

Or . . . "Agent Score"?

I suppose . . .

Name your variable **Agent Score** and click **OK**.

Variable name

Agent Score

● for all sprites ○ for this sprite only

OK Cancel

The new variable should appear in the code menu area, with a check next to it.

☑ Agent Score

4 Agents are evaluated on time. The longer an agent stays hidden, the better. We will create a timer to count how long it takes Zorg to find Agent X.

Find these four blocks and drag them into Agent X's script space:

when ▢ clicked

forever

wait 1 secs

change ▼ by 1

5 Match ETAMI's code.

COPY THE CODE

when ▢ clicked
forever
  wait 1 secs
  change Agent Score ▼ by 1

TEST

6

TEST: Click 🏁 to test the score variable.
SUCCESS: The score gets higher and higher.
Basically, you win!
ERROR: There's no score. How will we know who is the ultimate dodge agent?
FIX: Click the check box to make sure Agent Score shows on the stage.

☑ Agent Score ✔   ☐ Agent Score ✘

ERROR: Agent Score changes so fast it hurts to look at it.
FIX: Make sure your **wait block** is inside the **forever loop**.

```
when 🏁 clicked
forever
  wait 1 secs
  change Agent Score by 1
```
✔

```
when 🏁 clicked
wait 1 secs
forever
  change agent-score by 1
```
✘

STOP THE SCRIPT! Click ⬛.

7

Test this again, Potential Agent X. There is a bug in your logic.

Run the test again and try to spot the bug.

8

The score gets bigger and bigger. Why doesn't it reset when I click the green flag?

You have not told it to.

Find `set ▼ to 0`.
Drag it into the **script space**.

Click on the drop-down arrow and choose **Agent Score**.

```
set ▼ to 0
     Agent Score
```

9

I'll put it here, because all these code blocks only happen once, at the beginning.

```
when 🏁 clicked
set agent-score to 0
set size to 50 %
go to x: 0 y: 0
```

Insert the new block into Agent X's setup script to match ETAMI's code:

COPY THE CODE

TEST

10

TEST: Click 🏁 to test if your bug fix worked.
SUCCESS: Agent score resets to 0! Wootage!
ERROR: It still starts from wherever you left it.
FIX: Make sure you've changed the drop-down menu.

`set Agent Score to 0` ✔   `set ▼ to 0` ✘

STOP THE SCRIPT!
Click ⬛.

Impressive work!

ACHIEVEMENT UNLOCKED!
VARIATOR
LEVEL 1

Data alarm! All agents must save their data.

Save as **Octododge08**.

REVISION 4:
*** AGENT X CAN'T RUN FOREVER. DESIGN AN ENDGAME FOR THE TRAINING SIMULATION. ***

1

So, the sim should end when Zorg catches up with Agent X.

That seems logical.

Click on **Zorg** and go to the script space.

2

You need to write some code to detect whether Zorg is touching Agent X. Start with these blocks.

Drag these three blocks into the script space:

if
touching ▼ ?
broadcast ▼ and wait

Click the drop-down arrow in the **touching block** and choose Agent X.

3

What's a **broadcast**?

It is how you pass messages between sprites. Agent Natterninja will explain more later in training.

Click on the **drop-down menu** in:

broadcast ▼ and wait

Click **new** in the drop-down menu.

broadcast ▼ and wait
new...

Call your message **end sim**.
Click **OK**.

Message name
end sim
OK   Cancel

4 Match ETAMI's code.

if touching Agent X ▼ ?
broadcast end sim ▼ and wait

COPY THE CODE

5

This code doesn't have a curvy golden starter block, so it will not function yet. You can create a new script with a new block or insert it where you think it is logical.

It seems to look the same as this other if block. They're both about detecting things.

Drop the new code blocks inside the **forever block** in Zorg's movement script. It goes under the old **if block**.

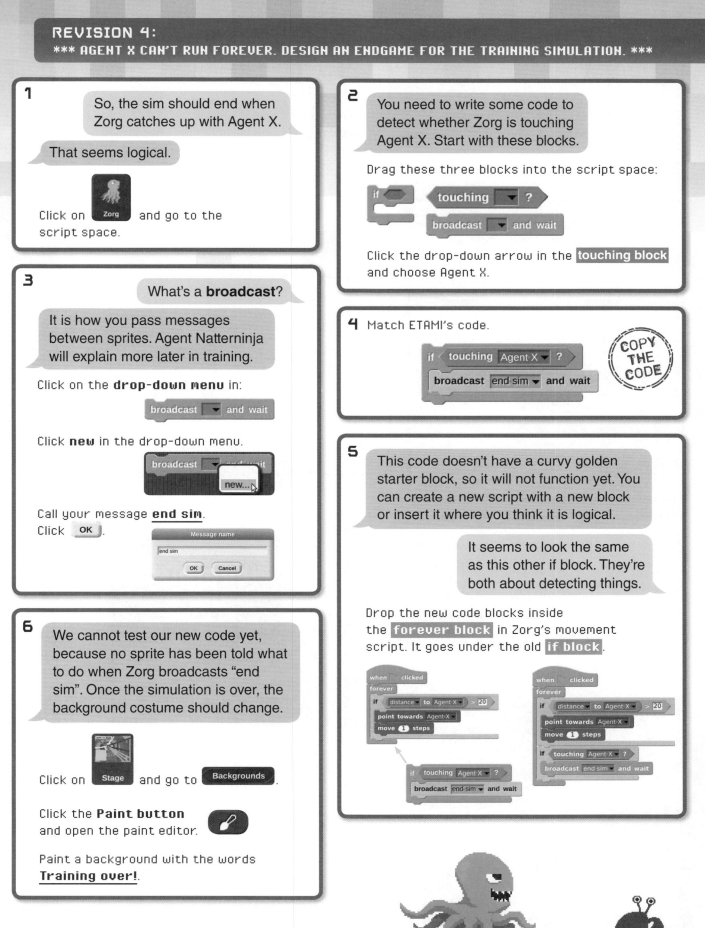

when ▢ clicked
forever
if distance ▼ to Agent X ▼ > 20
point towards Agent X ▼
move 1 steps

if touching Agent X ▼ ?
broadcast end sim ▼ and wait

when ▢ clicked
forever
if distance ▼ to Agent X ▼ > 20
point towards Agent X ▼
move 1 steps
if touching Agent X ▼ ?
broadcast end sim ▼ and wait

6

We cannot test our new code yet, because no sprite has been told what to do when Zorg broadcasts "end sim". Once the simulation is over, the background costume should change.

Click on **Stage** and go to **Backgrounds**.

Click the **Paint button** and open the paint editor.

Paint a background with the words **Training over!**.

EXPERIMENT

7

Make it as colorful as you like (or not!). Play around with the buttons, colors, and sliders to see what they do. You can hit `undo` if you make a mistake or `clear` to start over.

Click `OK` when you're done.

8

Everything should have a logical name.

Right-click on the new **background costume** button.

Choose **rename**.

Call your background **Training Over** and click `OK`.

rename background

Training Over

OK   Cancel

You should have two background costumes:

distractopia

RAWING OVER!

Training Over

9

Now that there are two backgrounds in the stage, I need more code, don't I?

Correct. Start with these blocks.

Go to `Scripts` and drag these three blocks into the script space:

when I receive ▼

switch to costume ▼

stop all ▼

10

I haven't used this curvy starter block before, have I?

No, you have not. This kind of block listens for a special message from other sprites. Agent Natterninja will explain later.

Match ETAMI's code.

COPY THE CODE

when I receive end sim ▼

switch to costume Training Over ▼

stop all ▼

TRAINING OVER

TEST

11

TEST: Click 🏴. Let Zorg catch Agent X. Don't worry: it's just a simulation!

SUCCESS: The background should start as **distractopia** when you click 🏴 and change to **Training Over** when Zorg and Agent X collide!

ERROR: The background doesn't change!

FIX: Make sure you have changed the drop-down menu on your `starter block`.

`when I receive end sim ▾` ✓

`when I receive ▾` ✗

ERROR: It takes a few seconds for it to switch.

FIX: Make sure you've used the right `broadcast block`.

`broadcast end sim ▾ and wait` ✓

`broadcast end sim ▾` ✗

STOP THE SCRIPT!

Click ⬤ .

This is some advanced coding, Potential Agent X!

Alert! Agents must save their data. Evil never rests!

Save as **Octododge09**.

ACHIEVEMENT UNLOCKED!

BROADCASTER

LEVEL 1

REVISION 5:
*** CALL IN SOME DIABOLICAL REINFORCEMENTS FOR ZORG! ***

1

I know how to do this one! We right-click and duplicate Zorg to make more enemy sprites.

Logical thinking, but in this case it is easier to **clone** instead of duplicate. The Echo agents will train you to know which is better to use when.

Cloning? Like making copies?

Correct. Duplicating is inefficient. Sprites can clone themselves.

Click on [Zorg] and go to [Scripts].

2

So many new blocks! I don't know what some do!

This is advanced coding, but you can build this. You have the technology.

Find these eight blocks and drag them into the script space:

`wait 1 secs`

`create a clone of myself ▾`

`show`

`hide`

`when I start as a clone`

`when I start as a clone`

`when I start as a clone`

`forever`

3 Your training simulation will get harder as more Zorg clones join the hunt for Agent X. You must change the scripts you have written for Zorg. First, replace some of the golden starter blocks.

Click and drag Zorg's movement script away from:

```
when clicked
```

```
when clicked

forever
  if  distance to Agent-X > 20
    point towards Agent-X
    move 1 steps
  if  touching Agent-X ?
    broadcast end sim and wait
```

Attach it to:

```
when I start as a clone
```

```
when I start as a clone
forever
  if  distance to Agent-X > 20
    point towards Agent-X
    move 1 steps
  if  touching Agent-X ?
    broadcast end sim and wait
```

Your script should look like this:

```
when I start as a clone
forever
  if  distance to Agent-X > 20
    point towards Agent-X
    move 1 steps
  if  touching Agent-X ?
    broadcast end sim and wait
```

4 Do the same for Zorg's setup script:

```
when clicked        when I start as a clone

go to x: -200 y: -140
set size to 50 %
```

Your script should look like this:

```
when I start as a clone
go to x: -200 y: -140
set size to 50 %
```

And for Zorg's costume script:

```
when clicked        when I start as a clone

forever
  next costume
  wait 0.2 secs
```

Your script should look like this:

```
when I start as a clone
forever
  next costume
  wait 0.2 secs
```

Insert **show** into your setup script.

```
when I start as a clone
show
go to x: -200 y: -140
set size to 50 %
```

5 Use a **when clicked** block and match ETAMI's code:

```
when clicked
hide
forever
  create a clone of myself
  wait 5 secs
```

COPY THE CODE

6 Clutter is very inefficient. You should delete the old blocks.

Drag any unused **when clicked** blocks into the **code menu area** to delete them. It'll keep ETAMI happy!

TEST

7

TEST: Click 🏴 and keep Agent X alive for more than 5 seconds.
SUCCESS: One Zorg appears when you click the green flag, and when the score gets to 5 another appears! DOOOOOODGE!
ERROR: There's no Zorg anymore!
FIX: Make sure `show` happens whenever a new clone starts.

```
when I start as a clone
show
go to x: -200 y: -140      ✔
set size to 50 %
```

```
when I start as a clone
go to x: -200 y: -140      ✘
set size to 50 %
```

ERROR: There's still no Zorg!
FIX: Make sure that the movement, costume, and start-up scripts all begin with: `when I start as a clone`

ERROR: There's no Zorg but there's lots of new Agent Xs!
FIX: Make sure you're cloning the right thing!

```
create a clone of myself ▾    ✔
```

```
create a clone of AgentX ▾    ✘
```

> We can use this training simulation, Potential Agent X. I will copy the code to my field-agent training database.

STOP THE SCRIPT! Click ⬤ .

> This training simulation is now Classified, Potential Agent X. Do not let it fall into the wrong hands!

Save as **Octododge10**.

ACHIEVEMENT UNLOCKED!
CLONER
1 LEVEL

> You have done well, Potential Agent X. There are not many recruits that make it this far so quickly. You have displayed the most valuable skill a VALID supercoder can have: the courage to try new things and learn from your mistakes. Finding a new supercoder is rare, but perhaps . . . Come. It is time for you to meet the other agents—the defenders of the galaxy—and continue your training.

NEW MESSAGE ✖

Go with ETAMI to meet the other VALID agents and learn to be a supercoder?

Y/H

EVENTS AND BROADCASTS

With Agent Natterninja

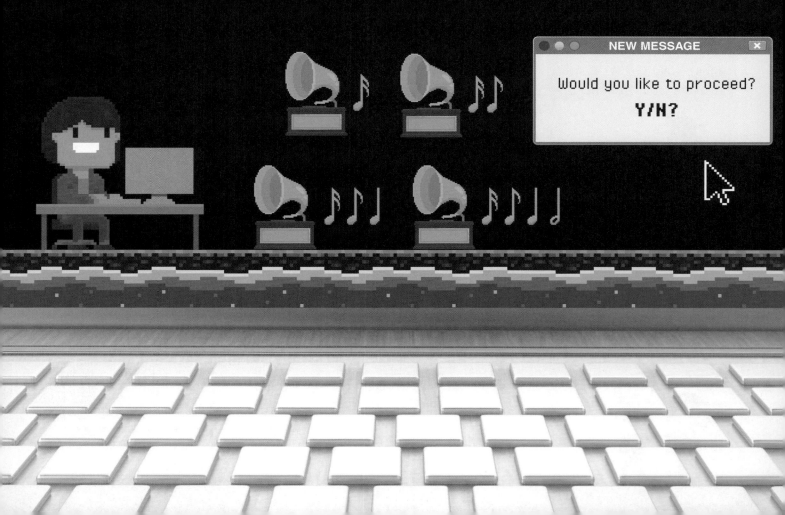

NEW MESSAGE ✕

Would you like to proceed?

Y/N?

You are a trainee at VALID, the agency responsible for the safety of Earth and the galaxy. So far, you've learned the galaxy is threatened. Several of VALID's top coders have disappeared in troubling circumstances. All signs point to an organization called CORUPT. The sooner you finish your training, the sooner you can help ETAMI and the VALID supercoders save the world. . . and their friends.

I have taught you all I can, Potential Agent X. Agent Natterninja will guide you through the next phase of your training. He is a field coder: our leading expert on events and broadcasts.

ETAMI! How's my favorite bucket of sparks today? I heard there's a new mini-agent in town.

INCORRECT. Potential Agent X is regulation human size. This is Agent Natterninja.

I've heard of you! Cool name.

Thanks. The other agents chose it because I have superfast reflexes.

INCOMPLETE INFORMATION.

. . . and I talk a lot . . . APPARENTLY. I'm from the Siren moon of Plaxxon. We're telepaths. Natural broadcasters. So, "Potential Agent X" passed the first test and is ready for the next stage of her training?

CORRECT. Her performance has been highly satisfactory.

High praise! I'm just back from a fact-finding mission to our Arctic data-warehouse. You were right, ETAMI. Our agent database has been copied. The report's in your home directory. I'll show Pax the ropes! Can I call you Pax?

That is alarming. I must analyze the data. Good work Agent Natterninja.

Is everything OK? That sounds serious.

Nothing we can do until ETAMI looks at my report. Ready to get started?

NEW MESSAGE

Go with Natterninja to continue your coder training?

Y/N

MISSION DOSSIER

>> LEARN THE FUNDAMENTALS OF BEING A VALID AGENT

You're ready to explore the complex world of events and broadcasts. Agent Natterninja will evaluate your field skills and check your reaction times, your creative problem solving, and your ability to work under pressure, all of which are vital skills needed in the battle against CORUPT.

LEVEL: 2
INSTRUCTOR: Agent Natterninja
BACKGROUND: Agent Natterninja grew up off-world on the Siren moon of Plaxxon: a mysterious planet whose inhabitants are highly regarded for their telepathic broadcasting skills. He's one of VALID's top field agents: a supercoder who uses his Siren mind-sending skills to fight for justice.

NATTERNINJA

MISSION OBJECTIVE 1: THE PLAN

Alright Pax, you're here to learn basic agent skills. We'll work on reaction times, flying spaceships, defusing bombs: that sort of thing. These require an in-depth knowledge of events and broadcasts.

I don't know what those are...

That's where I come in! Not to brag, but I'm one of the best. Broadcasting is my passion. We'll begin with events and get to the broadcast-y jazz later. I've written some mission plans for you.

What's a mission plan?

Every mission needs a goal, a plan, and a truly amazing codename.

To write code? Why?

Coding is complicated. It's easy to lose track of what you're trying to do. Suddenly you have a washing machine that cooks blueberry waffles. Nobody wants that: not the clothes, not the waffles. Every coding project needs a plan. A full agent writes their own. I'll help for now, but it's good to practice while you're training.

PROJECT OUTLINE

NAME:
WALKER

GOAL:
TO GET GARTZ WALKING WITH KEYPRESSES

REQUIREMENTS:
1. PAINT A COSTUME FOR GARTZ.
2. ACTIVATE THE COSTUME WITH **SPACEBAR**.
3. MOVE LEFT AND RIGHT WITH **A** AND **D**.
4. MOVE UP AND DOWN WITH **W** AND **S**.

MISSION OBJECTIVE 2: PAINT FOR ME, MAESTRO!

1 Open a web browser on your computer. Type **snap.berkeley.edu/run** in your browser bar. Hit enter. If you have a Snap! account, log in, otherwise acquire an adult to help make an account.

2 First we need a background and a costume.

Click **Stage**. Go to **Backgrounds**.
Click [ ]. Choose **Backgrounds** to open the **backgrounds selector**.
Double-click any background to import it.
Click **Cancel** to close the background selector.
Right-click the **background costume**.
Rename it **alliswell**.

3 We'll model this on Gartz. She's Plutonian, so she's round and green.

Click **Sprite**. Click the sprite **name field**.

Gartz
☑ draggable

Rename it **Gartz**.
Go to **Costumes**.
Create a new costume by clicking [🖌].

4 Painting sprites is hard. Drawing with a mouse is a TOTAL pain, but there's a trick. Think about what you're drawing, then break it into shapes you can make with the fill tools.

Gartz is mostly circular . . .

Exactly!

Click the **green part** of the **color bar** to find a green you like.

Use [●] to draw a big circular shape in the **paint screen** for the body.

5 When you're painting costumes, fill as much of the paint screen as possible. Just leave room for legs, flippers, feelers, mohawks—

Won't Gartz be too big? When she's animated, she'll move off the screen!

You can adjust the size in code later, so your sprites are right for whatever you need. Most sprites end up with a size adjustment in their setup script.

Make [●] white by clicking **white** on the **tone bar**.
Draw an eyeball on the upper right of your alien.

6 Make [●] black by clicking **black** on the **tone bar**.

Draw a pupil.

Click **purple** on the **color bar** to set the color to purple. Change the **line thickness** to **10** with the **brush size slider**.

Brush size

10

7 It's starting to look like Gartz! Here's a shortcut. Draw the mouth and make sure the lines go right to the edge.

Use [◻] or [🖌] to draw a triangular mouth and three purple feelers pointing up.

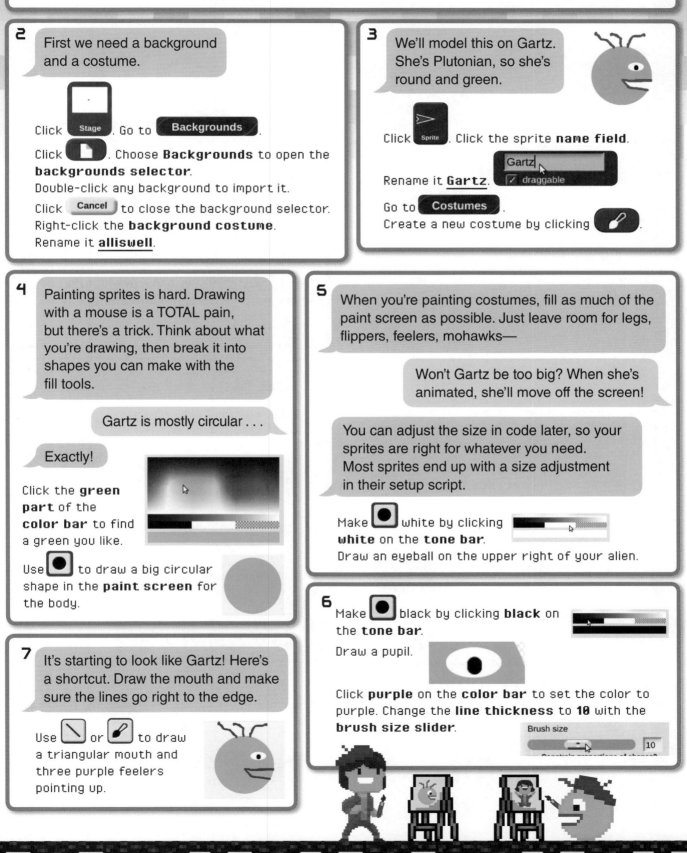

8 Here's a neat trick! Erasing freehand is a pest. Instead, set the fill tool to transparent and use it as an eraser!

Click . To make transparent, click the **checkered** part of the **tone bar**.

Click inside the mouth to erase the green.

9 Awesomebeans!

Right? So much easier. Close this and we'll make a copy.

Click OK. Right-click the costume. Choose **duplicate** to make a copy.

edit
rename
duplicate
delete
export
Untitled

10 The copy must look different to make the animation work.

Right-click the copy. Choose **edit**.

Click. Erase Gartz's bottom lip.

Use to erase Gartz's feelers but leave some purple dots to show where they start.

If you make a mistake or erase too much, use undo.

11 Let's use the eyedropper tool to make sure she stays the same colors.

Click. Click the purple part of the mouth.

Click or. Using the **brush size slider,** change the **line thickness** to **10**.

Brush size 10

12 She'll need a brand-new lip, OK?

Draw a new bottom lip that's lower than the old one. Draw three replacement feelers. Start at the purple dots, but draw down instead of up.

You've really captured her essential GREENNESS.

Save as **Walker01**.

13 For my next trick!

Click. Click the **checkered part** of the **tone bar** to make transparent.

Use to erase any extra bits of green in her mouth and to clean up.

Click OK to save your costume. Right-click each costume. **Rename** them **walk1** and **walk2**.

walk1
walk2

ACHIEVEMENT UNLOCKED!
PAINTMASTER
LEVEL 1

MISSION OBJECTIVE 3: THE WONDERS OF LEFT AND RIGHT

We need a setup script for Gartz.

What's a setup script?

I hoped you'd ask! It's code that sets up a sprite at the beginning of a mission. 99.99% of sprites need a setup script. It does things like set the size and position on screen, remove any injuries from the last mission, that sort of thing.

Injuries?

I mean . . . effects . . . Like, if something accidentally dyes your sprite blue, then it explodes, you start the beginning of the next mission with a non-blue unexploded sprite. So, Gartz needs a setup script. Like 99.99% of sprites!

1 Click **Scripts**.

Find and drag these blocks into the **script space**.

when ☐ clicked

set size to 100 %

go to x: 0 y: 0

2 The **go to block** is in most setup scripts. Sprites move around during missions, so when we reset, they should go back to their starting position. Finity will teach you about XY coordinates, but this block starts Gartz in the center of the stage.

Coolbeans! I need to change the **set size block**, right?

Sure do! As you pointed out, Gartz is bigger than big right now! Change the numbers in the **set size block.** The smaller the number, the smaller the Gartz.

In the **set size block**, click the **text field**. Type **40**.

3 Click the block to run and test the code by itself. Play with the number: try to make Gartz about half a thumb-size.

Connect the blocks to make a **setup script** that looks like this:

```
when green flag clicked
go to x: 0 y: 0
set size to 40 %
```

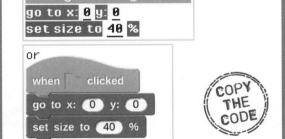

or

when ☐ clicked

go to x: 0 y: 0

set size to 40 %

COPY THE CODE

TEST ∿

4

TEST: Click 🚩 to test your new sprite.
SUCCESS: Gartz moves to the center of the screen and is about half the size of a thumb.
ERROR: Gartz is HUGE! Or tiny! Whatever the size, it's wrong!
FIX: Change the number in the **set size block**. Small numbers shrink; big numbers embiggen (totally a word!).

STOP THE SCRIPT! After each test, click 🛑 to stop the scripts running. Otherwise, things get weiiird. . .

Look at you with your testing! Glitchbane will LOVE you!

OK, now it's the real deal. We're talking events!

What is an ev—

What's an event?! Fantastic question! Events are things a user might do that can change what's going on in a mission.

Like touching an enemy?

Kind of! We're mainly talking about keyboard and mouse events. You move the mouse, you click a sprite, you press a key on the keyboard. There's a bunch of different events you can do, and a double bunch of ways of dealing with them. Some events have their own golden starter blocks, so we'll start with those.

5 Find and drag this block into the **script space**.

`when space ▼ key pressed`

6 This works just like the starter blocks you know, but instead of happening at the beginning of the mission, it happens—

When the user hits the spacebar?!

Yes! Isn't that great?!

Amazebeans!

Find and drag these blocks into the **script space**.

`forever`   `wait 1 secs`   `next costume`

In the `wait 1 secs block`, click the **text field**. Type **0.2**.

7 Connect the blocks to make an **animation script** that looks like this:

```
when space key pressed
forever
    wait 0.2 secs
    next costume
```

or

```
when space ▼ key pressed
forever
    wait 0.2 secs
    next costume
```

COPY THE CODE

8

TEST: Click 🏁. Then press the spacebar.
SUCCESS: Nothing happens when you click 🏁. When you press spacebar, Gartz changes!
ERROR: Gartz changes super slowly. It's like watching a Tucksonian Megasnail race.
FIX: Make sure you haven't left out the decimal point in the `wait block`.

`wait 0.2 secs` ✓   `wait 2 secs` ✗

STOP THE SCRIPT! Click ⬤. Give Gartz a break.

Save as **Walker02**.

9 Let's make our walker walk!

Find and drag these blocks into the **script space**.

`move 10 steps`

`when space ▼ key pressed`   `point in direction 90 ▼`

In the `when key pressed block`, choose **d**.

10

Can I have two events running at once? Will it know which key I pressed?

Yeppers! When you press **spacebar**, it sets off the animation script, which keeps on running. When you press **d**, it's a separate event running a totally separate script.

In the **point in direction block**, click the drop-down arrow. Choose **(90) right**. Connect the blocks to make a **movement script** that matches:

```
when d key pressed
point in direction 90
move 10 steps
```

or

```
when d ▼ key pressed
point in direction 90 ▼
move 10 steps
```

COPY THE CODE

14

Does Gartz walk upside down?

No! We can't change the laws of physics, but there is a quick fix.

There are three buttons next to the picture of Gartz above the **script space**. These are the **orientation buttons**. They control the directions sprites can face. Some sprites can freewheel in any direction, but Gartz can only go left and right.

Click the middle button to stop Gartz flipping.

ACHIEVEMENT UNLOCKED!
EVENT COORDINATOR

LEVEL 1

11

TEST: Click ▶. Press **spacebar** to activate Gartz. Press the **d** key to test right movement.
SUCCESS: The alien moves right!
ERROR: The d does nothing!?
FIX: Check your start block is set to **d**!

`when d ▼ key pressed` ✓   `when space ▼ key pressed` ✗

STOP THE SCRIPT! Click ⬤.

12 Find and drag these blocks into the **script space**.

```
when space ▼ key pressed

point in direction 90 ▼

move 10 steps
```

13 In the **when key pressed block**, choose **a**. In the **point in direction block**, click the drop-down arrow. Choose **(-90) left**. Connect the blocks to make a **movement script** matching:

```
when a ▼ key pressed
point in direction -90 ▼
move 10 steps
```

COPY THE CODE

TEST

15

TEST: Click ▶. Press the spacebar to activate Gartz. Press the **a** key to test left movement
SUCCESS: The alien moves left!
ERROR: Gartz only goes right. Sad times.
FIX: Check the minus sign is in the movement script.

```
when a ▼ key pressed
point in direction -90 ▼
move 10 steps
```
✓
```
when a ▼ key pressed
point in direction 90 ▼
move 10 steps
```
✗

STOP THE SCRIPT! Click ⬤.

Save as **Walker03**.

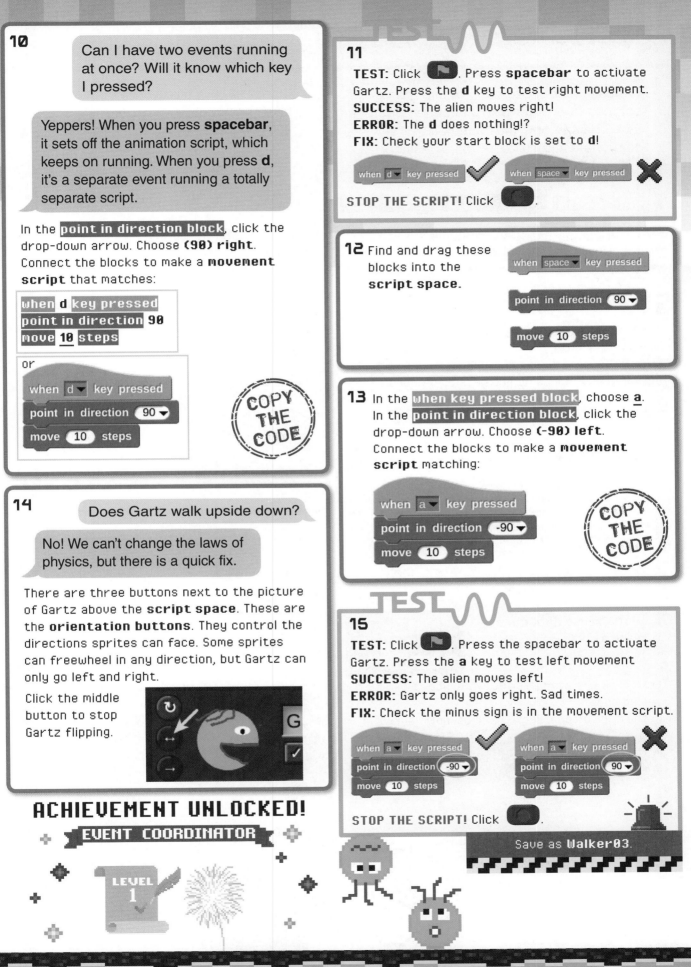

BONUS MISSION OBJECTIVE: A DIFFERENT WAY TO MOVE

1

We used step movement for left and right, but there's another way that supercoders use. You can also move sprites using coordinates. Let's do a bonus mission!

Find and drag these blocks into the **script space**.

`when space ▼ key pressed`   `change size by 10`   `change y by 10`

In the **when key pressed block**, click on the drop-down arrow. Choose **s**.

2

Let's change the size so that when Gartz moves up, it looks like she's going further away.

And closer when she moves down?

Yup!

In the **change size by block**, click the **text field** and type **1**.
In the **change y by block**, click the text field and type **-10**.
Connect the blocks to make a **movement script** matching:

```
when s key pressed
change size by 1
change y by -10
```

or

```
when s ▼ key pressed
change size by 1
change y by -10
```

COPY THE CODE

3 TEST

TEST: Click 🏴. Click **spacebar** to get Gartz moving. Then hit **s**.
SUCCESS: Gartz moves down! And she gets bigger!
ERROR: Gartz moves up AND gets bigger. She's defying the laws of nature.
FIX: Check you added minus in the **change y by block**.

`change y by -10` ✓   `change y by 10` ✗

STOP THE SCRIPT! Click 🔴.

4

I see what you mean about size.

Right? Looks real!

Right-click the new **movement script**. Choose **duplicate** to make a copy.

```
make a co[py]
and pick it [up]
help...
duplicate
when [key pressed]
delete
script pic...
```

Left-click the **script space** to place the copied code.
In the copied code, click the drop-down arrow in the **when key pressed block**. Choose **w**.
In the **change size by block**, type **-1**.
In the **change y by block**, type **10**.

```
when w ▼ key pressed
change size by -1
change y by 10
```

5 TEST

TEST: Click 🏴. Press **spacebar** to get Gartz moving. Try out **w** and **s**.
SUCCESS: Gartz moves up when you hit **w** and down when you hit **s**! It's like a beautiful alien dance of flappy feelers!

Could I use that for left and right too?

Abso-tooting-lutely!
Just use the x coordinate rather than the y coordinate. Neat, right?

STOP THE SCRIPT! Click 🔴.

Save as **Walker04**.

MISSION DOSSIER

>> DEFUSE STINKY BOMBS

Stinkbombs!? YUCK! Overcome your disgust to defuse them with mouse events and broadcasts.

LEVEL: 2
INSTRUCTOR: Agent Natterninja

MISSION OBJECTIVE 1: SAVING THE WORLD ONE MOUSE-CLICK AT A TIME

PROJECT OUTLINE

NAME:
BOMB DEFUSAL

GOAL:
DEFUSE STINKY BOMBS WITH MOUSE-CLICKS

REQUIREMENTS:
1. MOUSE-CLICK TO CHANGE COSTUME
2. MOUSE-CLICK TO CHANGE THE BACKGROUND WITH A BROADCAST.

1 Open a web browser and go to **snap.berkeley.edu/run** or start a new project by clicking [ ]. Choose **new**.

2 OK, you've done keypress events. Next is mouse events. They're a little more complicated, because you've got lots more options with a mouse.

Do I?

Yeppers! You can click it, move it without clicking, hold it down, click a sprite—you get the idea. I'll show you some and you can try out more later. Let's get set up.

Click **Stage**. Go to **Backgrounds**. Click [ ]. Choose **Backgrounds** to open the **backgrounds selector**. Double-click any background to import it. Click **Cancel** to close the background selector. Right-click the **background costume**. Choose **rename**. Call it **greatday**.

3
Where do we start?

Pax, I'm glad you asked. We start, as all good musical numbers do, with a c—

A costume?!

I was going to say "click," as in mouse click. But yeah, a costume too.

Click **Sprite**. Click the sprite **name field**.

Rename the sprite **S-bomb**.

Go to **Costumes**. Create a new costume by clicking [ ].

Use the paint tools to draw a stinkbomb with a big, red C (for CORUPT) on it.

Click **OK**.

Save as **Bombclicker01**.

4 Right-click the **costume**. Rename it **stinkbomb**. Right-click the **stinkbomb** costume. Choose **duplicate** to make a copy. Right-click the **stinkbomb(2)** costume. Choose **edit**.

Use [ ] or [ ] with different shades of green to draw a big, slimy, exploded mess. Don't forget stink lines!

Click **OK** to save your stinky costume. Right-click the new costume. **Rename** it **slimesplode**.

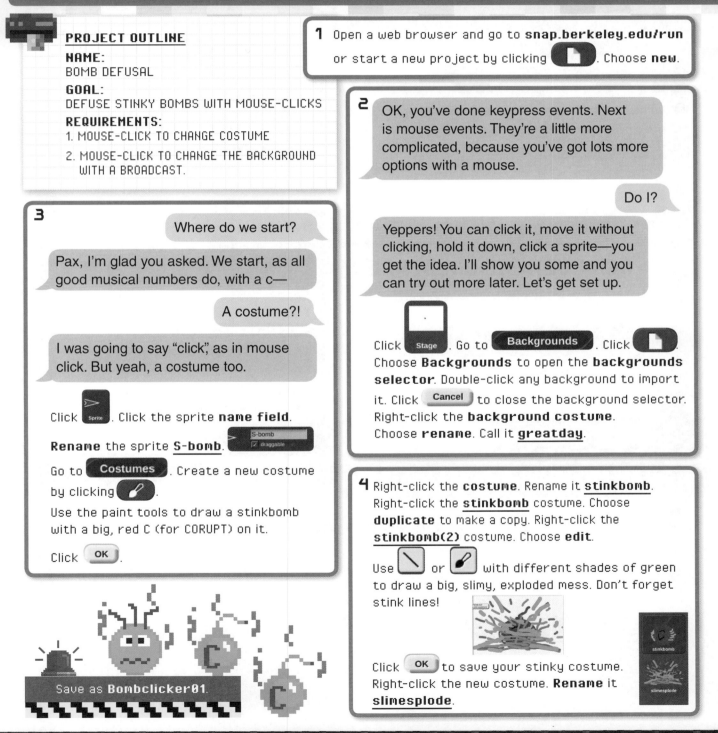

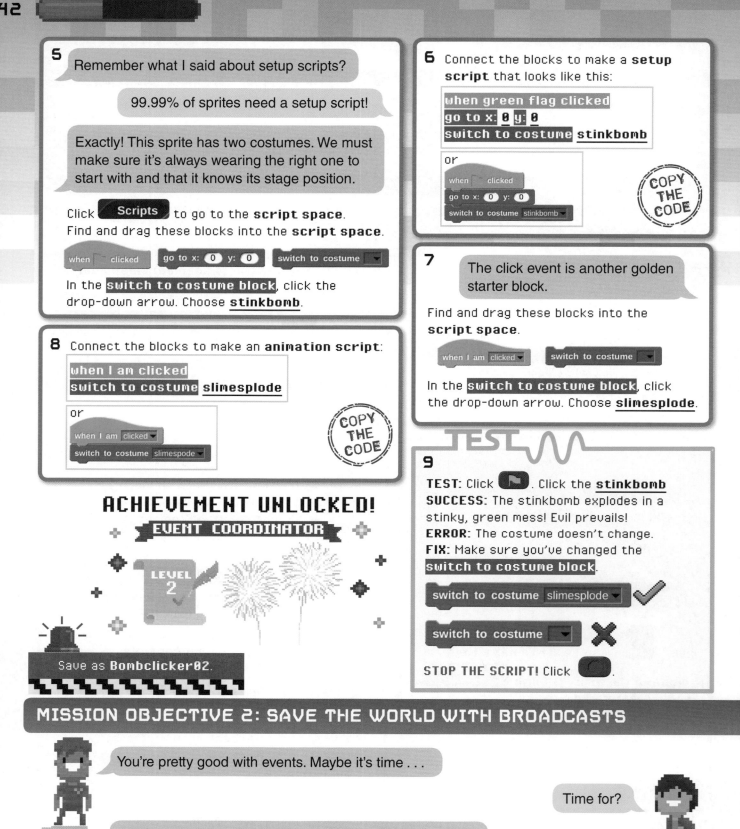

5

Remember what I said about setup scripts?

99.99% of sprites need a setup script!

Exactly! This sprite has two costumes. We must make sure it's always wearing the right one to start with and that it knows its stage position.

Click **Scripts** to go to the **script space**. Find and drag these blocks into the **script space**.

when [ ] clicked   go to x: ⓪ y: ⓪   switch to costume ▾

In the **switch to costume block**, click the drop-down arrow. Choose **stinkbomb**.

6 Connect the blocks to make a **setup script** that looks like this:

```
when green flag clicked
go to x: 0 y: 0
switch to costume stinkbomb
```

or

```
when [ ] clicked
go to x: 0 y: 0
switch to costume stinkbomb
```

COPY THE CODE

7

The click event is another golden starter block.

Find and drag these blocks into the **script space**.

when I am clicked ▾   switch to costume ▾

In the **switch to costume block**, click the drop-down arrow. Choose **slimesplode**.

8 Connect the blocks to make an **animation script**:

```
when I am clicked
switch to costume slimesplode
```

or

```
when I am clicked
switch to costume slimespode
```

COPY THE CODE

ACHIEVEMENT UNLOCKED!

EVENT COORDINATOR

LEVEL 2

Save as **Bombclicker02**.

TEST

9

TEST: Click [▶]. Click the **stinkbomb**
SUCCESS: The stinkbomb explodes in a stinky, green mess! Evil prevails!
ERROR: The costume doesn't change.
FIX: Make sure you've changed the **switch to costume block**.

switch to costume slimesplode ▾ ✓

switch to costume ▾ ✗

STOP THE SCRIPT! Click [ ].

MISSION OBJECTIVE 2: SAVE THE WORLD WITH BROADCASTS

You're pretty good with events. Maybe it's time . . .

Time for?

Broadcasts! I've been waiting for this. Do you know I can broadcast my thoughts directly into your brain?

Really?

Paaaaax, listen to Agent Natterninja! He is very wiiissse . . .

That is . . . AMAZEBEANS!

Right? It comes in handy out in the field. When a sprite sends a broadcast, it's just sending a group message to all the other sprites and the stage in case they need to do anything.

1

What do you use broadcasts for?

Lots of things! When you finish a game, it should come up with a "game over" screen, right?

Right!

Let's use a broadcast at the end of our bomb-defusal game.

Click the **S-bomb button**. Go to Costumes .

2 Let's put the explosion costume in the endgame background so it only shows up if our mission fails. After all, we're VALID agents: we try to prevent unnecessary stinkiness, right?

Click the **slimesplode costume**. Drag it into the **code menu area** to delete it. Click the **stinkbomb costume** to make sure the bomb shows up.

3 We need a new setup script for this sprite.

Go to Scripts . Click and drag your **setup script** into the **code menu area** to delete it. Your **setup script** starts with **when green flag clicked**.

Click Variables

Click Make a variable . Call it **SCORE**. Click OK .

4 Find and drag these blocks into the **script space**.

when ⚑ clicked   set size to (100) %

show   set [▾] to [0]

In the **set to 0 block**, click the drop-down arrow. Choose **SCORE**.
In the **set size to block**, click the **text field**. Type **30**.

5 Connect the blocks to make a new **setup script** matching:

when green flag clicked
set SCORE to 0
set size to 30%
show

or

when ⚑ clicked
set SCORE ▾ to 0
set size to 30 %
show

COPY THE CODE

HINT ✕

You might have to change the numbers in your **set size block**, depending on how big the original stinkbomb was. Smaller bombs make the game harder but train better spies; larger bombs make it easier but create less alert spies.

OK

6

TEST: Click 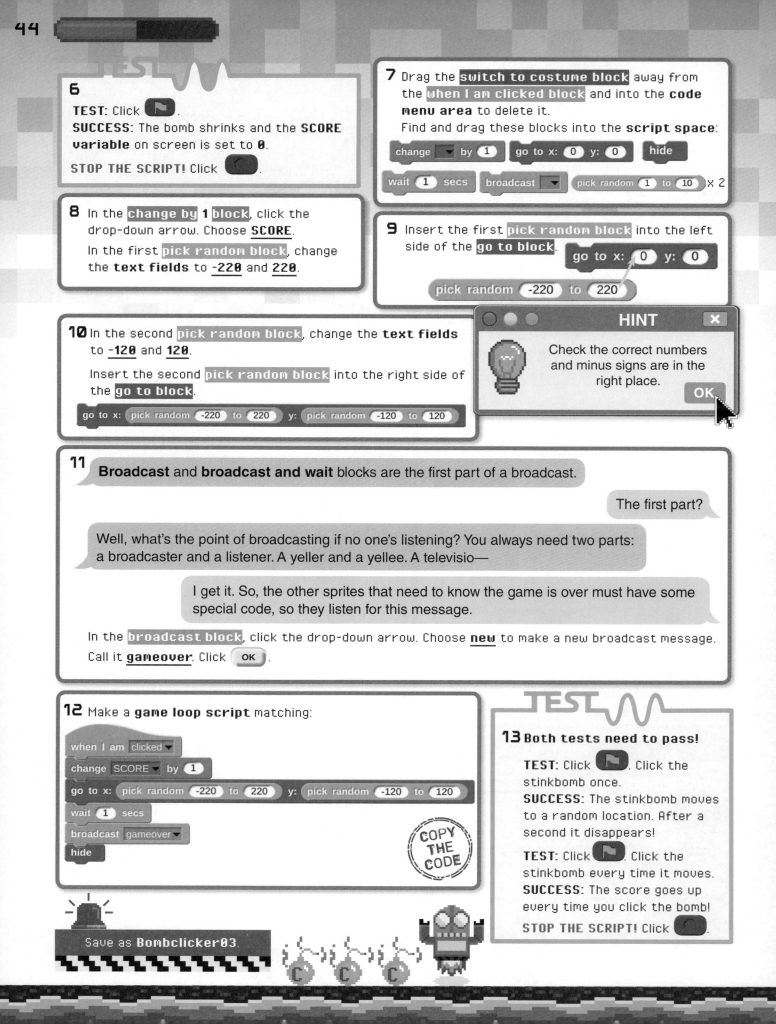 .
SUCCESS: The bomb shrinks and the **SCORE variable** on screen is set to **0**.

STOP THE SCRIPT! Click .

7 Drag the **switch to costume block** away from the **when I am clicked block** and into the **code menu area** to delete it.
Find and drag these blocks into the **script space**:

`change ▼ by 1`   `go to x: 0 y: 0`   `hide`

`wait 1 secs`   `broadcast ▼`   `pick random 1 to 10` × 2

8 In the **change by 1 block**, click the drop-down arrow. Choose **SCORE**.

In the first **pick random block**, change the **text fields** to **-220** and **220**.

9 Insert the first **pick random block** into the left side of the **go to block**.

`go to x: 0 y: 0`

`pick random -220 to 220`

10 In the second **pick random block**, change the **text fields** to **-120** and **120**.

Insert the second **pick random block** into the right side of the **go to block**.

`go to x: pick random -220 to 220 y: pick random -120 to 120`

HINT

Check the correct numbers and minus signs are in the right place.

OK

11

Broadcast and **broadcast and wait** blocks are the first part of a broadcast.

The first part?

Well, what's the point of broadcasting if no one's listening? You always need two parts: a broadcaster and a listener. A yeller and a yellee. A televisio—

I get it. So, the other sprites that need to know the game is over must have some special code, so they listen for this message.

In the **broadcast block**, click the drop-down arrow. Choose **new** to make a new broadcast message.
Call it **gameover**. Click OK .

12 Make a **game loop script** matching:

`when I am clicked ▼`
`change SCORE ▼ by 1`
`go to x: pick random -220 to 220 y: pick random -120 to 120`
`wait 1 secs`
`broadcast gameover ▼`
`hide`

COPY THE CODE

13 Both tests need to pass!

TEST: Click 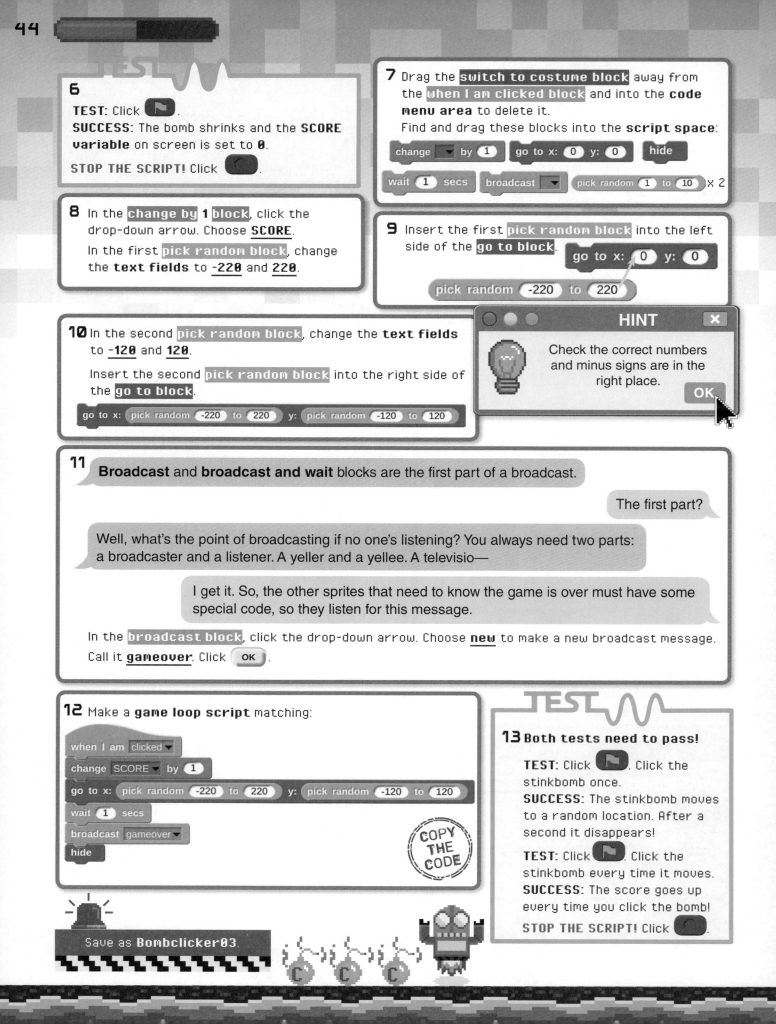 . Click the stinkbomb once.
SUCCESS: The stinkbomb moves to a random location. After a second it disappears!

TEST: Click . Click the stinkbomb every time it moves.
SUCCESS: The score goes up every time you click the bomb!

STOP THE SCRIPT! Click .

Save as **Bombclicker03**.

14 Click [Stage] go to [Backgrounds].
Right-click your **background**. Choose **duplicate** to make a copy.
Right-click the new costume. Choose **edit**.

16 Now we must set up the other end of our broadcast.

The listener!

Click [Scripts]. Find and drag these blocks into the **script space**:

when clicked

when I receive ▼

switch to costume ▼ x 2

17 In the **when I receive block**, choose **gameover**. In the **switch to costume blocks**, click the drop-down arrows. Change one costume to **greatday** and the other to **slimescape**.

18 Connect the blocks so you have a **setup script** and an **endgame script** to match:

when green flag clicked
switch to costume greatday
and
when I receive gameover
switch to costume slimescape

or

when clicked
switch to costume greatday ▼
and
when I receive gameover ▼
switch to costume slimescape ▼

COPY THE CODE

ACHIEVEMENT UNLOCKED!

BROADCASTER

LEVEL 2

15 Over the copied background, use [✎] or [╲] and different shades of green to paint another huge exploded, slimy stinkbomb.

When you're done, use [▢] or [✎] to write **GAME OVER** in big letters over your slime pile.

GAME OVER!!

Click [OK] to save your slime! Right-click the new **costume. Rename it slimescape**.

TEST

19
TEST: Click [⚑]. Then click the **stinkbomb** once.
SUCCESS: If you don't click the stinkbomb for a second, it explodes in a shower of grossness!

STOP THE SCRIPT! Click [◯].

Save as Bombclicker04.

CHALLENGE

20 Listening for a broadcast is kind of like an event. It's waiting for a thing to happen before it runs the code.

You got it!

What else can you use it for?

Lots of things! You can use it to make levels in your mission or to control timing between sprites. It will come up again!

Build your reflexes to practice for flight training. See how high you can get your score before the stinkbomb explodes.

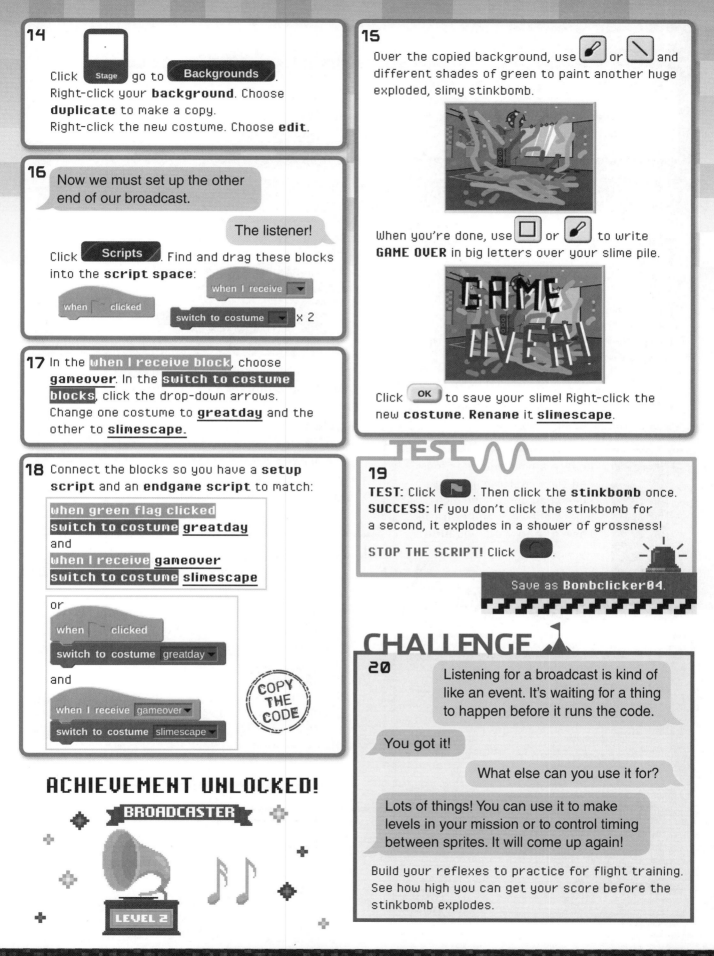

MISSION DOSSIER

>> QUICK THINKING AND CLICKING

One last test. Natterninja will check your reaction times to see how quickly you can pick a bad alien from good.

LEVEL: 2
INSTRUCTOR: Agent Natterninja

MISSION OBJECTIVE: ALIENS OF THE DDD

PROJECT OUTLINE

NAME:
THINKQUICK

GOAL:
USE THE MOUSE-DOWN EVENT TO SCROLL THROUGH THE DIGITAL DATABASE OF DIRTBAGS (DDD) AND TEST YOUR REFLEXES.

REQUIREMENTS:
1. DRAW THREE ALIENS FOR YOUR PROTOTYPE DDD
2. MAKE A SCROLL FUNCTION TO QUICKLY FIND THE RIGHT DIRTBAG.

1 Open a web browser and go to **snap.berkeley.edu/run** or start a new project by clicking [ ]. Choose **new**. Click the sprite **name field**. Name the sprite **ddd**.

Click [Sprite] go to [Costumes]

2 Create a new costume by clicking [🖌].
Click the **green part** of the **color bar** to find a green you like.

Use [⬤] to draw a big green alien body. Experiment with tools and colors to draw a green alien with eight legs.
Click [OK] when you're finished.

3 Create a new blue and a new red alien costume, making sure they don't have eight legs. Right-click and **rename** them **green**, **red**, and **blue**.

green
red
blue

Save as **DDD01**.

4 Here's a different way of waiting for events. We may need to check if a mouse-button or key is pressed on the go. The starter blocks we've used to wait for events are handy, but this way lets you check if someone is holding down the mouse-button.

Click [Scripts]. Find and drag these blocks into the **script space**.

wait 1 secs
when clicked
mouse down?
next costume
if
forever

5 In the **wait 1 secs block**, type **0.1**. Connect the blocks to make an **animation script**:

```
when green flag clicked
forever
    if mouse down?
        next costume
        wait 0.1 secs
```

or

```
when clicked
forever
    if mouse down?
    next costume
    wait 0.1 secs
```

COPY THE CODE

We're totally not evil!

Dirtbag Blue   Dirtbag Green   Dirtbag Red

TEST

6

TEST: Click 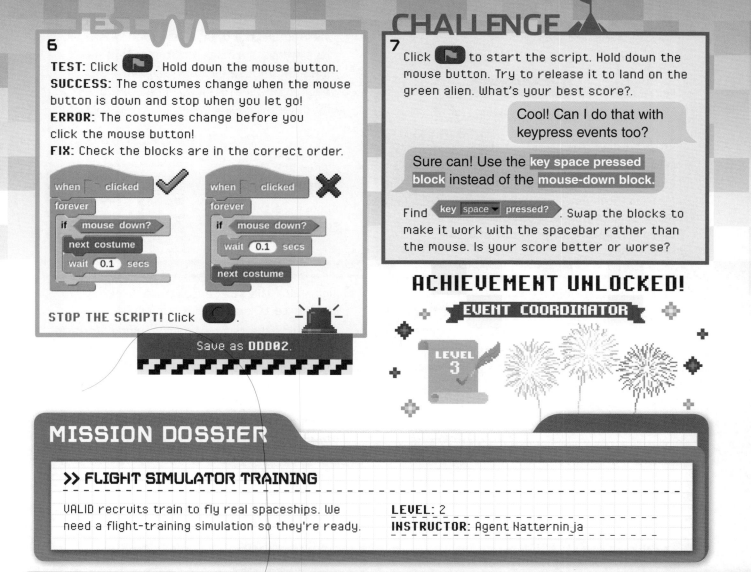. Hold down the mouse button.
SUCCESS: The costumes change when the mouse button is down and stop when you let go!
ERROR: The costumes change before you click the mouse button!
FIX: Check the blocks are in the correct order.

```
when [flag] clicked   ✔
forever
  if < mouse down? >
    next costume
    wait (0.1) secs
```

```
when [flag] clicked   ✘
forever
  if < mouse down? >
    wait (0.1) secs
    next costume
```

STOP THE SCRIPT! Click [stop].

Save as **DDD02**.

CHALLENGE

7

Click [flag] to start the script. Hold down the mouse button. Try to release it to land on the green alien. What's your best score?.

Cool! Can I do that with keypress events too?

Sure can! Use the **key space pressed block** instead of the **mouse-down block.**

Find < key [space ▾] pressed? > . Swap the blocks to make it work with the spacebar rather than the mouse. Is your score better or worse?

ACHIEVEMENT UNLOCKED!

EVENT COORDINATOR

LEVEL 3

MISSION DOSSIER

>> FLIGHT SIMULATOR TRAINING

VALID recruits train to fly real spaceships. We need a flight-training simulation so they're ready.

LEVEL: 2
INSTRUCTOR: Agent Natterninja

MISSION OBJECTIVE 1: BUILD A TRAINING COURSE. IN SPACE!

PROJECT OUTLINE

NAME:
FLIGHT SIMULATOR

GOAL:
BUILD A MULTI-LEVEL FLIGHT SIMULATOR TRAINING MODULE.

REQUIREMENTS:
1. BUILD A BASIC FLIGHT COURSE WITH A START GATE AND A DESTINATION GATE.
2. USE BROADCASTS TO SIGNAL ENDGAME AND LEVEL CHANGES.
3. BUILD MULTIPLE LEVELS OF INCREASING DIFFICULTY.
4. ADD A SCORING SYSTEM TO RATE PILOTS' PERFORMANCE.

Are you ready for space flight?

So ready!

Not worried about black holes? Cosmic rays? Micro-meteorites? The cold vacuum of interstellar space?

I wasn't before . . .

1 Open a web browser and go to **snap.berkeley.edu/run** or start a new project by clicking 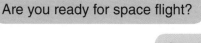. Choose **new**.

2 We need lots of stars.

Click [Stage]. Go to [Backgrounds].

Make a new background by clicking 🖌.

Use 🪣 and 🖌 to draw a starry space background.
Click **OK** when you're done.
Right-click the new background. **Rename** it **space**.
Right-click **space**. Click **duplicate** to make a copy.

3 We're making a multi-level game where levels have a similar background. To save time and mouse-clicks, we'll save a basic background that we'll duplicate and use for other levels later.

Good! Drawing stars is a pain.

Right-click the new **space(2)** costume.

Choose **edit**. Use ⬛ to draw a beginners' course. Make it wide!

4 The course starts at VALID HQ. Use ⬤ to draw a green circle at one end. Add a darker green V for VALID. Draw a red circle at the other end of the course for a red interstellar jump gate. Click **OK**.

Right-click the new background. Rename it **level1**.

5 Right-click the **space costume**. Click **duplicate** twice to make two copies.

Right-click the two new backgrounds. **Rename** them **gameover** and **tryagain**.

Right-click the new backgrounds. Choose **edit**. On **gameover**, write the message **GOOD FLYING AGENT**! Decorate it!

On **tryagain**, write the message **Oops! Practice and try again**.

6 Click [Scripts]. Find and drag these blocks into the **script space**.

when ⚑ clicked   when I receive ▢ x 2
switch to costume ▢ x 3   stop all ▾ x 2

Connect a **switch to costume block** under each golden starter block.

In the **when I receive blocks**, click the dropdown arrow. Click **new** to make two new broadcast messages. Call one **gameover** and the other **tryagain**.

7 Put the blocks together to make three scripts:

```
when green flag is clicked
switch to costume level1
and
when I receive gameover
switch to costume gameover
stop all
and
when I receive tryagain
switch to costume tryagain
stop all
```

or

```
when clicked
switch to costume level1
and
when I receive gameover▾
switch to costume gameover▾
stop all▾
and
when I receive tryagain▾
switch to costume tryagain▾
stop all▾
```

COPY THE CODE

ACHIEVEMENT UNLOCKED!

PAINTMASTER

LEVEL 2

Save as DDD03.

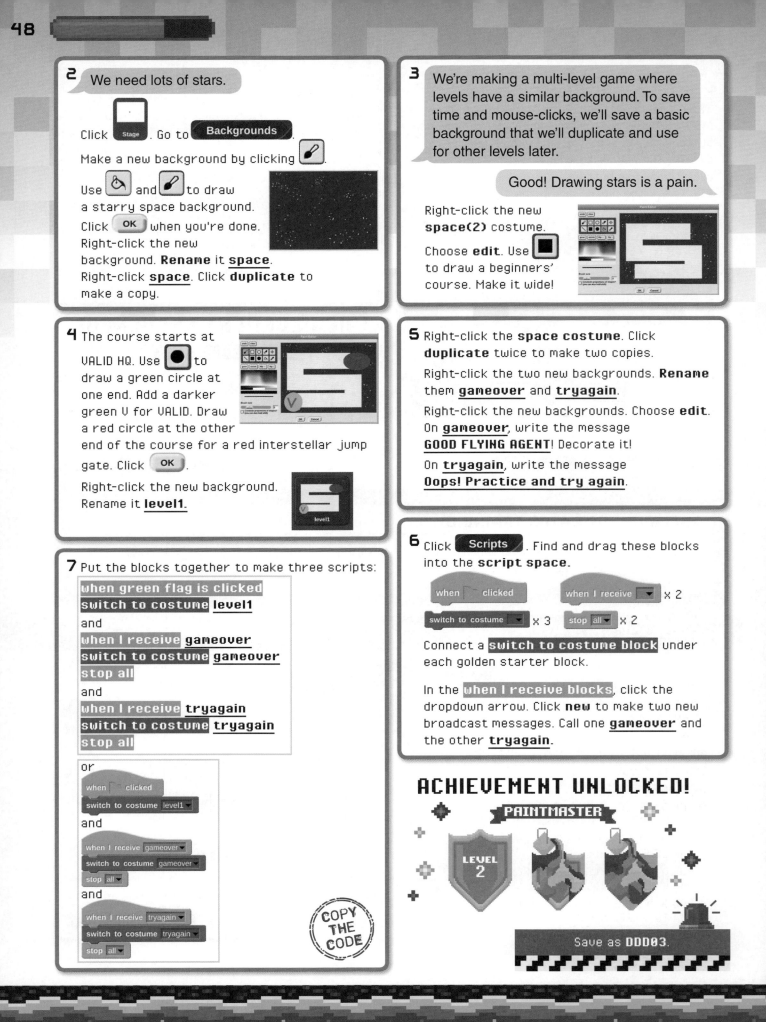

MISSION OBJECTIVE 2: BUILD A SHINY SPACESHIP AND FLY AWAY

1 Drawing spaceships isn't as hard as stars. VALID's training ships come in all shapes and sizes. Look for base shapes and use the line and fill tools to fill the gaps.

Click [Sprite]. Click the sprite **name field**. Name the sprite **spaceship**. Go to [Costumes]. Create a new costume by clicking [brush].

2 The easiest way to paint an amazing spaceship is using shapes. Pax's ship looks like this:

Pax used [■], [\], [▢], [fill], and [●]. She used [undo] a lot to fix her mistakes! Pax clicked [eyedropper] then clicked on her ship to copy that color.

As you work, click [OK] to save and then keep on editing.

3 Use [■] and [▢] to draw the basic shapes.

Then use [\] to draw wings.

Use [fill] to fill in the colors.

Add detailing to your ship. It can look however you want, as long as it flies!

4 In code, like real life, you must calibrate your spaceship properly. Otherwise it'll jump right into a passing space tourist.

Click [⊕]. Click and drag the gray circle so it's in the middle of your ship. Click [OK]. Right-click the new costume. Rename it **Training ship**.

5 Now, 99-

99.99% of sprites need a setup script?

Pax, I'm so proud! You remembered.

Click [Scripts]. Find and drag these blocks into the **script space**.

[when 🏳 clicked] [go to x: 0 y: 0] [broadcast ▼]
[point in direction 90 ▼] [set size to 100 %] [show]

In the **point in direction block**, click the drop-down menu. Choose **(90) right**.
In the **set size block**, click the **text field**. Type **10**.

6 The spaceship must fit inside the VALID circle on your screen and fly easily through the course without touching the edges.

Try typing different numbers, then click the block to test if it looks right. In the **go to block**, click the **text field**. Change the numbers so your spaceship starts in the VALID starting circle of the level 1 background.

EXPERIMENT

7 To start your spaceship in the right spot, experiment with numbers in the range x:(-170 to -200) and y:(-130 to -150, or 130 to 150 if HQ is in the top corner).

HINT

Remember: if you click the single **go to block**, you can test your numbers without running the whole script.

OK

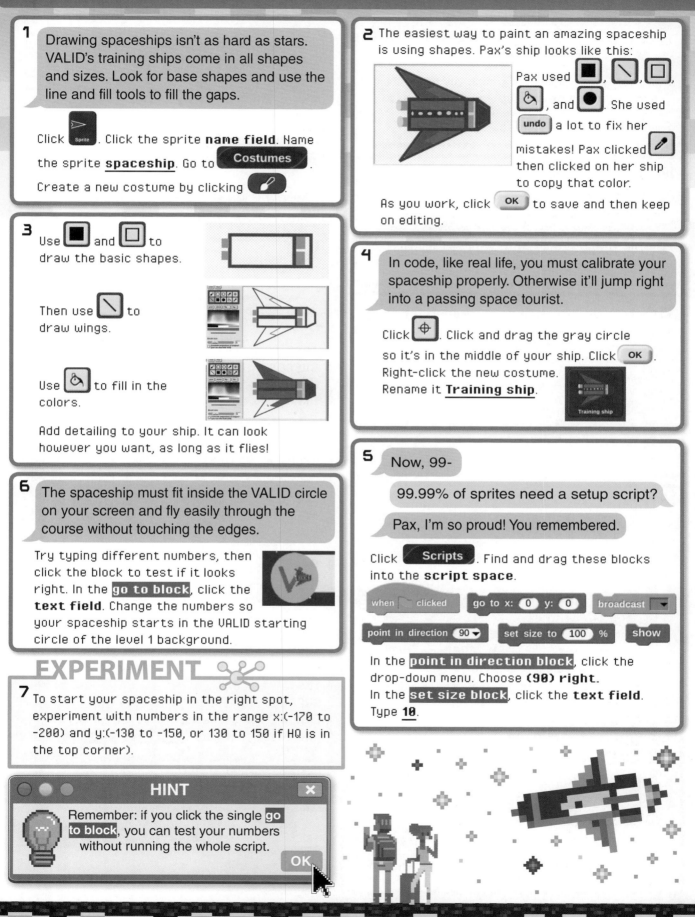

8 The setup script needs to send a broadcast to itself to start the first level. We'll make a gameplay script in your spaceship that runs when it hears that broadcast.

In the **broadcast block**, click the drop-down arrow. Choose **new**. Call the new broadcast message **level1**. Click OK.

9 Connect the blocks to make your **setup script**. Your **go to** coordinates can be different to Pax's.

```
when green flag is clicked
set size to 10 %
go to x-180 y-120
point in direction 90
show
broadcast level1
```

or

```
when       clicked
set size to 10 %
go to x: -180 y: -120
point in direction 90
show
broadcast level1
```

COPY THE CODE

10 Find and drag these blocks into the **script space**.

```
move 10 steps
when space key pressed      point in direction 90
```

In the **when key pressed block**, click the drop-down arrow. Choose **d**.

11 Connect the blocks to make a **movement script**.

```
When d key pressed
point in direction 90
move 10 steps
```

or

```
when d key pressed
point in direction 90
move 10 steps
```

COPY THE CODE

12

TEST: Click 🏁. Hit **d**.
SUCCESS: The spaceship moves to the right!
ERROR: The spaceship moves up or down or left.
FIX: Check the ship is pointing the right way.

```
point in direction 90 ✓      point in direction -90 ✗
```

STOP THE SCRIPT! Click [ ].

Save as **Takeoff01**.

13 Our movement scripts all use the same blocks, so let's copy them. We'll have to change the fields or each key will send the ship in the same direction.

In the **script space**, right-click the **when key pressed block**. Choose **duplicate**. Do it three times, making three copies.

```
when d ke...   help...        make
point in direc  duplicate      and p
move 10 s      delete
               script pic...
```

Change each script so you have three more **movement scripts** that match:

```
When a pressed
point in direction -90
move 10 steps
```

```
When s pressed
point in direction 180
move 10 steps
```

```
When w pressed
point in direction 0
move 10 steps
```

COPY THE CODE

14

TEST: Press **w**.
SUCCESS: The spaceship goes up!
TEST: Press **a**.
SUCCESS: The spaceship moves left!
TEST: Press **s**.
SUCCESS: The spaceship comes down!
TEST: Press **d**.
SUCCESS: The spaceship moves right!
ERROR: Your spaceship moves the wrong way.
FIX: Check that your **point in direction blocks** and **when key pressed blocks** match Pax's movement scripts.
STOP THE SCRIPT! Click [ ].

Save as **Takeoff02**.

15 Remember I told you about gameplay scripts?

They start when the setup script finishes and send out a broadcast.

Exactly. A gameplay script controls the flow of a game. It usually checks to see if the player has won or lost. Our gameplay script will check if the spaceship has gone outside the course or if it's flown to the jump gate and won.

Find and drag these blocks into the **script space**.

when I receive ▼   hide   forever   if

touching ■ ?   broadcast ▼

16 In the **when I receive block**, click the drop-down arrow. Choose **level1**.
In the **touching block**, click the **color square**. Click the background of the **stage**. The color square should match the **space** background. In the **broadcast block**, click the drop-down arrow. Choose **tryagain**.

17 Connect the blocks to make a **gameplay script** that matches:

when I receive level1 ▼
forever
if touching ■ ?
broadcast tryagain ▼
hide

COPY THE CODE

TEST

18

TEST: Click 🏴. Fly your spaceship out into the black. Twice!
SUCCESS: You crash and burn! The background changes to **tryagain** and your ship disappears. Click 🏴 to try again.
ERROR: The background changes before you get to space! Or it doesn't change at all!
FIX: Make sure your color square is the same color as the space background (not the flight track or the stars).
ERROR: On the second test, the spaceship doesn't show up.
FIX: Make sure you have a **show block** in your **start-up script**.
STOP THE SCRIPT! Click 🔴.

19 In the **gameplay script**, right-click the **if block**. Click **duplicate** to make a copy. Drag the new code and connect it **inside** the **forever block**, after the **if block**.

when I receive level1 ▼
forever
if touching ■ ?
broadcast tryagain ▼
hide

if touching ■ ?
broadcast tryagain ▼
hide

20 In the **touching block**, click the **color square**. Click the **red interstellar jump gate**. The color square should be red. In the **broadcast block**, click the drop-down arrow. Choose **gameover**.

when I receive level1 ▼
forever
if touching ■ ?
broadcast tryagain ▼
hide
if touching ■ ?
broadcast gameover ▼
hide

TEST

21

TEST: Click 🏴. Fly from VALID HQ to the jump gate without touching the edges.
SUCCESS: When you get to the jump gate, a **gameover** screen appears!
STOP THE SCRIPT! Click 🔴.

ACHIEVEMENT UNLOCKED!

BROADCASTER

LEVEL 3

Save as **Takeoff03**.

MISSION OBJECTIVE 3: KICK IT UP A NOTCH FOR LEVEL 2

OK, that was a training mission. Let's up the difficulty for level 2.

Like, make the course longer?

There are a lot of options. You could add more corners, as they're hard to fly around. You could make it a bit narrower. The key is to find a balance so that it's possible, but not **too** possible.

1
Click **Stage**. Go to **Backgrounds**
Right-click the **space** costume.
Click **duplicate** to make a copy.
Right-click the **space(2)** costume.
Click **edit**.

2 Design a level-2 track with lots of corners. It must start in the same place (VALID HQ).
Use ■ to build a more advanced track.

3
Use ● to make a green circle in the same place as before. It will end at a different jump gate, so add an orange circle at the end of the track.
Click **OK**.
Right-click the new background.
Rename it **level2**.

level2

4 Go to the **script space**. Find and drag these blocks into the **script space**.

when I receive ▼   switch to costume ▼

5 In the **when I receive block**, click the drop-down arrow. Choose **new** to make a new broadcast message. Call it **level2**.
Click **OK**.
In the **switch to costume block**, click the drop-down arrow. Choose **level2**.
Connect the blocks.

when I receive level2 ▼
switch to costume level2 ▼

COPY THE CODE

6 Click the **spaceship sprite button**. In the **touching block** that controls the **gameover** broadcast, click the **color square**.

if touching ■ ?
broadcast gameover ▼
hide

Then click the **orange jump gate** on the stage. The **color square** should be orange.

7 Find and drag these blocks into the **script space**.
if
go to x: 0 y: 0
broadcast ▼
touching ■ ?

8 Click ⚑. Then press ⬜ to start and stop your game. The **level1** background should display on stage.
In the new **touching color block**, click the **color square**. Then click the red jump gate on the stage.
The **color square** should be red. Click **Stage** and click on the level2 background. Click on the spaceship sprite and go to scripts.
In the **go to block**, change the numbers so the ship starts at VALID HQ (the green circle). Remember your numbers might be different from Pax's code on the next page!

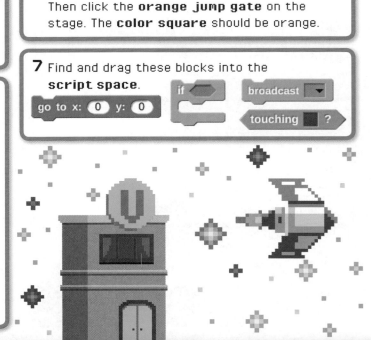

9 In the **broadcast block**, choose **level2**. Connect the blocks to match:

```
if touching [  ]
    go to x: -180 y: -120
    broadcast level2
```

or

```
if   touching [  ] ?
    go to x: -180  y: -120
    broadcast level2 ▼
```

TEST

11

TEST: Click 🏁. Fly to the first red jump gate.
SUCCESS: The red jump gate leads to level 2! HUGE SUCCESS!
ERROR: The red jump gate makes the ship disappear.
FIX: Every time you add a level, you must change the **gameplay script** so the **gameover** broadcast gets sent after the final level.

```
if  touching [  ] ?
    broadcast gameover ▼
    hide
```
✓

```
if  touching [  ] ?
    broadcast gameover ▼
    hide
```
✗

STOP THE SCRIPT! Click ⬤.

Save as **Takeoff04**.

10 Drag and connect the new code inside the **forever block** but after the last **if block**.

```
when I receive level1 ▼
forever
    if  touching [  ] ?
        broadcast tryagain ▼
        hide
    if  touching [  ] ?
        broadcast gameover ▼
        hide
    if  touching [  ] ?
        go to x: -180  y: -120
        broadcast level2 ▼
```

COPY THE CODE

ACHIEVEMENT UNLOCKED!

◆ **BROADCASTER** ◆

LEVEL 4

MISSION OBJECTIVE 4: RATE YOUR FLIGHT

1

When I made the training sim with ETAMI, I added a score. Should I do that here?

To see who's winning? Faster? Happier?

It's space flight training: I want to see if I'm getting better!

Click (Variables). Click (Make a variable). Name the variable **score**. Find and drag these blocks into the **script space**.

```
when ▢ clicked

repeat until ⬡

wait 1 secs

change ▼ by 1

score

broadcast ▼

set ▼ to 0

⬡ = ⬡
```

2

We need to set the score at the beginning. Do I add it to the setup script or keep all the scoring code in one script?

That is an amazingly good question. It could go in either. It is part of setup, but since we'll make a script that is entirely about scoring, it also makes sense to put it there. It does make it a bit easier to find later.

In the **set to 0 block**, click the drop-down arrow. Choose **score**. Click the **text field**. Type **20**.

```
set score ▼ to 20
```

Click and drag the **score block** into the left side of the **= block**. In the right side, type **0**.

```
score = 0
```

3 Click and drag the **= block** into the **blank hexagon** in the **repeat until block**.

```
repeat until < score = 0 >
```

4 In the **change by 1 block**, click the drop-down arrow. Choose **score**. Click the **text field**. Type **-1**.

In the **broadcast block**, click the drop-down arrow. Choose **tryagain**.

5 Connect the blocks to make a **scoring script**:

```
when green flag is clicked
set score to 20
repeat until score = 0
    wait 1 secs
    change score by -1
broadcast tryagain
```

or

```
when [flag] clicked
set score to 20
repeat until < score = 0 >
    wait 1 secs
    change score by -1
broadcast tryagain
```

COPY THE CODE

6 Find and drag these blocks into the **script space**.

```
change [ ] by 1        set [ ] to 0
```

7 In the **set to 0 block**, click the drop-down arrow. Choose **score**.

Drag the **set score block** inside the **gameplay script**. Insert it before the **broadcast tryagain block**.

```
if < touching [ ] ? >
    set score to 0
    broadcast tryagain
    hide
```

8 In the **change by 1 block**, click the drop-down arrow. Choose **score**. Click the **text field**. Type **10**.
Right-click the **change score by 10 block**. Choose **duplicate** to make a copy.

9 Click and drag one of the **change score by 10 blocks**. Insert it before the **broadcast level2 block**.

```
if < touching [ ] ? >
    go to x: -180 y: -120
    change score by 10
    broadcast level2
```

10 Insert the other **change score by 10 block** before the **broadcast gameover block**.

```
if < touching [ ] ? >
    change score by 10
    broadcast gameover
    hide
```

TEST

11
Both tests need to pass!

TEST: Click 🏳. Fly your hardest!
SUCCESS: The score starts at 20, then counts down as you fly! When you go through a jump gate, the score increases by 10.

TEST: Click 🏳. Let the score run down to 0.
SUCCESS: When the score reaches 0, the **tryagain** screen comes up.
ERROR: The game goes straight to the **tryagain** screen.
FIX: Make sure you set the score correctly.

```
set score to 20  ✓        set [ ] to 0  ✗
```

STOP THE SCRIPT! Click 🔴.

Save as **Takeoff05**.

MISSION OBJECTIVE 5: LEVEL 3—TEARS IN THE FABRIC OF SPACETIME

1 One thing you'll find in space is debris. It can make the trip from HQ to the jump gate hard. Let's add some obstacles.

Click **Stage**. Go to **Backgrounds**.
Right-click the **space costume**.
Click **duplicate** to make a copy.
Right-click the **new costume**. Click **edit**.

2 Let's make our obstacles out of our background so we don't need to set up a whole new script to check for space-trash.

Design a level-3 track with lots of corners. It must start in the same place (VALID HQ).

When you're done, use 🖋 to pick up the background color. Then use 🪣 and 🖌 to create obstacles the same color as the space background.

Use ⬤ to make a green circle in the same place as before. The end is a different jump gate, so add a light blue circle at the end of the track.

Click **OK**. Right-click the new background.
Rename it **level3.**

level3

3 Go to the **script space**. Find and drag these blocks into the **script space**.

when I receive ▼   switch to costume ▼

4 In the **when I receive block**, click the drop-down arrow. Choose **new** to make a new broadcast message. Call it **level3**. Click **OK**.
In the **switch to costume block**, click the drop-down arrow. Choose **level3**.
Connect the blocks.

5 Click the **spaceship sprite button**. In the **touching color block** that controls the **gameover** broadcast, click the **color square**.

if touching ⬜ ?
change score ▼ by 10
broadcast gameover ▼
hide

Click the **light blue jump gate** on the stage. The **color square** should be light blue.

6 Click **Stage**. Go to **Backgrounds**.
Click **level2** to make it appear on the stage.
Click the **spaceship sprite button**.
Go to the **script space**. Find and drag these blocks into the **script space**.

go to x: 0 y: 0   broadcast ▼   if
touching ⬛ ?

7 In the new **touching color block**, click the **color square**. Then click the **orange jump gate** on the stage. The **color square** should be orange.
Drag the **touching color block** into the hexagonal space in the **if block**.
In the **go to block**, change the numbers so the spaceship starts at HQ (the green circle).
In the **broadcast block**, click the drop-down arrow. Choose **level3**.

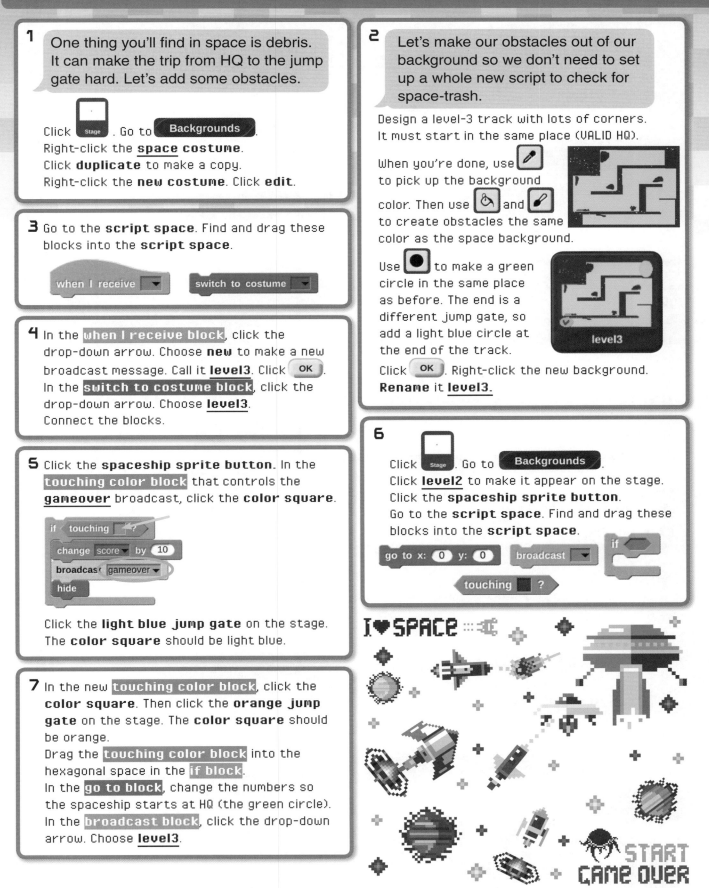

I ♥ SPACE

START
GAME OVER

8 Connect the blocks to match:

```
if touching [   ]
    go to x: -180 y: -120
    broadcast level3
```

Drag the new code inside the **forever block**, but after the last **if block**.

9 Drag this block into the script space.

```
change [  ▼  ] by 1
```

Click the drop-down arrow. Choose **score**.
Click the **text field**. Type **10**.
Click and drag the new **change score by 10 block**. Insert it before the **broadcast level3 block**.

COPY THE CODE

TEST

10

Both tests need to pass!

TEST: Click 🏴. Fly to the red jump gate, then the orange jump gate.

SUCCESS: The orange jump gate leads to level 3! Woot!

TEST: Fly through level 3 and make it to the light blue final jump gate.

SUCCESS: Made it! You're a leaf on the wind!

ERROR: You can't win on level 3. Maybe you're not cut out to be a pilot.

FIX: Go back to the stage and edit your level-3 track. It should be hard, but not impossible.

STOP THE SCRIPT! Click ⬤.

Save as **Takeoff06**.

ACHIEVEMENT UNLOCKED!
CODEMASTER
LEVEL 5

Oh. . . this isn't good! There's a message from ETAMI on the supercoder frequency. There's been another coder-napping!

Can I help?

I must go. My broadcasting skills could help. You've done well, Pax. I'll take you to Glitchbane. She'll head up the investigation from here. You may be able to help her.

Anything!

Let's bounce, Pax! No time to lose!

NEW MESSAGE

Go to help Agent Glitchbane with the investigation?

Y/N

BUG HUNTS AND PREDICATES

with Agent Glitchbane

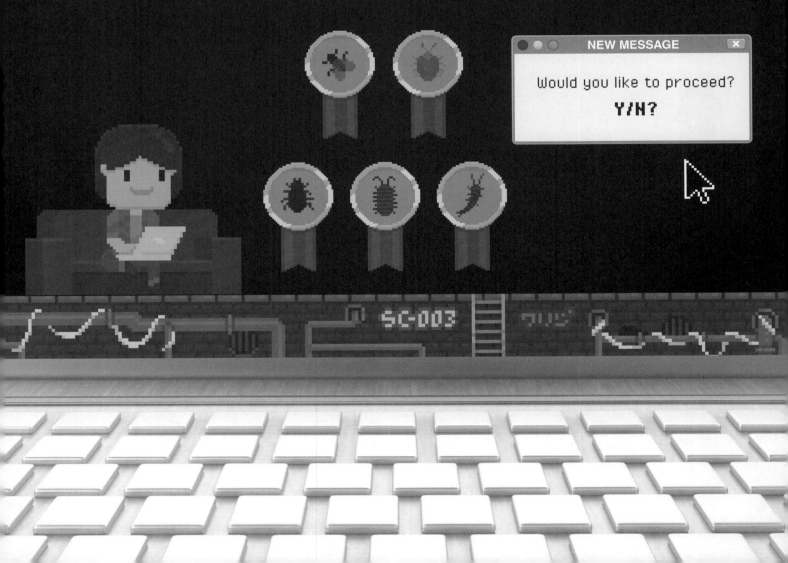

NEW MESSAGE

Would you like to proceed?

Y/N?

You are a trainee at VALID, the agency tasked with holding back the intergalactic threat known as CORUPT. In your second session, you learned two things from Agent Natterninja:

1. Broadcasts are powerful coding tools.

2. Another VALID coder is missing, and the agents are worried.

To continue your training, Natterninja is taking you to meet Agent Glitchbane, who will teach you about something called "predicates".

Natterninja, who's the newbie?

This is Pax. She can help track down our missing agents.

She has clearance for that?

Pax, don't mind Glitchbane—she's a Booliotic detective. She hunts down bugs so she's suspicious of everyone, but inside she's a giant softie. I'll see you two later.

Hi. What did he mean by Booliotic?

It's my home planet: Booliote 5. Booliotes have an exceptional sense of true and false. That's why I'm a detective. I can tell if someone is lying just by looking at them. So, how are you with predicates? True, false, ifs, elses?

I. . .

Hmm. I'll show you. Can you help with this investigation, Newbie?

I want to find those missing agents. I'll help however I can.

Strap on your logic shoes and fire up Snap!, Newbie!

NEW MESSAGE

Go with grumpy Glitchbane and help track down the missing agents?

Y/N

MISSION DOSSIER

>> IMPROVE SECURITY FOR GLITCHBANE'S OFFICE

Conquer predicates with Agent Glitchbane, the master of true and false. Before investigating the agents' disappearance, you must beef up security.

LEVEL: 3

INSTRUCTOR: AGENT GLITCHBANE

BACKGROUND: Glitchbane is VALID's bug-hunting lead investigator. A skilled alien supercoder from Booliote 5, she uses her mind-reading skills to spot the difference between truths and lies. She's a little grumpy, but loyal to the core.

GLITCHBANE

MISSION OBJECTIVE 1: PREVENT UNAUTHORIZED ACCESS

PROJECT OUTLINE

NAME: LOCKDOWN

GOAL: PREVENT UNAUTHORIZED ACCESS TO GLITCHBANE'S OFFICE.

REQUIREMENTS: 1. A LOCK FOR THE DOOR
2. A PASSWORD SYSTEM TO UNLOCK THE DOOR

1 Open a web browser. Type **snap.berkeley.edu/run** into your browser bar and hit enter. If you have a Snap! account, log in. If not, acquire a (human) adult to help you make an account.

2 First, have a look at the `if block`. You can't go past a good `if block` with a nice *predicate*, which is something that can be **true** or **false**. `If blocks` and predicates are how a computer decides what to do. In Snap!, we use `operator blocks` to write a predicate. The predicate goes in the hexagon in the `if block`. When you click the **green flag** to run the code, the computer checks if the predicate is **true** or **false**. If it's **true**, the code **inside** the block runs. If it's **false**, the computer ignores it.

Click `Control`. Find the `if blocks`.

3 We'll use an `if block` and predicates to check the password. If it matches, the door opens. Otherwise it stays locked.

Click ⬜. Click `Backgrounds`.

Stage

Click 🖌️.

Draw two different backgrounds: a locked office door and an unlocked door. Click `OK`.

Right-click each background. **Rename** them **locked** and **unlocked**.

4 Sprites? Where we're going, we don't need *sprites*...

Right click 🏴 Sprite. Choose **delete**

show
duplicate
clone
delete
parent...
export...

5 We need a variable for the password. The Introspecter will explain about variables, but for now follow my lead.

Click `Variables`. Then click `Make a variable`

Name the variable **password**. Click `OK`.

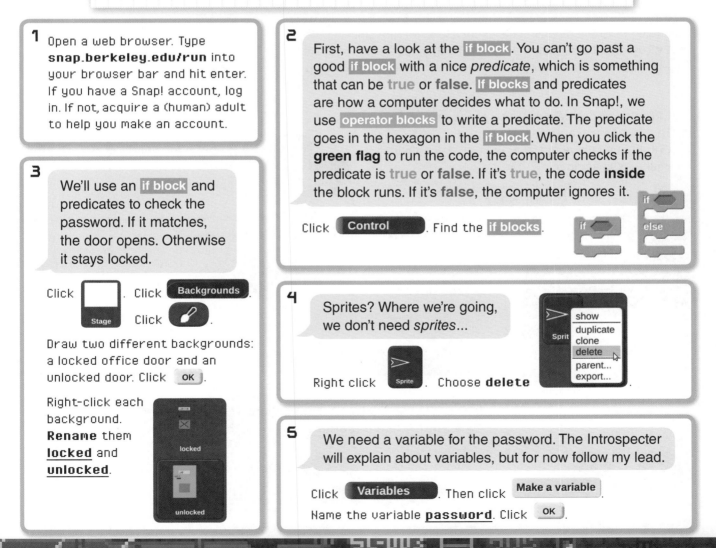

6 We need a good **setup script**.

Find and drag these blocks into the **script space**.

```
when [flag] clicked
```

```
set [ ▼ ] to [0]
```

```
switch to costume [ ▼ ]
```

7 In the **set to 0 block**, click the drop-down arrow. Choose **password**.

Click the **text field**. Type **GORP**.

```
set password ▼ to GORP
```

GORP? Really?

Gorp and Roppleblast are Booliote 5's moons.

In the **switch to costume block**, click the drop-down arrow. Choose **locked**.

```
switch to costume locked ▼
```

8 What's wrong with GORP?

Nothing! It's great . . .

Connect the blocks to make a **setup script** to match:

```
when green flag is clicked
  set password to GORP
  switch to costume locked.
```

or

```
when [flag] clicked
  set password ▼ to GORP
  switch to costume locked ▼
```

COPY THE CODE

TEST

9

TEST: Click [Backgrounds]. Click the **unlocked** costume. Click [flag].
SUCCESS: The background changes to **locked**. The **password** field on the stage is set to GORP. Security is getting tight!
ERROR: The background doesn't change. Anyone could get in!
FIX: Check you've changed the drop-down menu to **locked**.

```
switch to costume locked ▼   ✓
```
```
switch to costume [ ▼ ]       ✗
```

ERROR: The password on the stage area shows a 0. That's a terrible password!
FIX: Check you've set the password properly in your setup script.

```
set password ▼ to GORP   ✓
```
```
set password ▼ to [0]    ✗
```

STOP THE SCRIPT! Click [ ].

Save as **Lockdown01**.

10 We need a way to open the door, right?

Sure do!

Find and drag these blocks into the **script space**.

```
when [flag] clicked        ask [what's·your·name?] and wait
```

In the **ask block**, click the **text field**. Type **What's the password?**

```
ask [What's·the·password?] and wait
```

Connect the block.

```
when [flag] clicked
  ask [What's·the·password?] and wait
```

COPY THE CODE

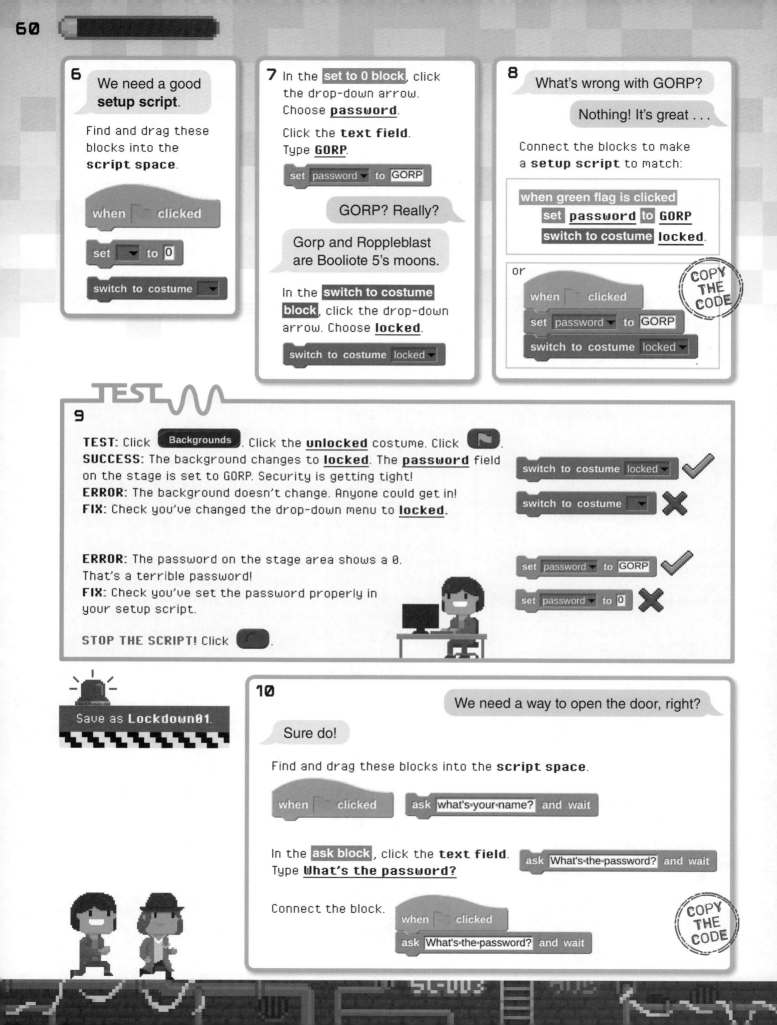

11 The computer checks if the password matches what is typed. Now our if block comes into play.

Find and drag these blocks into the **script space**.

`if`

`answer` `password`

`□ = □` `switch to costume ▼`

12 In the **switch to costume block**, click the drop-down arrow. Choose **unlocked**.

Drag the **answer block** into the left side of the **equals block**. Drag the **password block** into the right side. `answer = password`

Drag the **equals block** into the hexagonal space in the **if block**. `if` ← `answer = password`

13 Don't get put off by the different blocks. Sometimes it helps to think about it a little differently.

Q: What's the password?

ANSWER = PW

TRUE → **OPEN THE DOOR**   FALSE → **DO NOTHING**

is the same as

ask **What's the password?** and wait
if answer = password
switch to costume **unlocked**
else
    do nothing

is the same as

```
when ⚑ clicked
ask What's·the·password? and wait
if ⟨ answer = password ⟩
  switch to costume unlocked ▼
```

That makes sense.

When code makes your head hurt, write it down, draw it, or read it out. Put it together and see how it works.

Connect the blocks in the **script space** to match Glitchbane's example.

COPY THE CODE

TEST

14 Both tests must pass for true success!

TEST: Click ⚑. Type the correct password.
SUCCESS: The door opens! AUTHORIZED!

TEST: Click ⚑. Type the wrong password.
SUCCESS: The door stays locked! UNAUTHORIZED!

ERROR: You typed the correct password, but you're still locked out!
FIX: Check the password is spelled correctly in your code block.

`set password ▼ to GORP` ✔
`set password ▼ to GROP` ✘

STOP THE SCRIPT! Click 🛑.

Save as **Lockdown02**.

ACHIEVEMENT UNLOCKED!
LOGICIAN
LEVEL 1

MISSION OBJECTIVE 2: NEW FEATURES REQUESTED!

You have top-secret files, but nothing happens if someone breaks into your office.

Hmm. We could blow up the building with a mega-blast photon charge, or flood the room with poison gas!

OMG, no! What if YOU forget the password? An alarm should go off or something!

OK, what about sleeping gas to catch the intruder?

REVISION LIST

1. **ADD AN ALARM TO ANNOUNCE UNAUTHORIZED ACCESS!**

2. **ADD SOUND TO ALERT ETAMI AND GLITCHBANE.**

3. **FILL THE ROOM WITH SLEEPING GAS TO PREVENT ESCAPE!**

REVISION 1:
*** ADD AN ALARM TO ANNOUNCE UNAUTHORIZED ACCESS! ***

1

We need a costume for when the alarm goes off.

Click **Backgrounds**.

Right-click the **locked** costume. Choose **duplicate** to make a copy.

Right-click the **locked(2)** costume. Choose **edit**. Add some flashing lights or a warning. Click **OK**.

Right-click the **locked(2) costume**. **Rename** it **alarm**.

2

Now I need to add a costume change!

Connect a **switch to costume block** at the end of your script.

In the **switch to costume block**, click the drop-down arrow. Choose **alarm**.

```
when ⚑ clicked
ask What's the password? and wait
if < answer = password >
    switch to costume unlocked ▾
switch to costume alarm ▾
```

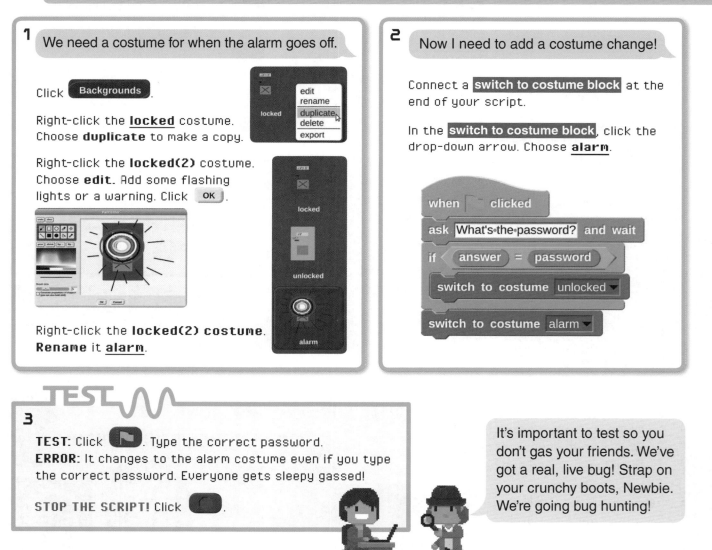

3

TEST: Click 🏳. Type the correct password.
ERROR: It changes to the alarm costume even if you type the correct password. Everyone gets sleepy gassed!

STOP THE SCRIPT! Click ⬭.

It's important to test so you don't gas your friends. We've got a real, live bug! Strap on your crunchy boots, Newbie. We're going bug hunting!

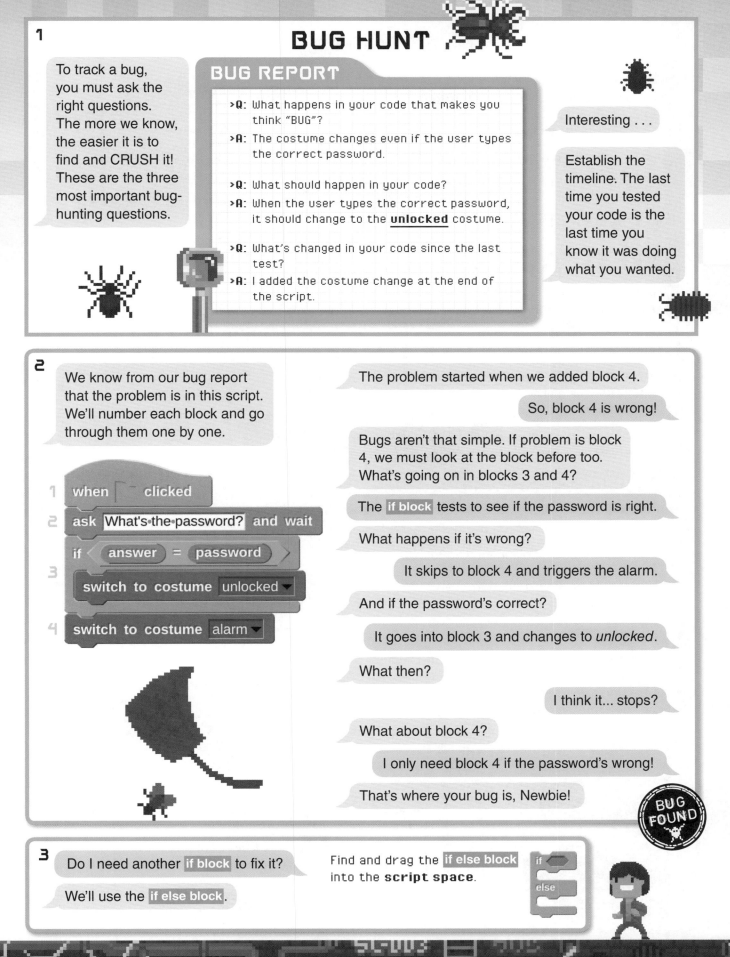

4

What does the **else** bit do?

Else is coder-speak for "otherwise." One thing happens if the predicate is **true**. Another happens if it's **false**.

Q: What's the password?

ANSWER = PW

TRUE → OPEN THE DOOR
FALSE → SOUND ALARM

is the same as

ask for a password
if answer equals password
    then open the door
else/otherwise
    sound alarm

is the same as

```
when ⚑ clicked
ask What's the password? and wait
if < answer = password >
    switch to costume unlocked ▾
else
    switch to costume alarm ▾
```

Change your code to match Glitchbane's.

Click and drag the empty **if block** into the **code menu area** to delete it.

COPY THE CODE

TEST

5

Both tests must pass for true success!

TEST: Click ⚑. Type **GORP**.
SUCCESS: The door opens! AUTHORIZED!

TEST: Click ⚑. Type **ROPPLEBLAST**.
SUCCESS: The alarm costume appears! Intruders caught in the act!

STOP THE SCRIPT! Click ⬤.

BUG FIXED

ACHIEVEMENT UNLOCKED!
BUG-HUNTER
LEVEL 2

Save as **Lockdown03**.

REVISION 2:
*** ADD SOUND TO ALERT ETAMI AND GLITCHBANE ***

1

SOUND! I've been looking forward to this!

This should be simple enough. We only need sound for a few seconds.

Find `repeat 10`. Drag it into the **script space**.

3 Drag and drop the alarm sound to match the code.

COPY THE CODE

```
when ⚑ clicked
ask What's the password? and wait
if < answer = password >
    switch to costume unlocked ▾
else
    repeat 10
        set instrument to 2 ▾
        play note 64 ▾ for 0.5 beats
        play note 72 ▾ for 0.5 beats
    switch to costume alarm ▾
```

EXPERIMENT

2

Click `Sound`. Use `set instrument to 1 ▾` and two `play note 60 ▾ for 0.5 beats` to create an alarm inside `repeat 10`.

Click a single script to check just that one.

Experiment with note numbers to make your own sounds, or try Glitchbane's ideas:

```
repeat 10
    set instrument to 2 ▾
    play note 64 ▾ for 0.5 beats
    play note 72 ▾ for 0.5 beats
```

TEST

4

TEST: Click ⚑. Type **ROPPLEBLAST**.
ERROR: The costume doesn't change until the noise stops! What the. . .?

STOP THE SCRIPT! Click ⬤.

I smell a BUG. Time to hunt!

1

BUG HUNT

BUG REPORT

>**Q**: What happens in your code that makes you think "BUG"?

>**A**: The costume doesn't show until **after** the sound stops.

>**Q**: What should happen in your code?

>**A**: The costume should change **before** the sound plays.

>**Q**: What's changed in your code since the last test?

>**A**: I added the **repeat 10 block** with the sound.

2

What happens in the **else block**?

It plays each note for 0.5 beats.

They repeat 9 more times. Then what?

Then it changes the costume! It waits until the sound finishes?

Got it! Your bug report had the answer: "The costume should change **before** the sound plays."

```
1  when   clicked
2  ask What's-the-password? and wait
3  if < answer = password >
4    switch to costume unlocked
   else
5    repeat  10
5A     set instrument to 2
5B     play note 64 for 0.5 beats
5C     play note 72 for 0.5 beats
6    switch to costume alarm
```

BUG FOUND

3

If I swap blocks 5 and 6, it should work!

Change the order of your code so

switch to costume alarm

runs BEFORE the alarm script.

```
when   clicked
ask What's-the-password? and wait
if < answer = password >
  switch to costume unlocked
else
  switch to costume alarm
  repeat  10
    set instrument to 2
    play note 64 for 0.5 beats
    play note 72 for 0.5 beats
```

4

TEST

TEST: Click 🏳. Type **ROPPLEBLAST**.
SUCCESS: The alarm costume appears and THEN the alarm sounds. Woot!
STOP THE SCRIPT! Click ⬤.

Awesomebeans!

BUG FIXED

Save as **Lockdown04**.

BUG-HUNTER
LEVEL 3

ACHIEVEMENT UNLOCKED!

REVISION 3:
*** FILL THE ROOM WITH SLEEPING GAS TO PREVENT ESCAPE! ***

1

The sleeping gas takes about 10 seconds to work.

So, they fall asleep as the alarm sounds, right?

Find **change ghost effect by 25**.

Drop it into:
```
repeat  10
  set instrument to 2
  play note 64 for 0.5 beats
  play note 72 for 0.5 beats
```
change ghost effect by 25

In the **change effect block**, click the drop-down arrow.

Choose **ghost**.

Click the **text field**. Type **10**.

2

If you change sprites or backgrounds using **Looks blocks**, you must clear them every time you hit the green flag.

Find and drag

clear graphic effects

into the **script space**.

Connect it at the beginning of the **setup script**:

```
when   clicked
clear graphic effects
set password to GORP
switch to costume locked
```

TEST

3

TEST: Click and type in the wrong password
SUCCESS: The alarm sounds as the screen fades to black. Night!
ERROR: It's a bit darker but everyone's awake!
FIX: Is the `change` `ghost` `effect block` in the right place?

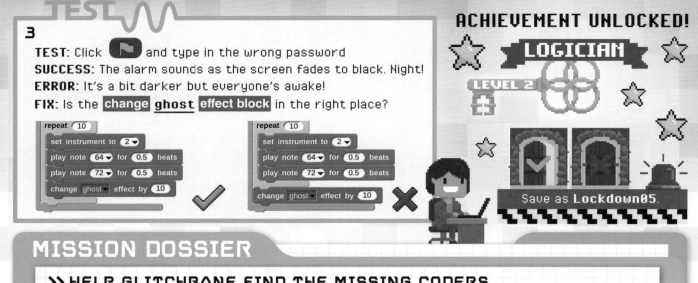

ACHIEVEMENT UNLOCKED!

LOGICIAN

LEVEL 2

Save as **Lockdown05**.

MISSION DOSSIER

›› HELP GLITCHBANE FIND THE MISSING CODERS

The missing VALID coder makes holographic armor. Glitchbane's "Just the Facts" (JTF) interview technique is used by lawmakers the galaxy over. Use it to interview witnesses, who saw an alien make off with the coder, get a description, and check the Digital Database of Dirtbags (DDD) for a match.

LEVEL: 3

INSTRUCTOR: AGENT GLITCHBANE

MISSION OBJECTIVE 1: JUST THE FACTS!

Natterninja says make a project plan. Let's call it. . .

THE INTERROGATOR 4000!

Okaaay. . . What's the goal?

Build a program to interrogate the witnesses and find the suspect in the DDD.

Awesomebeans. How?

Use the questions in my JTF database to interrogate the witnesses! Discover what they saw! Then build a mugshot and send it to the DDD.

PROJECT OUTLINE

NAME:
INTERROGATOR 4000

GOAL:
BUILD A PROGRAM TO INTERROGATE WITNESSES AND FIND THE SUSPECT IN THE DDD.

REQUIREMENTS:
1. ASK GLITCHBANE'S LIST OF QUESTIONS.
2. SCAN THE DDD FOR A MATCH
3. DISPLAY MATCH ON SCREEN

MISSION OBJECTIVE 2: ASK ME YOUR QUESTIONS, BRIDGEKEEPER!

1 Open a web browser. Type **snap.berkeley. edu/run** into your browser bar and hit enter. If you have a Snap! account, log in. Otherwise acquire an adult to help you make an account.

2 Click `Stage`.

Click `Backgrounds`.

Go to the **page menu**. Click **Backgrounds**.

Double-click two different backgrounds. Click **Cancel**.

Project notes...
New   ^N
Open...   ^O
Save   ^S
Save As...
Import...
Export project...
Export summary...
Import tools
Libraries...
Backgrounds...
Sounds...

Right-click each background. Choose **rename**. Name one **interrogation** and one **match found**.

edit
rename
duplicate
delete
export

Night City w

3 Right-click the **match found** background. Choose **edit**. Use

Brush size

and [slider] 5 to paint **MATCH FOUND** on the **match found** background.

interrogation
MATCH FOUND
match found

4 Find and drag these blocks into the **script space**:

when [flag] clicked   when I receive [▼]

switch to costume [▼] × 2

5 In the when I receive block, click the drop-down arrow. Click **new** to create a new broadcast message. Call it **profile complete**. Click **OK**.

In a switch to costume block, click the drop-down arrow. Choose **interrogation**.

In the other switch to costume block, click the drop-down arrow. Choose **match found**.

6 Connect your blocks to create two scripts:

when [flag] clicked
switch to costume Interrogation [▼]

when I receive profile complete [▼]
switch to costume match found [▼]

7 We need an interrogator.

Click [Sprite]. In the sprite **name field**, name the sprite **interrogator**. Click [Costumes]. Then click [brush].

Paint the interrogator. She can be human or alien and any color you like.

When you're done, click **OK**. Right-click the costume. **Rename** it **interrogator.**

8 Find and drag these blocks into the **script space**:

show
when [flag] clicked   go to x: 0 y: 0

Connect the blocks to make a **setup script**.

EXPERIMENT

9 If your interrogator is too big or small, use set size to 100 % in your **setup script**. Lower numbers make it smaller; higher numbers make it bigger!

when [flag] clicked
show
go to x: 0 y: 0
set size to 90 %

TEST

10 How do you start an interrogation?

Find these blocks. Connect them at the end of your script.

say Hello! for 2 secs × 2

Change the **say blocks** to:

We need to get a description to match to our Digital Database of Dirtbags.

Answer carefully. And remember! Just the facts!

COPY THE CODE

when [flag] clicked
show
set size to 90 %
go to x: 0 y: 0
say We·need·to·get·a·description·to·match·to·our·Digital·Database·of·Dirtbags for 2 secs
say Answer·carefully.·And·remember!·Just·the·facts! for 2 secs

11 **TEST:** Click and drag the interrogator to any location on the stage. Click [flag].

SUCCESS: The interrogator moves to the center and reads each line for two seconds.

ERROR: It's so fast I can't read it!

FIX: Change the number of seconds. If it disappears faster than you can read it aloud, it's too fast.

STOP THE SCRIPT! Click [stop].

Save as **Interrogator01.**

12 Each question needs an `ask block` and a `broadcast block`.

Find and connect these blocks to the bottom of the **setup script**.

`ask what's-your-name? and wait` × 6

Change each **text field** to a "JTF" question.

> ➤ Aliens are blue, purple, pink, red, yellow, or green. What color was the alien you saw?
> ------------------------------------
> ➤ Most aliens have between 1 and 6 legs. How many legs were there?
> ------------------------------------
> ➤ Did the alien have markings? Spots? Stripes? Nothing?
> ------------------------------------
> ➤ Aliens have between 1 and 6 eyes. How many eyes did the alien you saw have?
> ------------------------------------
> ➤ What about its head? Did the alien have ears? Or antennae?
> ------------------------------------
> ➤ OK, did it have big, shiny teeth?

13 Find and drag these blocks into the **script space**.

`broadcast ▼` × 7

Click the drop-down arrow in each `broadcast block`. Create a new message for each:

`broadcast` **color**
`broadcast` **legs**
`broadcast` **markings**
`broadcast` **eyes**
`broadcast` **head**
`broadcast` **teeth**
`broadcast` **profile complete**

Insert the matching `broadcast block` after each question. The **profile complete** `broadcast` goes at the end.

14 How do you test these? Nothing happens when we ask questions.

I'll show you a trade secret.

In the `sensing blocks` code menu area, click the **check box** next to ☑ `answer`.

The answer shows on the stage.

`answer`

15

The sprites can see what's typed but we need to send a message to tell them when there's a new answer.

That's why we broadcast after each question!

Exactly! Run your code and see the answer change.

TEST: Click 🏴.
SUCCESS: All the questions come up! The answers appear in the answer box!
ERROR: There's a question missing.
FIX: Add any missing questions. Without them, it's hard to get a match!

STOP THE SCRIPT! Click ⬤.

16 When we're done, we'll fade out the interrogator.

Find and drag these blocks into the **script space**.

`when I receive ▼` `hide`

In the `when I receive block`, click the drop-down arrow. Choose **profile complete**.

Connect the `hide block`.

17

TEST: Click 🏴.
SUCCESS: The interrogator disappears after the questioning!

STOP THE SCRIPT! Click ⬤.

Save as **Interrogator02**.

1
Click ▶ to make a new sprite.

Click the new sprite's **name field**.
Name it **body**.

body
☑ draggable

2
Most aliens are naturally round. We're on a blue planet, so let's make this alien blue.

Go to Costumes .
Create a new costume by clicking 🖌.

Click the **check box**. ☑ Constrain proportions of shapes? (you can also hold shift)

Choose a blue in the **color bar**.

3
Click ⬤ . Click in the middle of the screen. Drag outwards to make a circle.

Click **OK** to save your costume.

Right-click the costume and **rename** it **blue**.

Save as **Interrogator03**.

4
Alrighty, we need a setup script, Newbie!

Find and drag these blocks into the **script space**.

when ⚑ clicked

hide

go to x: 0 y: 0

point in direction 90 ▾

5
Connect the blocks to make a **setup script**. Check the values in the blue blocks match this code.

when ⚑ clicked
go to x: 0 y: 0
point in direction 90 ▾
hide

COPY THE CODE

HINT ✕

If the sprite is wonky or in the wrong place, right-click it in the costume tab and choose **edit**.

Click ⊕ . Move the cross into the center of your circle.

Click **OK**.

blue
edit
rename
duplicate
delete
export

OK

6
Add a script to show the results at the end.

Find and drag these blocks into the **script space**:

when I receive ▾   show

Click the drop-down menu. Change the broadcast to **profile complete**.

when I receive profile complete ▾
show

Connect the blocks.

7
Are you ready for the fun part?

Find and drag these blocks into the **script space**:

when I receive ▾

set ghost ▾ effect to 0   answer   if ◇

In the **when I receive block** and the **set effect block**, click the drop-down arrows. Choose **color**.

8

We'll change the suspect's color based on what the witness says. This might take a few tries.

Do or do not! There is no try! That's a movie quote!

From a non-coder! Figure out why and try again. That's a supercoder quote!

Click **Looks**.

Click **show** to make the **body sprite** visible.

10

Now for lots of green hexagons, which are **operators**. They're the backbone of an **if block**.

I've used the equals before!

That block is an **equality**. It's true if both sides of the equals sign are the same. It's like math: if I say it had 2+4 legs, I'm saying it had 6 legs, because 2+4=6.

Weird thing to say, but yeah, 6 legs is the same as 2+4 legs!

Click **Operators**.

Find and drag the **equality operator** into the **script space**.

TEST

12

Let's run a quick test.

TEST: Click 🏳. Type **purple**.
SUCCESS: The purple body appears!

STOP THE SCRIPT! Click ⬤.

body

EXPERIMENT

9

Computers use numbers for colors. Changing the numbers in your **set color block** changes your sprite's color. Its costume is blue, so blue is color 0. Try to make it purple.

Change the number in **set color effect to 0**. Click it to run just this block. The body sprite will change color.

What number makes it purple? Purple is close to blue, so try lower numbers first.

Cool! So if I can change it in the block, I don't have to make a new costume for every color?

Nope! We can just write a script!

11

If our witness says the alien is purple, we'll change the body sprite to purple.

If the answer is the same as "purple", then let's set the color effect to 20.

Good choice.

Q: What color was the alien you saw?

ANSWER = **purple**

TRUE / FALSE

set color effect to 20 | do nothing

is the same as

What color was the alien you saw?
**if answer is the same as purple
then set color effect to 20
else/otherwise**
do nothing

is the same as

```
if < answer = purple >
  set color ▼ effect to 20
```

Connect the blocks to make the script.

Attach it under **when I receive color ▼**

COPY THE CODE

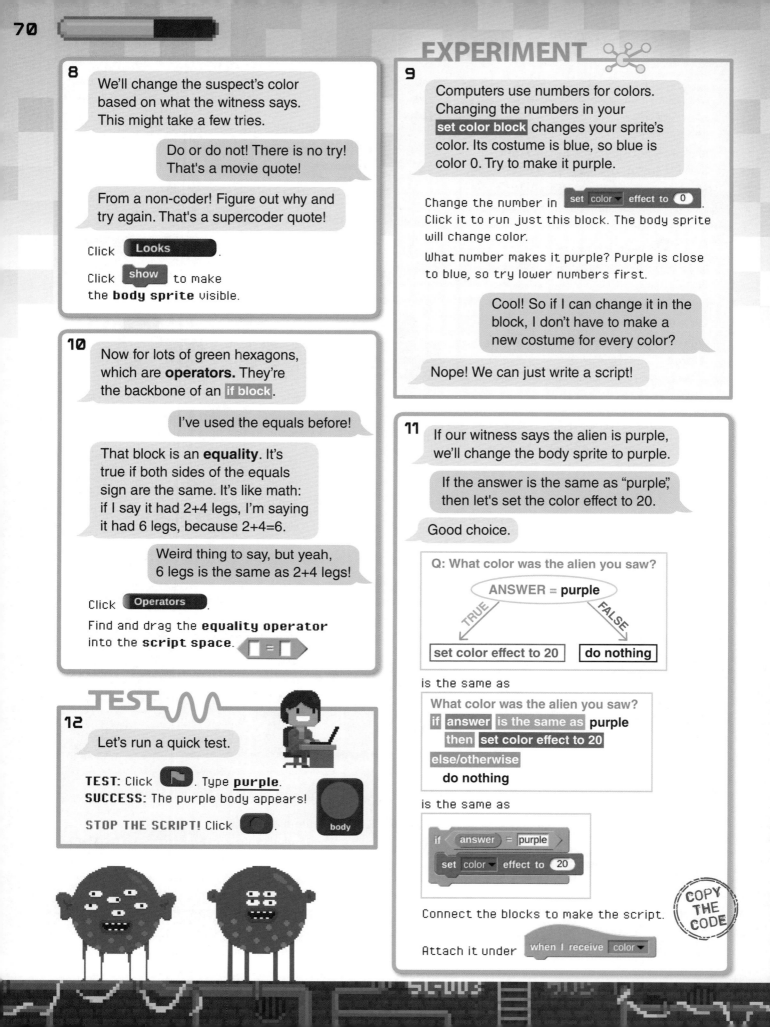

13 Next color, Newbie!

Find and drag these blocks into the **script space**:

if

⬡ = ⬡

answer

set ghost effect to 0

Put them together to say:
**if answer = blue
set color effect to 0**

Attach the new blocks to the bottom of your script.

when I receive color ▾
if ⟨ answer = purple ⟩
  set color ▾ effect to 20
if ⟨ answer = blue ⟩
  set color ▾ effect to 0

TEST

14

TEST: Click 🏳.
Type **purple** for the body.

SUCCESS: The body sprite is purple!

TEST: Click 🏳.
Type **blue** for the body.

SUCCESS: The body sprite is blue!

STOP THE SCRIPT! Click ⬤.

body

Save as **Interrogator04**.

HINT

Only right-click the block you want to duplicate! If you click too high, you'll copy the starter block. If you click the inner blocks, you'll only copy those!

OK

---

15 Right-click the **if block** you created. Choose **duplicate**.

Attach the duplicated block to the bottom of your script.

when I receive color ▾
if ⟨ answer = purple ⟩
  set color ▾ effect to 20
if ⟨ answer   blue ⟩
  help...   ct to 0
  relabel...
  duplicate

---

16 Duplicate the **if blocks** until you have six blocks in your script.

when I receive color ▾
if ⟨ answer = purple ⟩
  set color ▾ effect to 20
if ⟨ answer = blue ⟩
  set color ▾ effect to 0
if ⟨ answer = blue ⟩
  set color ▾ effect to 0
if ⟨ answer = blue ⟩
  set color ▾ effect to 0
if ⟨ answer = blue ⟩
  set color ▾ effect to 0
if ⟨ answer = blue ⟩
  set color ▾ effect to 0

---

17 Change the **if blocks** to test for blue, purple, pink, red, yellow, or green.

Change the new **answer = blue blocks**, so each blocks checks for a different color.

when I receive color ▾
if ⟨ answer = purple ⟩
  set color ▾ effect to 20
if ⟨ answer = blue ⟩
  set color ▾ effect to 0
if ⟨ answer = red ⟩
  set color ▾ effect to 0
if ⟨ answer = pink ⟩
  set color ▾ effect to 0
if ⟨ answer = yellow ⟩
  set color ▾ effect to 0
if ⟨ answer = green ⟩
  set color ▾ effect to 0

TEST

18

TEST: Click 🏳. Type **red**.
ERROR: It doesn't change!

STOP THE SCRIPT! Click ⬤.

Why doesn't it change?

1 BUG HUNT

You handle this, Newbie.

BUG REPORT

>Q: What happens in your code that makes you think "BUG"?

>A: When I type red, the body sprite is blue or purple.

>Q: What should happen in your code?

>A: The color should turn red!

>Q: What's changed in your code since the last test?

>A: I duplicated four **if blocks** and changed them for when someone types "pink", "red", "yellow", or "green".

It was working last test. Blue and purple work.

Are you sure? A bug can turn good code bad . . .

INVESTIGATE FURTHER

2

TEST 1: Click 🚩. Type **blue**.
TEST 2: Click 🚩. Type **purple**.
SUCCESS: They work!

STOP THE SCRIPT! Click ⬤.

It's my job to ask: are you sure you typed it correctly?

Mostly. . .

There's an easy way to check. Look in the answer variable on the stage. It shows the last thing that was typed. The error happened when you typed "red". Try again.

HINT

If `answer` isn't visible on the stage area, click `Sensing`. Click the check box next to answer.

✔ `answer`   OK

3

TEST: Click 🚩.
Type **red**.

It's "red" on the stage!

Maybe it's spelled wrong in the code blocks? The answer and code wouldn't be the same: they wouldn't be equal!

Nope. It's r-e-d in the code block and r-e-d in the answer.

You're right. The bug is somewhere else. Let's break it down.

5

TEST: Click 🚩. Type **red**.
SUCCESS: The body changes to sort of red. . . but NOT blue or purple!

STOP THE SCRIPT! Click ⬤.

The rest probably have the same problem!

Duplicating code makes sneaky bugs.

4

Line 1 compares the answer with the word "red".

```
1  if  answer  =  red
2  set color ▾ effect to  0
```

That works. It's the same as the blue and purple code, and they work. Line 2 changes the color effect, but how?

Computers use numbers for colors. Blue is 0, purple is 20.

What's red?

Around 65 to 75.

A-ha! This code IS doing what I told it to! When I type "red", the code happens, but it doesn't change it to red because the number is wrong!

Pax, you've cracked the case!

Change the number in the **set color effect block** to **75**.

```
set color ▾ effect to  75
```

BUG FOUND

EXPERIMENT

6

```
when I receive color ▼
if   answer = purple
  set color ▼ effect to 20
if   answer = blue
  set color ▼ effect to 0
if   answer = red
  set color ▼ effect to 75
if   answer = pink
  set color ▼ effect to 45
if   answer = yellow
  set color ▼ effect to 95
if   answer = green
  set color ▼ effect to 130
```

Change the numbers in each **if block** so the body is always the right color. Experiment with different colors.

TEST

7

Make sure all colors are right.

Before each test, click 🏴.
TEST: First, answer **purple**.
  Answer **blue**.
  Answer **red**.
  Answer **pink**.
  Answer **yellow**.
  Answer **green**.

SUCCESS: The colors match what's typed. Color BOSS!

BUG FIXED

Save as **Interrogator05**.

ACHIEVEMENT UNLOCKED!
BUG-HUNTER
LEVEL 4

HINT

To run individual blocks by themselves without running the whole script, click

`set color ▼ effect to 90`

OK

QUESTION 2: HOW MANY LEGS WERE THERE?

1

Can it have more than two legs? You have two . . .

That's to blend in on Earth. I normally have four. DDD aliens have between 1 and 6 legs. Let's draw more costumes.

Right-click the **body sprite button**. Choose **duplicate** to create a copy.

```
body
  show
  duplicate
  clone
  delete
  parent...
  export...
```

2

Rename it before we get six bodies and one leg.

Click 🔘 . Click sprite **name field**. Rename the **body(2) sprite legs**.

```
legs
✓ draggable
```

3

We need most of the body code for our legs code. We use the body costume as a base so our legs have a starting position, a color, and face the same way as the body.

Click the **legs sprite button**.
Click **Costumes**.

Right-click the **blue costume**. Choose **duplicate**.

```
  show
  duplicate
  clone
  delete
  parent...
  export...
```

Right-click the new costume. Choose **edit** to bring up the **paint editor**.

4

Draw a leg in a different blue to the body. Start inside the body circle and finish under it.

You can use ╲ or 🖌 .

Make it thicker with: `Brush size [====] 5`

Erase the body using 🪣 in transparent mode.

To use transparent mode, click the checkered part of: ▆▆▆▆▆▆░░░
If you make a mistake, click **undo**.

Once you've drawn a leg, click **OK** to save.
Right-click your leg.
Rename your leg costume **one**.

```
blue(2)
  edit
  rename
  duplicate
  delete
  export
```

5 Good. There's five more to make but we know what we're working with.

Or "walking" with?

...

Right-click 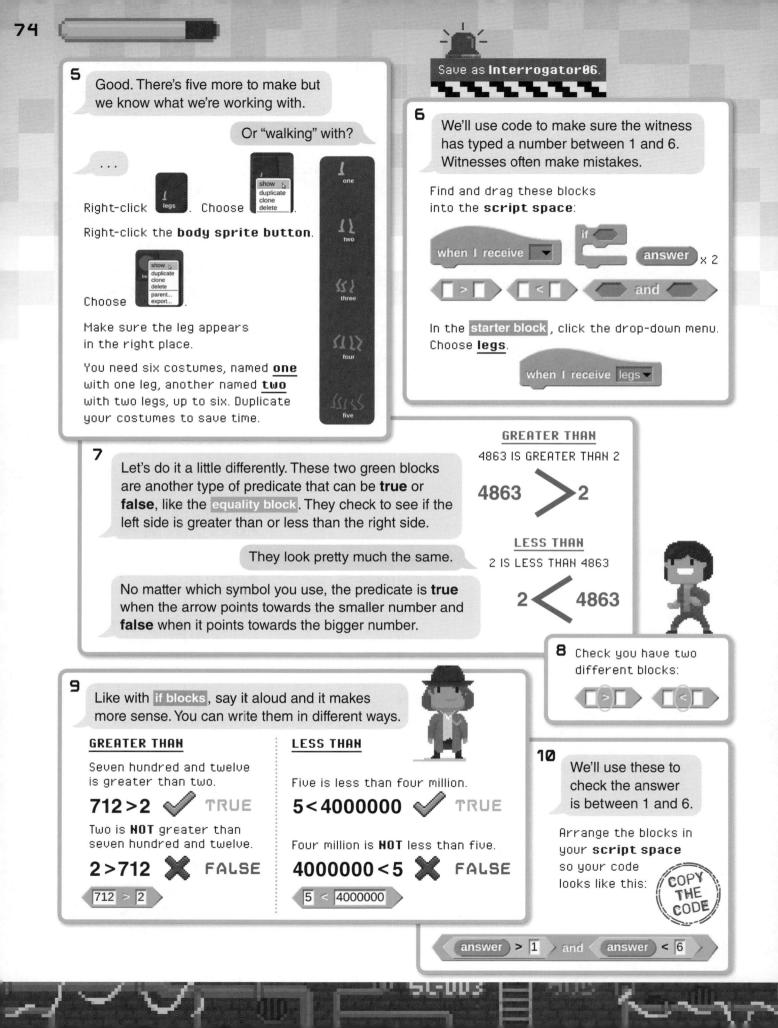 . Choose **show**.

Right-click the **body sprite button**.

Choose **show**.

Make sure the leg appears in the right place.

You need six costumes, named **one** with one leg, another named **two** with two legs, up to six. Duplicate your costumes to save time.

one
two
three
four
five

Save as **Interrogator06**.

6 We'll use code to make sure the witness has typed a number between 1 and 6. Witnesses often make mistakes.

Find and drag these blocks into the **script space**:

when I receive ▼   if   answer × 2

☐ > ☐   ☐ < ☐   and

In the **starter block**, click the drop-down menu. Choose **legs**.

when I receive legs ▼

7 Let's do it a little differently. These two green blocks are another type of predicate that can be **true** or **false**, like the **equality block**. They check to see if the left side is greater than or less than the right side.

They look pretty much the same.

No matter which symbol you use, the predicate is **true** when the arrow points towards the smaller number and **false** when it points towards the bigger number.

GREATER THAN
4863 IS GREATER THAN 2

4863 > 2

LESS THAN
2 IS LESS THAN 4863

2 < 4863

8 Check you have two different blocks:

☐ > ☐   ☐ < ☐

9 Like with **if blocks**, say it aloud and it makes more sense. You can write them in different ways.

GREATER THAN

Seven hundred and twelve is greater than two.

712 > 2 ✓ TRUE

Two is **NOT** greater than seven hundred and twelve.

2 > 712 ✗ FALSE

712 > 2

LESS THAN

Five is less than four million.

5 < 4000000 ✓ TRUE

Four million is **NOT** less than five.

4000000 < 5 ✗ FALSE

5 < 4000000

10 We'll use these to check the answer is between 1 and 6.

Arrange the blocks in your **script space** so your code looks like this:

COPY THE CODE

answer > 1   and   answer < 6

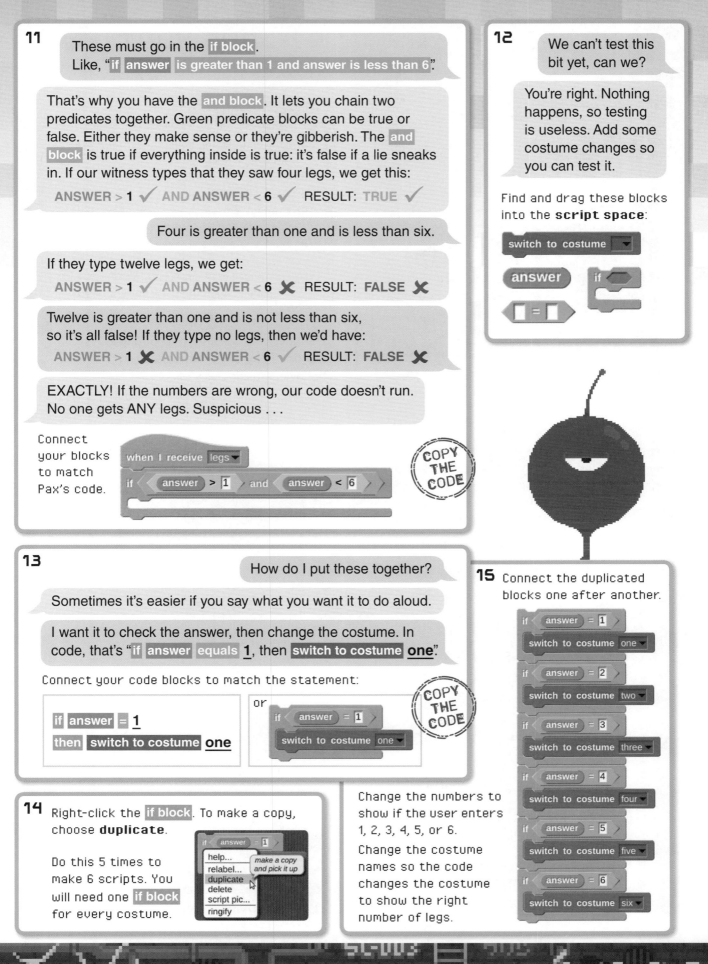

11 These must go in the if block.
Like, "if answer is greater than 1 and answer is less than 6".

That's why you have the and block. It lets you chain two predicates together. Green predicate blocks can be true or false. Either they make sense or they're gibberish. The and block is true if everything inside is true: it's false if a lie sneaks in. If our witness types that they saw four legs, we get this:

ANSWER > 1 ✓ AND ANSWER < 6 ✓ RESULT: TRUE ✓

Four is greater than one and is less than six.

If they type twelve legs, we get:

ANSWER > 1 ✓ AND ANSWER < 6 ✗ RESULT: FALSE ✗

Twelve is greater than one and is not less than six, so it's all false! If they type no legs, then we'd have:

ANSWER > 1 ✗ AND ANSWER < 6 ✓ RESULT: FALSE ✗

EXACTLY! If the numbers are wrong, our code doesn't run. No one gets ANY legs. Suspicious . . .

Connect your blocks to match Pax's code.

when I receive legs
if ⟨ ⟨ answer > 1 ⟩ and ⟨ answer < 6 ⟩ ⟩

COPY THE CODE

12 We can't test this bit yet, can we?

You're right. Nothing happens, so testing is useless. Add some costume changes so you can test it.

Find and drag these blocks into the **script space**:

switch to costume ▾

answer   if ⬡

☐ = ☐

13 How do I put these together?

Sometimes it's easier if you say what you want it to do aloud.

I want it to check the answer, then change the costume. In code, that's "if answer equals 1, then switch to costume one".

Connect your code blocks to match the statement:

if answer = 1
then switch to costume one

or

if ⟨ answer = 1 ⟩
switch to costume one ▾

COPY THE CODE

14 Right-click the if block. To make a copy, choose **duplicate**.

Do this 5 times to make 6 scripts. You will need one if block for every costume.

if ⟨ answer = 1 ⟩
help...   make a copy
relabel...   and pick it up
duplicate
delete
script pic...
ringify

15 Connect the duplicated blocks one after another.

if ⟨ answer = 1 ⟩
switch to costume one ▾
if ⟨ answer = 2 ⟩
switch to costume two ▾
if ⟨ answer = 3 ⟩
switch to costume three ▾
if ⟨ answer = 4 ⟩
switch to costume four ▾
if ⟨ answer = 5 ⟩
switch to costume five ▾
if ⟨ answer = 6 ⟩
switch to costume six ▾

Change the numbers to show if the user enters 1, 2, 3, 4, 5, or 6.
Change the costume names so the code changes the costume to show the right number of legs.

16 Click the top `if block` and drag them all inside the `when I receive` `legs` script.

```
when I receive legs
if  answer > 1  and  answer < 6
    if  answer = 1
        switch to costume one
    if  answer = 2
        switch to costume two
    if  answer = 3
        switch to costume three
    if  answer = 4
        switch to costume four
    if  answer = 5
        switch to costume five
    if  answer = 6
        switch to costume six
```

TEST

17

TEST: Click 🏳.
Type **1** for legs.
ERROR: It has no legs!

STOP THE SCRIPT!
Click ⬤.

TEST

2

Before each test, click 🏳.

TEST: First, answer **2**. **RESULT:** The sprite has two legs!
Answer **3**. **RESULT:** The sprite has three legs!
Answer **4**. **RESULT:** The sprite has four legs!
Answer **5**. **RESULT:** The sprite has five legs!
Answer **6**. **RESULT:** The sprite has no legs!

STOP THE SCRIPT! Click ⬤.

There's a problem with 1 and 6.

3

Lines 4, 5, 6, and 7 work.

They're the same as lines 3 and 8, so it's not them either.

Line 2 then.

What happens if the user types 1?

It checks if the answer is greater than 1. Wait! Is 1 greater than 1?

If two things are equal, they can't be greater than or less than.

6 doesn't work because 6 isn't **less than 6**! Change it to "greater than 0 and less than 7"!

1

BUG HUNT

A bug! Let's crush it!

BUG REPORT

> **Q:** What happens in your code that makes you think "BUG"?
> **A:** I answer **1 leg** and none appear!
> **Q:** What should happen in your code?
> **A:** The legs sprite should change to costume one with **one** leg
> **Q:** What's changed in your code since the last test?
> **A:** I've drawn legs costumes, used > and < symbols, and added costume changes.

1 should be a valid answer! Strange … I wonder if any other numbers are behaving suspiciously?

Test the other numbers?

```
1  when I receive legs
2  if  answer > 1  and  answer < 6
3      if  answer = 1
           switch to costume one
4      if  answer = 2
           switch to costume two
5      if  answer = 3
           switch to costume three
6      if  answer = 4
           switch to costume four
7      if  answer = 5
           switch to costume five
8      if  answer = 6
           switch to costume six
```

BUG FOUND

Change the numbers.

```
when I receive legs
if  answer > (1)  and  answer < (6)
```

4

TEST: Click 🏳. Answer **1**.
SUCCESS: A one-legged sprite appears!

TEST: Click 🏳. Answer **6**.
SUCCESS: A six-legged sprite appears!

STOP THE SCRIPT! Click ⬤.

BUG FIXED

ACHIEVEMENT UNLOCKED!
BUG-HUNTER
LEVEL 5

Save as **Interrogator07**.

QUESTION 3: DID THE ALIEN HAVE MARKINGS? SPOTS? STRIPES? NOTHING?

1

Alien markings are like human fingerprints. This could break the case wide open. We'll add a question about the marking color, but only if they answer "stripes" or "spots".

We need an **if block**?

And a predicate called an **or block**.

Click [interroga]. Then click **Scripts**.

Find and drag these blocks into the **script space**:

if | or | [ ] = [ ] x 2
broadcast ▾ | answer x 2
ask what's your name? and wait

2

Or blocks work a bit like **and blocks**, but instead of both sides having to be true, only one side does. Use this when there is more than one correct answer. If the witness types "stripes", we get:

ANSWER = **STRIPES** ✓ OR ANSWER = **SPOTS** ✗ RESULT: TRUE ✓

And if the witness types "spots", we get:

ANSWER = **STRIPES** ✗ OR ANSWER = **SPOTS** ✓ RESULT: TRUE ✓

Exactly! But if the witness types "nothing", we have:

ANSWER = **STRIPES** ✗ OR ANSWER = **SPOTS** ✗ RESULT: FALSE ✗

3

Click and drag the **answer blocks** into the left sides of the **equals blocks**. Type **stripes** and **spots** in the right sides.

Click and drag the **equals blocks** into the left and right fields of the **or block**.

In the **ask block**, type **What color were they?**.

In the **broadcast block**, click the drop-down arrow. Choose **new** to make a new **broadcast message**. Call it **marking color**. Click **OK**.

Connect the blocks to match:

```
if < answer = stripes > or < answer = spots >
    ask What color were they? and wait

broadcast marking color ▾
```

COPY THE CODE

4

Insert the block into your script after the **broadcast markings block**.

```
when 🏳 clicked
show
set size to 90 %
go to x: 0 y: 0
say We need to get a description to match to our Digital Database of Dirtbags for 2 secs
say Answer carefully. And remember! Just the facts! for 2 secs
ask Aliens are blue, purple, pink, red, yellow, or green. What color was the alien you saw? and wait
broadcast color ▾
ask Most aliens have between 1 and 6 legs. How many legs were there? and wait
broadcast legs ▾
ask Did the alien have markings? Spots? Stripes? Nothing? and wait
broadcast markings ▾
if < answer = stripes > or < answer = spots >
    ask What color were they? and wait
broadcast marking color ▾
```

COPY THE CODE

TEST

5

TEST: Click 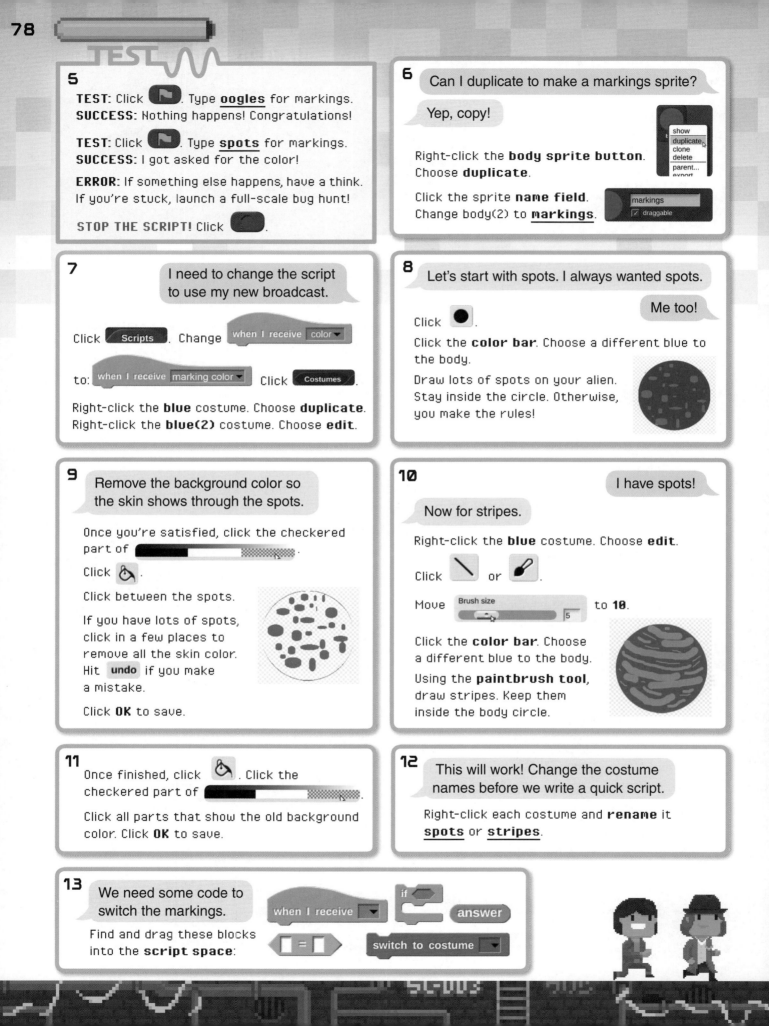. Type **oogles** for markings.
SUCCESS: Nothing happens! Congratulations!

TEST: Click . Type **spots** for markings.
SUCCESS: I got asked for the color!

ERROR: If something else happens, have a think. If you're stuck, launch a full-scale bug hunt!

STOP THE SCRIPT! Click .

6

Can I duplicate to make a markings sprite?

Yep, copy!

Right-click the **body sprite button**. Choose **duplicate**.

show
duplicate
clone
delete
parent...
export

Click the sprite **name field**. Change body(2) to **markings**.

markings
✓ draggable

7

I need to change the script to use my new broadcast.

Click **Scripts**. Change **when I receive color ▾**

to: **when I receive marking color ▾** Click **Costumes**

Right-click the **blue** costume. Choose **duplicate**. Right-click the **blue(2)** costume. Choose **edit**.

8

Let's start with spots. I always wanted spots.

Me too!

Click ●.

Click the **color bar**. Choose a different blue to the body.

Draw lots of spots on your alien. Stay inside the circle. Otherwise, you make the rules!

9

Remove the background color so the skin shows through the spots.

Once you're satisfied, click the checkered part of .

Click .

Click between the spots.

If you have lots of spots, click in a few places to remove all the skin color. Hit **undo** if you make a mistake.

Click **OK** to save.

10

I have spots!

Now for stripes.

Right-click the **blue** costume. Choose **edit**.

Click \ or .

Move **Brush size** 5 to **10**.

Click the **color bar**. Choose a different blue to the body.

Using the **paintbrush tool**, draw stripes. Keep them inside the body circle.

11

Once finished, click . Click the checkered part of .

Click all parts that show the old background color. Click **OK** to save.

12

This will work! Change the costume names before we write a quick script.

Right-click each costume and **rename** it **spots** or **stripes**.

13

We need some code to switch the markings.

Find and drag these blocks into the **script space**:

when I receive ▾   if

answer

[ ] = [ ]   **switch to costume ▾**

14 In the `when I receive block`, click the drop-down arrow. Choose **markings**.

Drag the `answer block` into the left side of the `equals block`. Type **spots** in the right side.

In the `switch to costume block`, click the drop-down arrow. Choose **spots**.

Connect the blocks to match:

```
when I receive  markings ▼
if  answer  =  spots
  switch to costume  spots ▼
```

COPY THE CODE

15 The code for stripes is the same, right?

Right-click the `if block`. **Duplicate** the new code. Make the changes for stripes.

Connect the duplicated block to the bottom of your script.

```
if  answer  =  stripes
  switch to costume  stripes ▼
```

TEST ∿

16

TEST: Click 🏳. Answer **stripes**.
SUCCESS: We have stripes! OMG!

TEST: Click 🏳. Answer **spots**.
SUCCESS: We have spots! COOL!

ERROR: No spots. No stripes. It's the worst. It might be time for a bug hunt!

STOP THE SCRIPT! Click ⬤.

You've done well finding bugs, Pax. Now it's time to run your own bug hunts when they're needed. Don't forget to do a bug report with the three bug-hunting questions!

Save as **Interrogator08**.

QUESTION 4: ALIENS HAVE BETWEEN 1 AND 6 EYES. HOW MANY EYES DID THE ALIEN YOU SAW HAVE?

1 Eyes tell you a lot. Let's see what the suspect's eyes tell us.

Right-click `legs`. Choose **duplicate**.

Click the sprite **name field. Rename** your sprite **eyes**.

2 We need costumes for the eyes. We'll borrow the body sprite's costume.

Click the **body sprite button**.

Click `Costumes`.

Click and drag the **blue** costume over the **eye** sprite.

3 The body costume appears when I click the eyes sprite!

Click the **eyes sprite button.** Check the **body costume** shows up.

Drag all the **legs costumes** into the **code menu area** to delete.

Right-click the **body costume.** Duplicate it until you have six copies.

Rename each copy, so there's **one, two, three, four, five**, and **six**.

4 Right-click costume **one**. Choose **edit**.

In the top half of the circle, draw one alien eye. The ⬤ and ╲ are handy here.

Once your eye is perfect, click 🪣. Click the checkered area of ▬▬▬▬▬▦.

Click in the blue body to remove the color. Click **OK**. Repeat for each costume until you have six eye costumes.

Drawing eyes is creepy.

True, but if it gets us closer to our bad guy, it's worth it.

Save as **Interrogator09**.

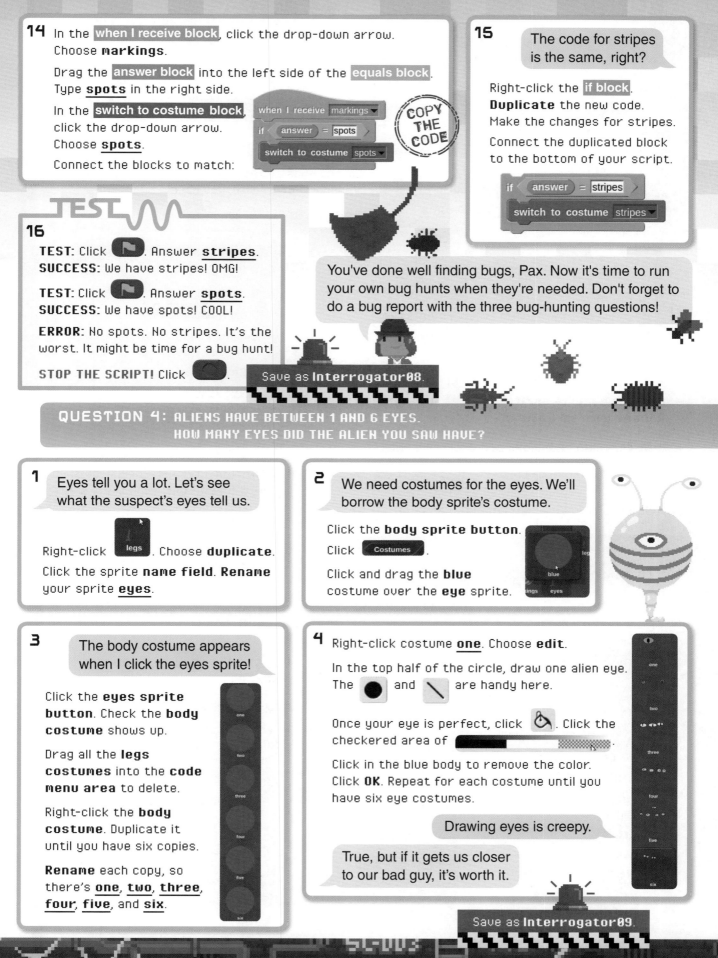

5 We duplicated this sprite. Let's check that everything's OK.

Go to the **script space**:

Click `when I receive color ▼`.

Drag the whole script into the code menu area to delete it.

In the `when I receive legs block`, click the drop-down arrow. Change **legs** to **eyes**.

TEST

6

Before each test, click 🏳.
TEST: First, answer **1**. Answer **2**.
Answer **3**. Answer **4**.
Answer **5**. Answer **6**.

SUCCESS: The correct number of eyes appears!

ERROR: The number of eyes doesn't match what's typed.

FIX: Check your costumes are named correctly and the eyes script is not listening for the **legs** broadcast. Otherwise, you need a bug hunt.

STOP THE SCRIPT! Click ⬤.

QUESTION 5: WHAT ABOUT ITS HEAD? DID THE ALIEN HAVE EARS? OR ANTENNAE?

1 Most aliens hear soundwaves with ears like humans or ultrasonically with antennae.

Right-click the **body** sprite.
Choose **duplicate** to make a copy.

Click the **body(2) sprite**. Click the sprite **name field**. **Rename** your sprite **head**.

We'll use the body color script for this sprite.

I just need a costume.

One costume for antennae and one for ears, Pax.

2 Click `Costumes`.

Right-click the **blue** costume.
Choose **duplicate** to make a copy.

Rename your costumes **ears** and **antennae**.

3 Edit the **ears costume**. Draw ears around the blue circle. Choose the **fill tool**. Click the checkered area of the **tone bar**. Click the body to remove the blue. Click **OK**.

Edit the antennae costume by drawing antennae on top of the body circle. Click **OK**.

4 Looking good! Now our code is simple.

Find and drag these blocks into the **script space**:

I think I know this!

`when I receive ▼`   `if ◄ ⬦` x 2   `[ ] = [ ]` x 2

`answer` x 2   `switch to costume ▼` x 2

TEST

6

TEST: Click 🏳. Type **ears** for head.
SUCCESS: Our suspect has ears!

TEST: Click 🏳.
Type **antennae** for head.

SUCCESS: Our suspect has waving antennae!

ERROR: No ears. No antennae. It's the worst. It might be time for a bug hunt!

STOP THE SCRIPT! Click ⬤.

I'm impressed. We're nearly there!

5 In the `when I receive block`, click the drop-down arrow. Choose **head**.

Drag the `answer blocks` into the right sides of the `equals blocks`. Type **ears** and **antennae** in the left sides.

In the `switch to costume blocks`, click the drop-down arrows. Choose **antennae** and **ears**.

COPY THE CODE

Connect the blocks to match:

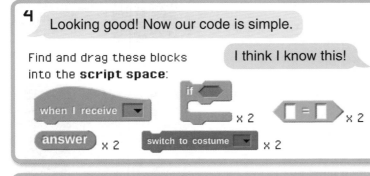

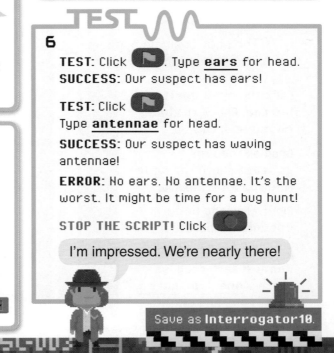

Save as **Interrogator10**.

QUESTION 6: OK, DID IT HAVE BIG, SHINY TEETH?

1 One last question. Then we'll run this program.

Right-click the **body** sprite. Choose **duplicate**.

Click the **body(2)** sprite. Click the sprite **name field**. Rename your sprite **teeth**.

Click **Costumes**. Rename your costume **no teeth**.

2 Right-click the **no teeth costume**. Choose **edit**.

Draw a mouth shape or lips in the bottom half of the screen.

Click the **fill tool**. Click the checkered area of the **tone bar**. Click the **blue body color** to remove it.

Click **OK**.

3 Once more with teeth!

Right-click the **no teeth costume**. Choose **duplicate**.
Right-click **no teeth(2)**. Rename it **teeth**.
Right-click the **teeth costume**. Choose **edit**.
Add teeth to the mouth. Click **OK**.

4 I think my code should look like:

```
when teeth is broadcast
if answer = yes
    switch to costume teeth
if answer = no
    switch to costume no teeth
```

5 It's almost identical to the head script. Can I copy that script without copying the whole sprite?

Sure!

Click the **head sprite button**.

Click and drag the script until it's over the **teeth sprite button** (it will be highlighted). Then drop it.

Click the **teeth sprite button**. See if your new script is there.

In the teeth sprite **scripts space**, change the drop-down menus to work for this sprite.

6 Make sure your code matches Pax's:

```
when I receive teeth
if answer = yes
    switch to costume teeth
if answer = no
    switch to costume no teeth
```

COPY THE CODE

7 TEST

TEST: Click 🚩. Type **yes** for teeth.
SUCCESS: Our alien munches anything!

TEST: Click 🚩. Type **no** for teeth.
SUCCESS: No teeth! Our alien eats jelly.
ERROR: Put on your bug-hunting boots!

STOP THE SCRIPT! Click ⬤.

Save as **Interrogator11**.

Amazing work! I'll start running our witnesses through the Interrogator 4000.

Will my code help find the coders?

It might be the breakthrough that cracks this case wide open, Pax. Soon we'll have some leads. Agent Finity will put together a field team.

NEW MESSAGE ✖

Help Agent Finity run her field team through some loops to rescue the coders?

Y/H

CO-ORDINATES AND LOOPS

with Agent Finity

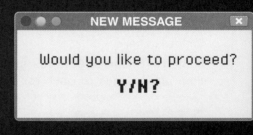

NEW MESSAGE

Would you like to proceed?

Y/N?

It's your fourth training session at VALID. You've learned about coding, broadcasts, predicates, and the mysterious world of bughunting.

You've also learned that CORUPT, a mysterious organization, is kidnapping coders. You've been working with Agent Glitchbane, VALID's lead investigator, to get to the bottom of the latest kidnapping. Maybe your work has turned up something useful. . .

ETAMI, I've been looking for you. Glitchbane sent me her report of the witness interrogations she did with the new recruit!

That would be me!

You worked on this code with Glitchbane? Thanks to this, we've got a suspected CORUPT agent in custody.

Pax does not have clearance for that information, Agent Finity.

Pfft! Pax is the only reason we have this information.

True. Protocols have already been broken.

Did the code get us any closer to the missing agents?

Maybe. We've found a coded message on our suspect. We think it's a landing point on a remote island owned by CORUPT.

Potential Agent X is not trained for field work, Agent Finity.

I can try!

No, too dangerous for a rookie. If my info pans out, we'll send in a team. They need us to be at the top of our game back here, Pax. Can you do that?

NEW MESSAGE ❌

Go with Finity to protect a team of highly specialized field agents on a covert op inside a suspected enemy stronghold?

Y/N

MISSION DOSSIER

>> DISCOVER THE POWER OF LOOPS

VALID has captured a mid-level CORUPT agent. His tracker links him to a remote deserted island. Satellite imagery shows a network of tunnels. A secret base? Help Agent Finity use loops to investigate.

LEVEL: 4

INSTRUCTOR: AGENT FINITY

BACKGROUND: Agent Finity is equally good in the field and behind a keyboard. Trained as a gymnast, she loves the fast-moving art of parkour and has a natural skill with the complex loops of programmatic flow.

FINITY

MISSION OBJECTIVE 1: COORDINATING OUR POSITION

PROJECT OUTLINE

NAME: X MARKS THE SPOT

GOAL: FIGURE OUT WHAT THE MYSTERIOUS NUMBERS SENT BY THE KIDNAPPED CODERS MEAN.

REQUIREMENTS: USE COORDINATES TO PLOT THE NUMBERS ON THE STAGE AND SEE IF THEY TURN UP ANYTHING.

1 One of the kidnapped coders has got a message to us. He's sent us some numbers that might be a safe place to land a boat. We'll map them out and see.

How do you map things in code?

Pax, time to learn about x and y coordinates!

2 Open a web browser on your computer. Type **snap.berkeley.edu/run** into your browser bar and hit **enter**. If you have a Snap! account, log in. Otherwise, acquire an adult to help you make one.

3 Coordinates are how we track position. I do a lot of field work and coordinates are SO important. Bring up a coordinate map for me.

Click **Stage** . Click ▢.
Choose **Backgrounds** to open the backgrounds importer.

Scroll down and double-click **XY Grid** to import it. Click **cancel** to close the backgrounds importer.

4 There are two main lines on the stage now. The orange line going from left to right is the x-axis. The blue line going up and down is the y-axis.

Like in the go to blocks?

Exactly! Both lines start in the middle at 0. That's why you say, "go to x:0 y:0" when you send a sprite to the middle of the stage. If you go left, the x coordinates get smaller, into the negatives. If you go right . . .

They get bigger?

Exactly! Same with y coordinates. If you go up, they get bigger. If you go down, they get smaller.

5 Let's turn on the readout to track them.

Click **Sensing** .

Click the check boxes next to the **mouse x block** and **mouse y block**.

☑ mouse x
☑ mouse y

6 Move your mouse in the stage area until the `mouse x block` and `mouse y block` match the coordinates on each line.

```
X: -100 Y: 100
X: -20 Y: -150
X: -240 Y: -100
X: 145 Y: 170
```

I think I found them all.

Pax, that looks like a cross! Let's map it out and see.

7 Click `Sprite`. Go to the **script space**.

Find and drag these blocks into the **script space**:

```
when ⚑ clicked
set pen color to ■
clear
pen up              x 2
go to x: (0) y: (0)     x 2
glide (1) secs to x: (0) y: (0)   x 2
pen down            x 2
```

8 In the `set pen color to block`, click the **color square**. Choose **bright red**.

In the `go to blocks`, type in the first and third sets of coordinates.

In the `glide blocks`, type in the second and fourth sets of coordinates.

9 Connect the blocks to make a mapping script to match:

```
when ⚑ clicked
set pen color to ■
clear
pen up
go to x: (-100) y: (100)
pen down
glide (1) secs to x: (-20) y: (-150)
pen up
go to x: (-240) y: (-100)
pen down
glide (1) secs to x: (145) y: (170)
```

COPY THE CODE

TEST

10 TEST: Click 🚩 .
SUCCESS: The sprite draws a red cross!
ERROR: No red cross. . .
FIX: Check that you have the right numbers in the right blocks in the right order.
STOP THE SCRIPT! After each test, click ⬤ to stop the scripts running!

Save as **Map01**.

It's like a big X!

I'll cross-reference it with the island. Where the lines meet, what are the coordinates?

Move your mouse to the cross point. Write out the coordinates:

X: _____ Y: _____

Perfect, thanks! It's not a boat landing point. It looks like a parachute drop-point!

MAP-READER

LEVEL 1

We'll airdrop a team onto the island. This op is complex. The timing must be just right. We'll run some intense loops. You've used loops before.

I have?

Sure! Loops are blocks that make things happen again and again. The code in them runs over and over. It's great for repetitive jobs. The ones in Snap! look like:

Oh yeah! I've seen these!

They repeat infinitely and only stop when you click the red button. These are my namesake. One day I left a robo-droid looping through code telling it to make a cheese sandwich. The lab overflowed with sandwiches! Forever loops run forever. Supercoders tend to go for these two instead:

`repeat 10` The **repeat block** is good when you know how many times your code must repeat. Like knowing you only want 10 sandwiches.

`repeat until` The **repeat until block** works with predicates. Like knowing you want sandwiches until everyone has one. Always think about which loop is the loop for you!

MISSION OBJECTIVE 2: COUNTDOWN TO THE DROP ZONE

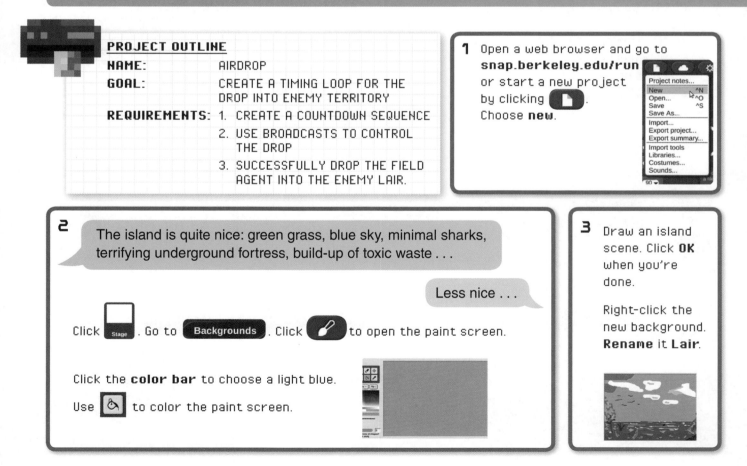

PROJECT OUTLINE

NAME: AIRDROP

GOAL: CREATE A TIMING LOOP FOR THE DROP INTO ENEMY TERRITORY

REQUIREMENTS:
1. CREATE A COUNTDOWN SEQUENCE
2. USE BROADCASTS TO CONTROL THE DROP
3. SUCCESSFULLY DROP THE FIELD AGENT INTO THE ENEMY LAIR.

1 Open a web browser and go to **snap.berkeley.edu/run** or start a new project by clicking [ ]. Choose **new**.

Project notes...
New   ^N
Open...   ^O
Save   ^S
Save As...
Import...
Export project...
Export summary...
Import tools
Libraries...
Costumes...
Sounds...

2 The island is quite nice: green grass, blue sky, minimal sharks, terrifying underground fortress, build-up of toxic waste . . .

Less nice . . .

Click [Stage]. Go to [Backgrounds]. Click [brush] to open the paint screen.

Click the **color bar** to choose a light blue.

Use [fill] to color the paint screen.

3 Draw an island scene. Click **OK** when you're done.

Right-click the new background. **Rename** it **Lair**.

4 We need to set up a timer to control the drop, or the team could end up in the ocean. Or worse.

Click [Sprite]. Click the sprite **name field**. Change the name to **countdown**.

`countdown`

Go to [Costumes]. Create a new costume by clicking 🖌.

5 Click the **color bar** to choose a color. Use the paint tools to draw a giant 10.

Click **OK** when you're done.

Right-click the new costume. Rename it **ten**.

Create nine extra costumes, with the numbers 9 to 1 in them. **Rename** them to match. They can be decorated in different colors and designs!

6 Should we make a confirmation message, so we can tell when the drop team has landed safely?

Good thinking!

Create a new costume by clicking 🖌.

Click the **color bar** to choose a color. Write **AGENT LANDED!** in big letters.

Click **OK** when you're done.

Right-click the new costume. **Rename** it **landed**.

landed

7 Click [Scripts]. Find and drag these blocks into the **script space**:

when [ ] clicked

go to x: 0 y: 0

switch to costume ▼

broadcast ▼

8 In the **switch to costume block**, click the drop-down arrow. Choose **ten**.

In the **broadcast block**, click the drop-down arrow. Choose **new** to make a new **broadcast message**. Call it **countdown!**. Click **OK**.

Save as **Drop01**.

9 Connect the blocks to make a **setup script**:

```
when green flag clicked
switch to costume ten
go to x: 0 y: 0
broadcast countdown
```

or

```
when [ ] clicked
switch to costume ten ▼
go to x: 0 y: 0
broadcast countdown! ▼
```

COPY THE CODE

10 I've looked at of your previous work with the other agents. If you hadn't used loops, your code would have been muuuuch longer. Let me show you what code is like without loops Pax!

Find and drag these blocks into the **script space**:

when I receive ▼   show   hide   broadcast ▼

wait 1 secs ×10   next costume ×9

11 In the **when I receive block**, click the drop-down arrow. Choose **countdown!**.

In the **broadcast block**, click the drop-down arrow. Click **new** to make a new **broadcast message**. Call it **dropzone**. Click **OK**.

12 Connect the blocks to make an **animation script** to match:

```
when I receive countdown!
show
wait 1 secs
next costume
wait 1 secs
next costume
wait 1 secs
next costume
wait 1 secs
next costume
wait 1 secs
next costume
wait 1 secs
next costume
wait 1 secs
next costume
wait 1 secs
next costume
wait 1 secs
next costume
wait 1 secs
hide
broadcast dropzone
```

or

```
when I receive countdown! ▼
show
wait 1 secs
next costume
wait 1 secs
next costume
wait 1 secs
next costume
wait 1 secs
next costume
wait 1 secs
next costume
wait 1 secs
next costume
wait 1 secs
next costume
wait 1 secs
next costume
wait 1 secs
next costume
wait 1 secs
hide
broadcast dropzone ▼
```

TEST

13

TEST: Click 🏳.
SUCCESS: The countdown starts at 10, counts down to 1.
ERROR: My countdown is super out of order!
FIX: Go to Costumes . Make sure your costumes are in sorted order, with **10** at the top and **landed** at the end.
ERROR: It's all in order but some low numbers don't show up.
FIX: Make sure your script starts with a `wait 1 secs block` after the `show`. Otherwise the costume will change too fast for the eye to see!

```
when I receive countdown! ▼
show
wait 1 secs
next costume
```
✔

```
when I receive countdown! ▼
show
next costume
wait 1 secs
next costume
wait 1 secs
```
✘

STOP THE SCRIPT! Click ⬤ .

This might be the longest script I've ever written . . .

It just might be. This is what happens when you don't use loops. Things get crazy.

It's just the same thing over and over!

We use computers to do repetitive jobs for squish-brains, right? It makes sense that a lot of the code is repeated. If I wanted you to tap your foot four times, I wouldn't say, "tap your foot, tap your foot, tap your foot, tap your foot".

You'd say, "tap your foot four times".

Exactly. Let's make this code much shorter and simpler by using a repeat 10 block.

14 Find and drag these blocks into the **script space**:

```
repeat 10
```
```
broadcast ▼
```
```
show    hide
```
```
wait 1 secs
```
```
when I receive ▼
```
```
next costume
```

15 In the `when I receive block`, click the drop-down arrow. Choose **countdown!**

In the `broadcast block`, click the drop-down arrow. Choose **dropzone**.

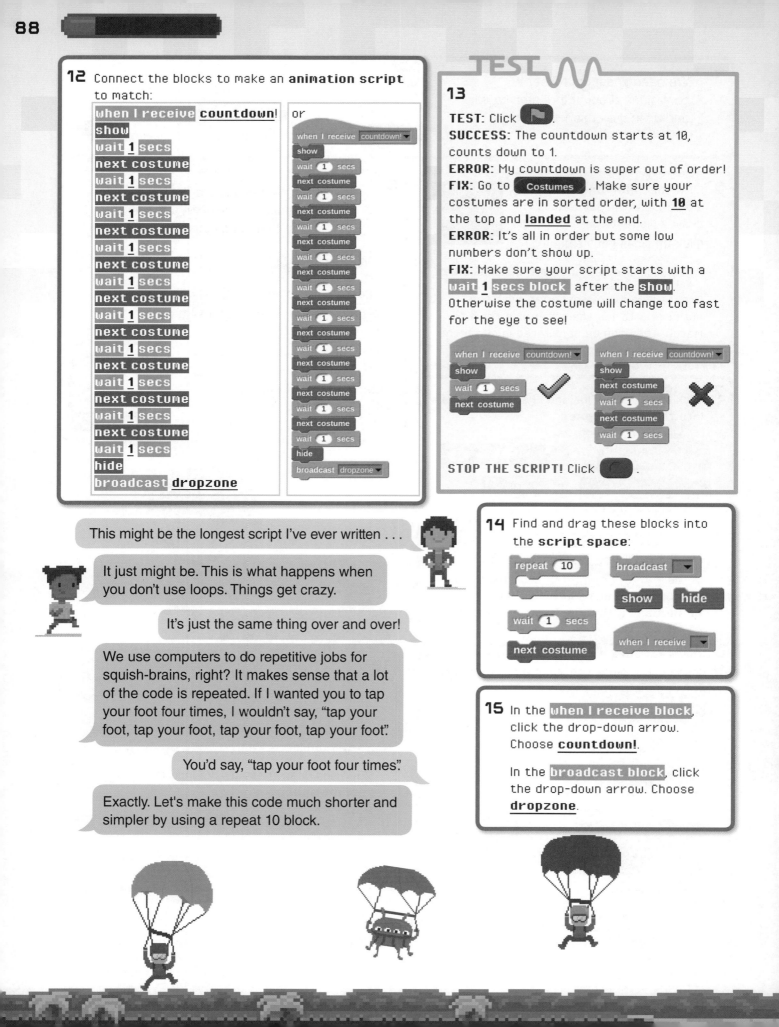

16 This can sometimes get tricky. Often the first or last loop needs some extra work. In this case, we've already set up our first costume ready to start, so we don't need to change it after the `wait 1 secs block`.

Connect the blocks to make a replacement **animation script** to match:

```
when I receive countdown
repeat 10
    show
    wait 1 secs
    next costume
    hide
broadcast dropzone
```

or

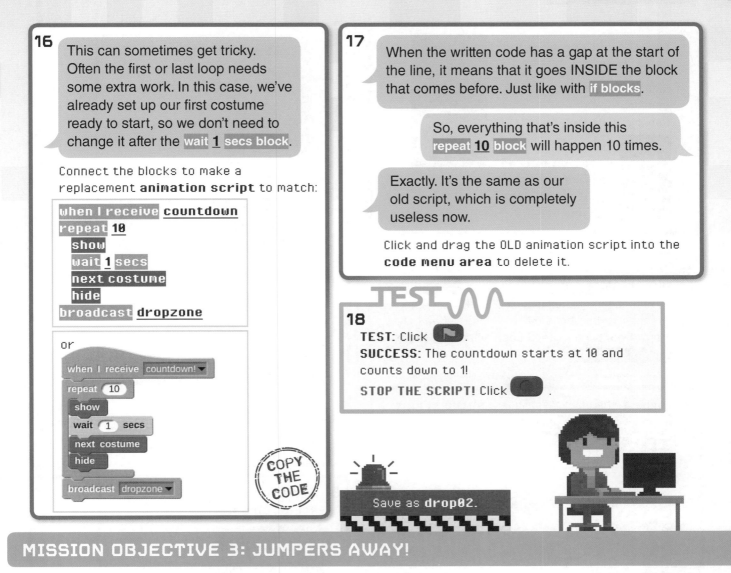

```
when I receive countdown!
repeat 10
    show
    wait 1 secs
    next costume
    hide
broadcast dropzone
```

COPY THE CODE

17 When the written code has a gap at the start of the line, it means that it goes INSIDE the block that comes before. Just like with `if blocks`.

So, everything that's inside this `repeat 10 block` will happen 10 times.

Exactly. It's the same as our old script, which is completely useless now.

Click and drag the OLD animation script into the **code menu area** to delete it.

TEST

18 **TEST:** Click 🏳.
SUCCESS: The countdown starts at 10 and counts down to 1!
STOP THE SCRIPT! Click ⭘.

Save as **drop02**.

MISSION OBJECTIVE 3: JUMPERS AWAY!

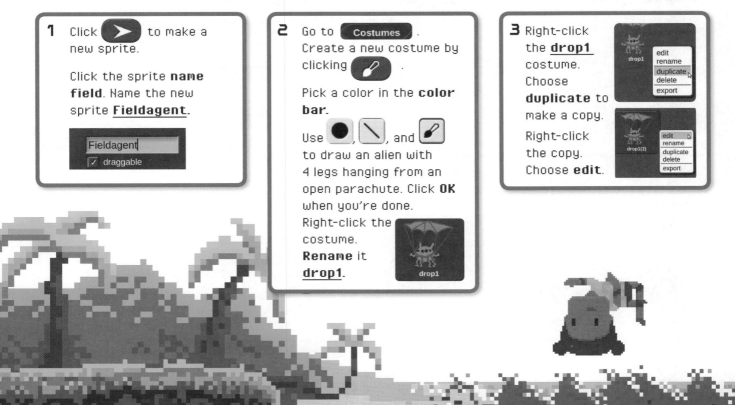

1 Click ▶ to make a new sprite.

Click the sprite **name field**. Name the new sprite **Fieldagent**.

Fieldagent
✓ draggable

2 Go to Costumes. Create a new costume by clicking 🖌.

Pick a color in the **color bar**.

Use ⬤, ＼, and 🖌 to draw an alien with 4 legs hanging from an open parachute. Click **OK** when you're done.

Right-click the costume. **Rename** it **drop1**.

drop1

3 Right-click the **drop1** costume. Choose **duplicate** to make a copy. Right-click the copy. Choose **edit**.

drop1
edit
rename
duplicate
delete
export

drop1(2)
edit
rename
duplicate
delete
export

4 Click `flip ↔` to reverse the image, then click **OK**.

Right-click the new costume.
Rename it **drop2**.

Click the **rotation button** to make sure the agent is the right way up.

EXPERIMENT

6 Click the `set size block` and the `go to block` to run them by themselves. Check your agent changes to be about 0.7 in (2 cm) tall and that it's not visible on the screen when you click the `go to block`.

7 Connect the blocks to make a **setup script**:

```
when green flag clicked
set size to 20 %
go to x: 0 y: 220
```

or

```
when  clicked
set size to 20 %
go to x: 0 y: 220
```

COPY THE CODE

EXPERIMENT

9 Click `glide 3 secs to x: 0 y: -100` to run it by itself. Make sure your agent ends up standing on the ground. Your ground might be higher or lower than Pax's. Increase or decrease the y: field until it looks right

10 Connect the blocks to make a **movement script** matching:

```
when I receive dropzone
glide 3 secs to x 0 y:-100
```

or

```
when I receive dropzone ▼
glide 3 secs to x: 0 y: -100
```

COPY THE CODE

5 First the easy, loopless bit. Our jumper needs a setup script. We want him to start in the middle of the screen at the top, so you need the right XY coordinates. What's the middle coordinate?

0.

So, we have x: 0 to start. The y-axis only goes to 180, so anything above 180 is fine for y.

I'll try 220.

Click `Scripts`.

Find and drag these blocks into the **script space**:

```
when  clicked
```
```
set size to 100 %
```
```
go to x: 0 y: 0
```

In the `set size block`, click the **text field**. Type **20**.

In the `go to block`, click the **text field**. Type y: **220**.

8 Find and drag these blocks into the **script space**:

```
when I receive ▼
```
```
glide 1 secs to x: 0 y: 0
```

In the `when I receive block`, click the **drop-down** arrow. Choose **dropzone**.

In the `glide block`, click the **text fields**. Change it to `glide 3 secs to x:0 y:-100`.

```
glide 3 secs to x: 0 y: -100
```

TEST

11
TEST: Click 🏳.
SUCCESS: When the countdown is over, the agent parachutes into the drop zone.
ERROR: Does something unexpected happen? Get out your bug-hunting shoes and sift through your code for clues, block by block.

STOP THE SCRIPT! Click ⭕.

12 Find and drag these blocks into the **script space**:

`next costume` ×6

`when I receive ▼`

`wait 1 secs` ×6

In the **when I receive block**, click the drop-down arrow. Choose **dropzone**.

In the **wait 1 secs blocks**, click each text field. Type **0.2**.

EXPERIMENT

14 The animation will make the costume of the **fieldagent sprite** move as it glides down. Currently it flickers six times and stops. **Duplicate** and connect the animation code so the **fieldagent sprite** is animated until it hits the ground. In Pax's code, it takes 18 repeats!

13 Connect the blocks to make an **animation script** to match:

```
when I receive dropzone
next costume
wait 0.2 secs
next costume
wait 0.2 secs
next costume
wait 0.2 secs
next costume
wait 0.2 secs
next costume
wait 0.2 secs
next costume
wait 0.2 secs
```

or

```
when I receive dropzone ▼
next costume
wait 0.2 secs
next costume
wait 0.2 secs
next costume
wait 0.2 secs
next costume
wait 0.2 secs
next costume
wait 0.2 secs
next costume
wait 0.2 secs
```

COPY THE CODE

15

So here I need to change this to be in a repeat 18 loop?

You could, but Natterninja would yell at me. The blocks we've used so far are great when you know for a fact how many times something must happen. If we're making 10 sandwiches, we need 10 loops; if we're making 4 sandwiches, we only need 4 loops. Here, we need to repeat the animation UNTIL the agent is on the ground. Right? **Repeat until**. . . And we use a broadcast to tell us when the agent has landed.

Find and drag these blocks into the **script space**:

`broadcast ▼`   `message`   `◀ ▢ = ▢ ▶`   `repeat until ◆`

16 In the **broadcast block**, click the drop-down arrow. Choose **new** to make a new broadcast message. Call it **landed**. Click **OK**.

Connect `broadcast landed ▼` to the end of the **movement script** to match:

```
when I receive dropzone ▼
glide 3 secs to x: 0 y: -100
broadcast landed ▼
```

COPY THE CODE

17 We can run our animation script until we get the broadcast message that the agent has landed, so we use a **repeat until block**. This is a predicate—they don't just work with **if blocks**, but a whole bunch of things. It would be impossible to code without them.

Click and drag the **message block** into the left side of the **= block**.

18 The **message block** stores the last broadcast message that was sent.

In the right side of the **= block**, click the text field. Type **landed**.

message **=** landed

Make sure you've spelled **landed** the same way as the broadcast. Capital letters matter. **LanDeD** is not the same as **landed**.

19 So that checks to see if the last broadcast sent was landed?

Exactly, and now we use that predicate to loop the code inside the **repeat block** until the broadcast message equals landed.

When the predicate will be true! Coolbeans.

Click and drag the **message = landed block** into the blank hexagon in the **repeat until block**.

repeat until ⟨ message **=** landed ⟩

20 Click and drag the bottom two blocks in the **animation script** into the **repeat until block**.

when I receive dropzone ▼
next costume
wait .2 secs
next costume
wait .2 secs
next costume
wait .2 secs
next costume
wait .2 secs
next costume
wait .2 secs
next costume
wait .2 secs

repeat until ⟨ message **=** landed ⟩

Drag the rest of the **next costume blocks** and **wait 0.2 secs blocks** from the old animation script into the **code menu area** to delete them.

21 Connect the **repeat until block** under the **when I receive dropzone block**.

when I receive block, **dropzone**
repeat until message = landed
    next costume
    wait 0.2 secs

or

when I receive dropzone ▼
repeat until ⟨ message **=** landed ⟩
    next costume
    wait 0.2 secs

COPY THE CODE

TEST

22
TEST: Click 🏳.
SUCCESS: The jumper waggles from side to side, all the way to the ground.
ERROR: An unexpected error occurred! Get out your bug-hunting questions and go through your code. What is each line doing? What SHOULD it be doing?

STOP THE SCRIPT! Click ⬤.

23 One last thing. We never want to lose track of our agents in the field, so let's add some code to send a message back to base when we're done.

Click the **countdown sprite button**.
Find and drag these blocks into the **script space**:

switch to costume ▼

when I receive ▼   show

24 In the **when I receive block**, click the drop-down arrow. Choose **landed**.
In the **switch to costume block**, click the drop-down arrow. Choose **landed**.

COPY THE CODE

when I receive landed
switch to costume landed
show

or

when I receive landed ▼
switch to costume landed ▼
show

Save as **Drop03**.

ACHIEVEMENT UNLOCKED!

LOOPER

LEVEL 2

MISSION DOSSIER

>> SCANBOT2020

Help the field team scan for the entrance to the underground base. Program the Scanbot2020 to plot a ten-sided search grid.

LEVEL: 4
INSTRUCTOR: Agent Finity

MISSION OBJECTIVE 1: LAY OUT A TEN-SIDED SEARCH PERIMETER

PROJECT OUTLINE

NAME: SCANBOT2020

GOAL: USE LOOPS TO DRAW A SEARCH GRID FOR THE FIELD AGENTS TO SWEEP.

REQUIREMENTS:
1. DRAW A TEN-SIDED SEARCH GRID FOR SCANBOT2020.
2. DRAW TEN TEN-SIDED SEARCH GRIDS FOR SCANBOT2020.
3. ADD COLOR AND SOUND TO HELP KEEP TRACK OF THE SEARCH PROGRESS.
4. BONUS: DESIGN SEARCH GRIDS BASED ON USER INPUT.

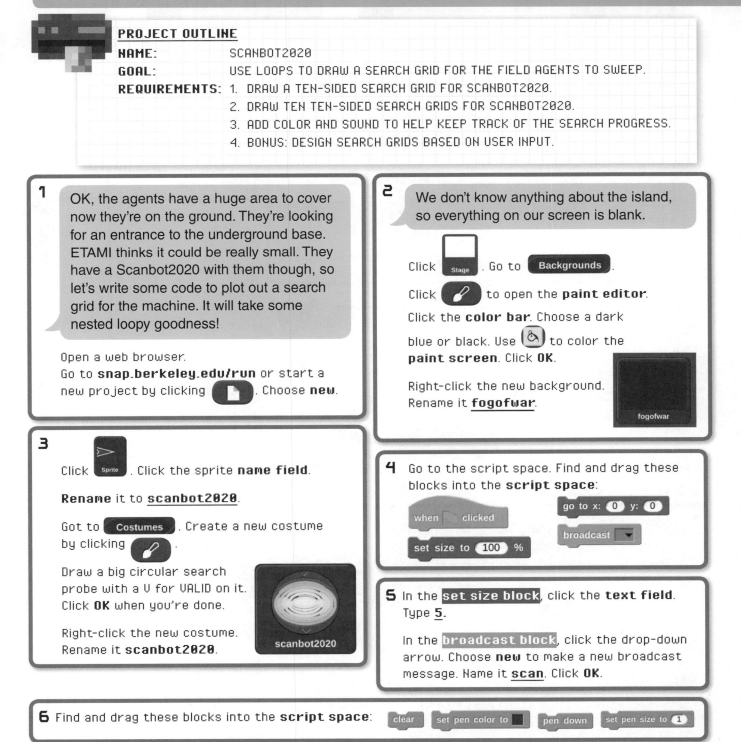

1 OK, the agents have a huge area to cover now they're on the ground. They're looking for an entrance to the underground base. ETAMI thinks it could be really small. They have a Scanbot2020 with them though, so let's write some code to plot out a search grid for the machine. It will take some nested loopy goodness!

Open a web browser.
Go to **snap.berkeley.edu/run** or start a new project by clicking [ ]. Choose **new**.

2 We don't know anything about the island, so everything on our screen is blank.

Click [Stage]. Go to [Backgrounds].

Click [ ] to open the **paint editor**.

Click the **color bar**. Choose a dark blue or black. Use [ ] to color the **paint screen**. Click **OK**.

Right-click the new background. Rename it **fogofwar**.

3 Click [Sprite]. Click the sprite **name field**.

Rename it to **scanbot2020**.

Got to [Costumes]. Create a new costume by clicking [ ].

Draw a big circular search probe with a V for VALID on it. Click **OK** when you're done.

Right-click the new costume. Rename it **scanbot2020**.

4 Go to the script space. Find and drag these blocks into the **script space**:

when [ ] clicked
go to x: 0 y: 0
set size to 100 %
broadcast ▼

5 In the **set size block**, click the **text field**. Type **5**.

In the **broadcast block**, click the drop-down arrow. Choose **new** to make a new broadcast message. Name it **scan**. Click **OK**.

6 Find and drag these blocks into the **script space**: clear · set pen color to ■ · pen down · set pen size to 1

7 In the **set pen color block**, click the **colored square**. Choose a bright color.

set pen color to ▣

In the **set pen size block**, click the text field. Type **2**.

set pen size to (2)

Save as **Scan01**.

8 Connect the blocks to make a **setup script**:

```
when ⚑ clicked
set size to (5) %
go to x: (0) y: (0)
set pen color to ▢
set pen size to (2)
pen down
clear
broadcast scan ▾
```

COPY THE CODE

9 Let's start with a **standard ten-sided search** and see what we find.

Find and drag these blocks into the **script space**:

```
when I receive ▾
repeat (10)
```

```
turn ↻ (15) degrees
( / )
move (10) steps
```

10 In the **when I receive block**, click the drop-down. Choose **scan**.

In the **/ block**, click the left **text field**. Type **360**. Click the right text field. Type **10**.

Drag the **/ block** into the **turn degrees block**.

```
turn ↻ (15) degrees
( 360 / 10 )
```

In the **move 10 steps block**, click the **text field**. Type **30**.

11 Connect the blocks together to make an **animation script**:

```
when I receive scan
repeat 10
  turn 360 / 10 degrees
  move 30 steps
```

COPY THE CODE

or

```
when I receive scan ▾
repeat (10)
  turn ↻ (360 / 10) degrees
  move (30) steps
```

Did it find anything?

No, but we're not done. As Glitchbane says, if at first you don't succeed, figure out why and try again! We need to decuple the search area.

Decupl—what?

It means multiply by 10. Make it 10 times bigger. Get ready to nest some loops Pax! That means loops **inside** loops!

12

TEST

TEST: Click ⚑ .

SUCCESS: A ten-sided polygon (a decagon) is drawn! Scanbot2020 is 10 times closer to finding the target!

STOP THE SCRIPT! Click ⬟ .

Save as **Scan02**.

MISSION OBJECTIVE 2: DECUPLE THE SEARCH PERIMETER

1 So, this loop runs the code inside it 10 times. Each time it loops, the Scanbot2020 turns with the power of geometry and draws a side of the search area. Now, imagine if the code inside a loop was *gasp* another loop!?

It would scan . . . a whole search area every time it looped?

Right-click the **repeat 10 block**. Choose **duplicate** to make a copy.

Drag to insert the duplicated blocks between the **turn 360 / 10 degrees** and **move 30 steps blocks**.

Click and drag the bottom **move block** into the **code menu** area to delete it.

```
when I receive scan ▾
repeat (10)
  turn ↻ (360 / 10) degrees
  move (30) steps
```

```
repeat (10)
  turn ↻ (360 / 10) degrees
  move (30) steps
```

2 Check that your code matches:

```
when I receive scan
repeat 10
    turn 360 / 10 degrees
    repeat 10
        turn 360 / 10 degrees
        move 30 steps
```

or

```
when I receive scan
repeat 10
    turn 360 / 10 degrees
    repeat 10
        turn 360 / 10 degrees
        move 30 steps
```

COPY THE CODE

Save as **Scan03**.

TEST

3
TEST: Click 🏳.
SUCCESS: Scanbot2020 scans TEN DECAGONS of space!

STOP THE SCRIPT! Click ⬤.

> That's amazing. And kind of pretty.

ACHIEVEMENT UNLOCKED!
LOOPER
LEVEL 3

MISSION OBJECTIVE 3: CHECK ALL FREQUENCIES

1
> It looks cool. I'm not sure why it works, though.

> There are easy ways to keep track of which loop is doing what. Let me show you.

Find and drag this block into the **script space**:

`change pen color by 10`

2
> We'll change the color of the line every time the outer loop runs.

Click and drag the **change pen color block** into the outer loop.

```
when I receive scan
repeat 10
    turn 360 / 10 degrees
    repeat 10
        turn 360 / 10 degrees
        move 30 steps
```
`change pen color by 10`

TEST

3
TEST: Click 🏳.
SUCCESS: Each decagon is a different color!

STOP THE SCRIPT! Click ⬤.

The 10 sides of each decagon are drawn by this code in the inner loop and the color stays the same. When it's finished, the outer loop changes the color and runs again.

```
when I receive scan
repeat 10
    turn 360 / 10 degrees
    change pen color by 10
    repeat 10
        turn 360 / 10 degrees
        move 30 steps
```

4
> What happens if we move the color change to the inner loop?

Click and drag the **change pen color block** into the inner loop.

```
when I receive scan
repeat 10
    turn 360 / 10 degrees
    change pen color by 10
    repeat 10
        turn 360 / 10 degrees
        move 30 steps
```

```
when I receive scan
repeat 10
    turn 360 / 10 degrees
    repeat 10
        turn 360 / 10 degrees
        change pen color by 10
        move 30 steps
```

TEST

5
TEST: Click 🏳.
SUCCESS: Each side of each decagon is a different color!

STOP THE SCRIPT! Click ⬤.

6 Now each side of each decagon is a different color, because the color change runs every time.

Coolbeans! I think I get it.

It's complicated stuff. You can do it with sound as well, though! Loops make some AMAZING music.

Drag these blocks into the **script space**:

`play note 60▾ for 0.5 beats` x2

TEST

9
TEST: Click 🏳.
SUCCESS: Scanbot2020 plays a sound when it draws a side of the shape and a different noise when it comes back to the center.
STOP THE SCRIPT! Click ⬤.

ACHIEVEMENT UNLOCKED!
LOOPER

LEVEL 4

Save as **Scan04**.

7 In each **play note block**, click the drop-down arrow. Choose a different number. (Pax likes 71 and 52 but it's up to you.) Change the second **text field** to **0.1**.

`play note 71▾ for 0.1 beats`

`play note 52▾ for 0.1 beats`

8 Click and drag one of the **play note blocks** into the outer loop and one into the inner loop of your **animation script**.

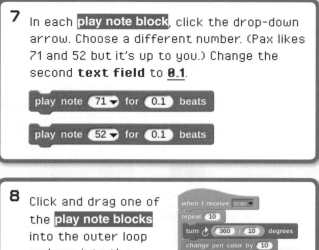

A-ha! That's so cool!

Every time it plays a note, that's the end of the inner loop. When the note changes, that's the end of the outer loop.

Amazebeans. Can you loop loops inside loops inside loops?

With loops, the sky's the limit, but more than two levels of nested loops tends to make your brain explode. It makes it hard to track bugs. Let's send this code to the Scanbot2020.

BONUS MISSION OBJECTIVE: INFINITE SCANS! MWAHAHAHAHA!

1 Find and drag these blocks into the **script space**:

`ask what's·your·name? and wait`

`answer` x 5   ⬭

2 In the **ask and wait block**, click the text field. Type **How many sides**?
Insert the **ask and wait block** after the golden starter block.
In the **/ block**, click the left text field. Type **100**. Drag an **answer block** into the right text field.
Drag the **/ block** into the **change pen color block**.

`change pen color by  100 / answer`

3 Click and drag the **answer block** to replace the number **10** all over the script.

COPY THE CODE

4

TEST: Click 🚩. Try number 3.

SUCCESS: Your scans scan three triangles!

STOP THE SCRIPT! Click ⬭ .

💡 Try it with any number from 3 to infinity. Higher numbers might take a while!

Save as **Scan05**.

MISSION DOSSIER

≫ LASER LOOPS

There's a field of lasers in operation! Help the team dodge their way through it.

LEVEL: 4

INSTRUCTOR: Agent Finity

MISSION OBJECTIVE 1: INITIATE A COUNTDOWN! 3, 2, 1, GO!

It looks like the Scanbot2020 has found something. The drop team is heading towards it, but it looks like there are laser fields in operation.

Laser fields?

Pretty standard. Our agents are pretty good at dodging them. I can show you; it might come in handy when you've finished your training.

Coolbeans!

PROJECT OUTLINE

NAME:
LASER DODGE

GOAL:

REQUIREMENTS:

1. INITIATE A COUNTDOWN
2. TURN ON THE LASER EMITTER
3. USE LOOPS TO DO A LASER BEAM SWEEP OF THE AREA
4. USE TWO SPRITES TO DODGE THE LASER AS LONG AS THEY CAN
5. DISPLAY THE NAME OF THE MOST SKILLED LASER DODGER ON SCREEN

1 We'll use our training sector to set up the laser emitter.

Click 📄 . Choose **new** to start a new project.

Click ⬜ . Go to
Stage → Backgrounds

Click 🖌 .

2 Click the **color bar** to choose a dark blue or black. Use 🪣 to color the **paint screen**.

Choose a lighter color and draw some stars to make a space background. Click **OK** when you're done.

Right-click the new background. **Rename** it **sector3.1415**.

sedctor3.1415

3 Go to the **script space**. Find and drag these blocks into the **script space**:

```
when 🚩 clicked
```

```
switch to costume ▾
```

In the **switch to costume block**, click the drop-down arrow. Choose **sector3.1415**.

4 Connect them together to make a **setup script**:

```
when green flag clicked
switch to costume sector 3.1415
```

or

```
when 🚩 clicked
switch to costume sector3.1415 ▾
```

COPY THE CODE

5 Remember how to make a countdown? It only needs to be from three this time.

Click 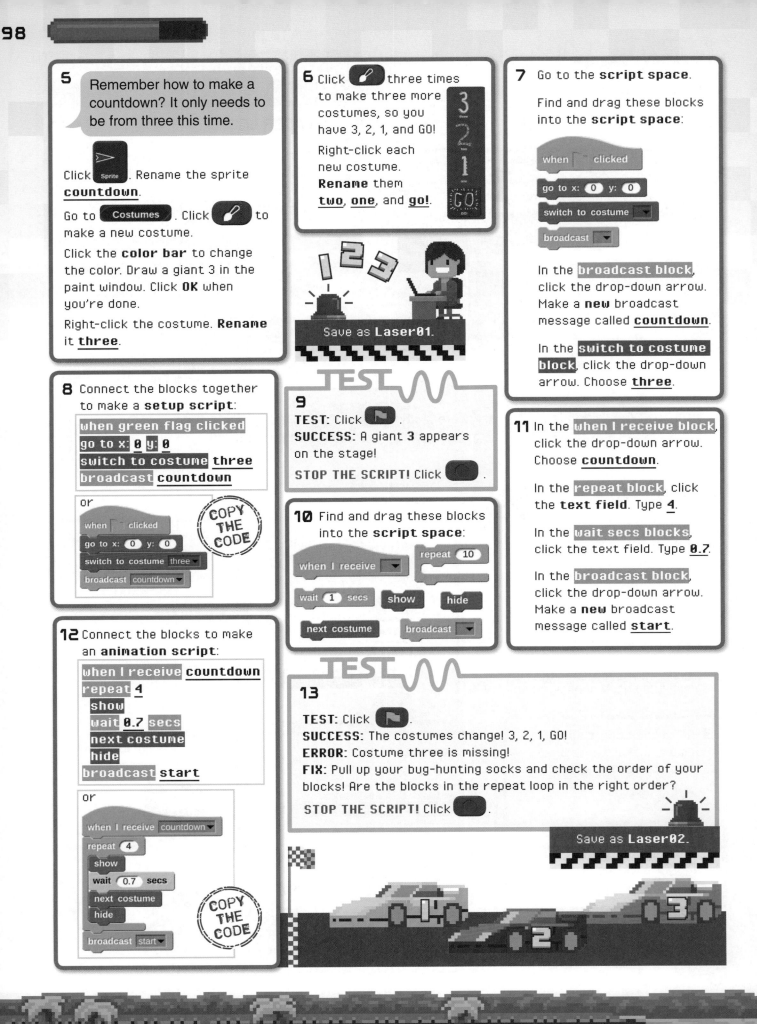 **Sprite**. Rename the sprite **countdown**.

Go to **Costumes**. Click ✎ to make a new costume.

Click the **color bar** to change the color. Draw a giant 3 in the paint window. Click **OK** when you're done.

Right-click the costume. **Rename** it **three**.

6 Click ✎ three times to make three more costumes, so you have 3, 2, 1, and GO!

Right-click each new costume. **Rename** them **two**, **one**, and **go!**.

Save as **Laser01**.

7 Go to the **script space**.

Find and drag these blocks into the **script space**:

```
when [ ] clicked
go to x: 0 y: 0
switch to costume [ ]
broadcast [ ]
```

In the **broadcast block**, click the drop-down arrow. Make a **new** broadcast message called **countdown**.

In the **switch to costume block**, click the drop-down arrow. Choose **three**.

8 Connect the blocks together to make a **setup script**:

```
when green flag clicked
go to x: 0 y: 0
switch to costume three
broadcast countdown
```

or

```
when [ ] clicked
go to x: 0 y: 0
switch to costume three ▾
broadcast countdown ▾
```

COPY THE CODE

9 **TEST:** Click ⚑.
SUCCESS: A giant **3** appears on the stage!
STOP THE SCRIPT! Click ⬤.

10 Find and drag these blocks into the **script space**:

```
when I receive [ ▾ ]     repeat 10
wait 1 secs    show    hide
next costume    broadcast [ ▾ ]
```

11 In the **when I receive block**, click the drop-down arrow. Choose **countdown**.

In the **repeat block**, click the **text field**. Type **4**.

In the **wait secs blocks**, click the text field. Type **0.7**.

In the **broadcast block**, click the drop-down arrow. Make a **new** broadcast message called **start**.

12 Connect the blocks to make an **animation script**:

```
when I receive countdown
repeat 4
  show
  wait 0.7 secs
  next costume
hide
broadcast start
```

or

```
when I receive countdown ▾
repeat 4
  show
  wait 0.7 secs
  next costume
hide
broadcast start ▾
```

COPY THE CODE

13

TEST: Click ⚑.
SUCCESS: The costumes change! 3, 2, 1, GO!
ERROR: Costume three is missing!
FIX: Pull up your bug-hunting socks and check the order of your blocks! Are the blocks in the repeat loop in the right order?

STOP THE SCRIPT! Click ⬤.

Save as **Laser02**.

MISSION OBJECTIVE 2: TURN ON THE LASER EMITTER

1 To generate the kind of security lasers our team is up against, we need a powerful laser emitter, which is normally a small, gray box with a bunch of lights on the side. When you're on a mission, it's the first thing you look for.

Click ▶ to make a new sprite.

Click the sprite **name field**. **Rename** the sprite **emitter**.

2 Go to Costumes . Create a new costume by clicking 🖌 .

Use the paint tools to draw a laser emitter. This one has two red buttons on the side. Click **OK** when you're done.

Untitled

Right-click the **costume**. Rename it **off**.

3 Right-click the **off** costume. Click **duplicate** twice to make two copies.

Right-click **off(2)** and **off(3)**. Rename them **on1** and **on2**.

4 Right-click **on1** and **on2**. Choose **edit** to open the paint editor and make changes.

Use 🖐 to edit both costumes so the lights are different colors. Click **OK** when done.

Find the three **rotation buttons** at the top of the screen. Click the **middle button** to make sure the emitter doesn't rotate.

5 Click Scripts .

Find and drag these blocks into the **script space**:

when ⚐ clicked   go to x: 0 y: 0
set size to 100 %   switch to costume ▾

In the **set size to block**, click the **text field**. Change it to **40%**.

EXPERIMENT

6 The number in the **set size box** always depends on how big your paint drawing is. The emitter should end up being about 0.4-0.8 in (1-2 cm) tall on your stage. Change the number in the **set size block** and click it to test the size until you get it right.

7 In the **switch to costume block**, click the drop-down arrow. Choose **off**. Connect the blocks to make a **setup script**:

when green flag clicked
go to x: 0 y: 0
set size to 40%
switch to costume off

or

when ⚐ clicked
go to x: 0 y: 0
set size to 40 %
switch to costume off ▾

COPY THE CODE

8 Find and drag these blocks into the **script space**:

when I receive ▾   show

repeat until ⬡   ⬡ or ⬡

                      hide

wait 1 secs × 2

switch to costume ▾ × 2

⬡ = ⬡ × 2   message × 2

In the **when I receive block**, choose **start**.

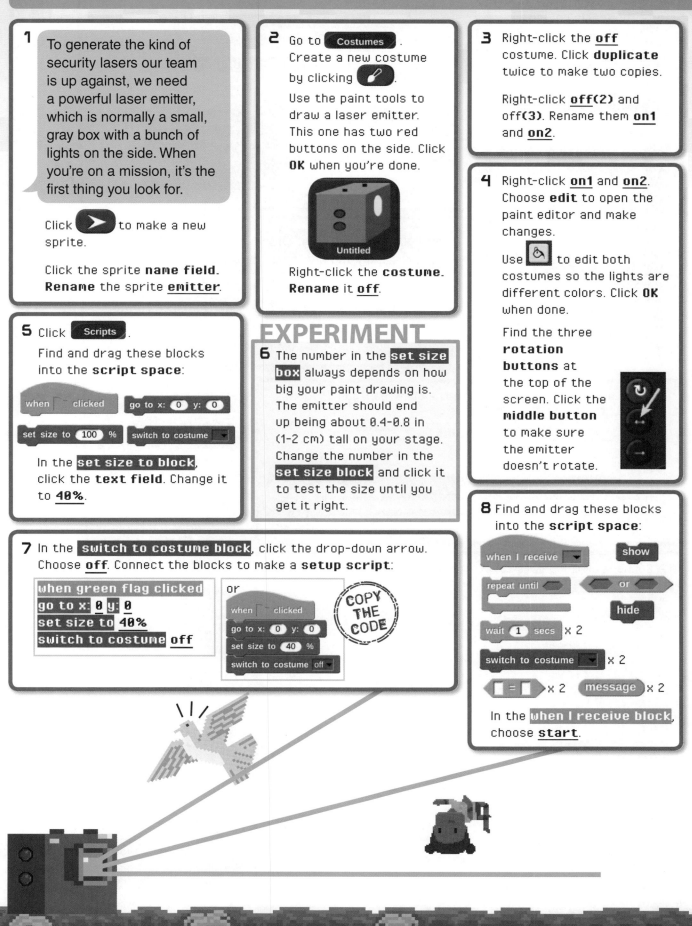

9 We haven't got any broadcasts yet, so I'm not sure what we're going to use for the predicates.

Leave it blank for now.

Connect some of the blocks of your **animation script**:

```
when I receive start
show
repeat until ____
hide
```

or

```
when I receive start ▼
show
repeat until ◁▷
hide
```

COPY THE CODE

10 In the `wait 1 secs blocks`, click the **text fields**. Change both to **0.2**.

In the `switch to costume blocks`, click the drop-down arrow. Change one to **on1** and the other to **on2**.

Connect the `switch to costume blocks` underneath the `wait blocks` to match:

```
wait 0.2 secs
switch to costume on1
wait 0.2 secs
switch to costume on2
```

or

```
wait 0.2 secs
switch to costume on1 ▼
wait 0.2 secs
switch to costume on2 ▼
```

COPY THE CODE

11 We'll run this simulation for two players, so there are two possible endgame broadcast messages: one for each player.

Drag the two `message blocks` into the left spaces in the `= blocks`.

In the right space of the `= blocks`, click the **text fields**. Type **a1wins** and **a2wins**.

Drag the `= blocks` into the blank hexagons in the `or blocks`.

12 Click and drag the `or block` into the blank hexagon in the `repeat until block`:

```
repeat until message = a1wins or message = a2wins
```

or

```
show
repeat until ⟨ message = a1wins ⟩ or ⟨ message = a2wins ⟩
hide
```

COPY THE CODE

13 Connect all the blocks together to make an **animation script**:

```
when I receive start
show
repeat until message = a1wins or message = a2wins
    wait 0.2 secs
    switch to costume on1
    wait 0.2 secs
    switch to costume on2
hide
```

or

```
when I receive start ▼
show
repeat until ⟨ message = a1wins ⟩ or ⟨ message = a2wins ⟩
    wait 0.2 secs
    switch to costume on1 ▼
    wait 0.2 secs
    switch to costume on2 ▼
hide
```

COPY THE CODE

TEST

14
TEST: Click ▶.
SUCCESS: The lights are red during the countdown, then flash!

STOP THE SCRIPT! Click ⬤.

I don't think the test passes. There's a hide block at the end that doesn't fire.

We had to stop it before it got to the end of the script. Broadcasts have two parts: the sending and the receiving.

Oh! We haven't set up the sending yet, so this loop . . .

Never finishes. Every loop MUST have a way of stopping!

Save as **Laser03**.

MISSION OBJECTIVE 3: DO A LASER BEAM SWEEP OF THE AREA

1 Click [>] to make a new sprite.

Click the sprite **name field**. Rename the sprite **laser**.

2 Go to [Costumes]. Create a new costume by clicking [🖌]. Use the paint tools to draw a laser beam from one side of the paint window to the other. Laser beams are long but thin.

3 When you're done, click [⊕]. Move it to the very beginning of your laser beam.

Click **OK** when you're done. Right-click the **costume**. Rename it **laserbeam**.

EXPERIMENT

4 Find and drag these blocks into the **script space**:

when [ ] clicked

hide

go to x: 0 y: 0

point in direction 90 ▾

5 The start of the laser beam should match up with the center of the emitter. The end should be off the stage. Click the `go to x: 0 y: 0 block` to check it's in the right position. If it's not, change the **text fields** in the `go to x: 0 y: 0 block`.

A higher number in the x: text field will move right; a lower value in the x: text field will move left.

A higher number in the y: text field will move up; a lower number will move it down.
Remember to click the block each time to see your changes.

> I needed different numbers here, so my code doesn't match exactly. Is that cool?

> Sure! Your code may look a little different to mine when you experiment. If it works, don't stress.

6 In the `point in direction block`, click the drop-down arrow. Choose **0**. Connect the blocks to make a **setup script**:

```
when green flag clicked
hide
go to x: 5 y: 5
point in direction 0
```

or

when [ ] clicked
hide
go to x: 5 y: 5
point in direction 0 ▾

COPY THE CODE

7 Click the **emitter sprite**.

Right-click the **start block** of the **animation script** in the emitter sprite. Choose **duplicate** to make a copy.

Drag the copy onto the **laser sprite button** and click to drop it.

8 Click the **laser sprite button**. The copied **animation script** should be in the **script space**.

Click and drag the blocks inside the `repeat until loop` into the **code menu area** to delete them.

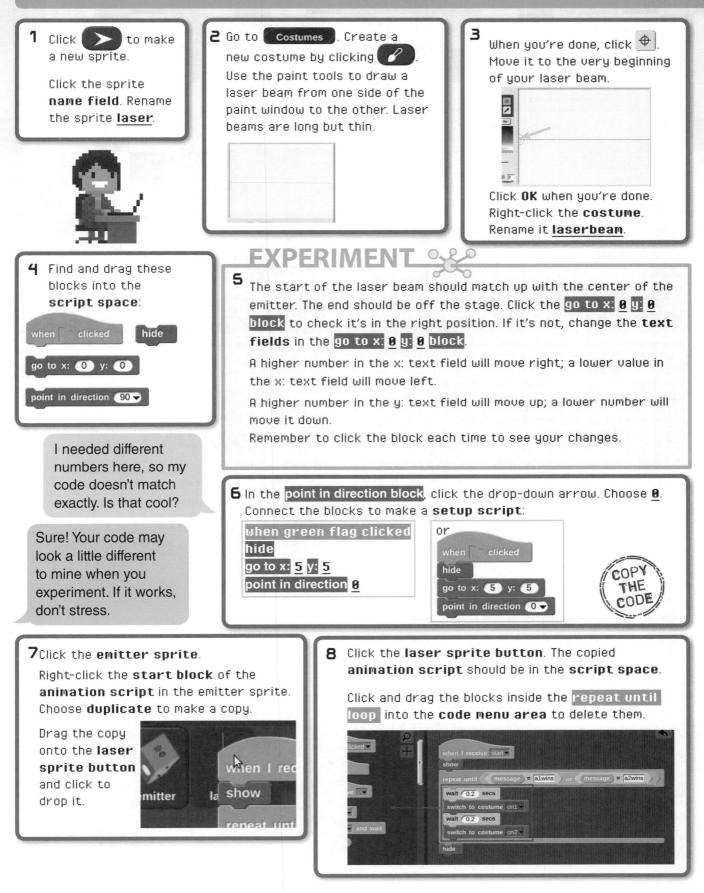

9 Find and drag this block into the **script space**:

turn ↺ **15** degrees

In the **turn degrees block**, click the **text field**. Type **1**.

10 Drag and connect the **turn 1 degrees block** inside the **repeat until block** in your **animation script**.

when I receive start ▾
show
repeat until ⟨ message = a1wins ⟩ or ⟨ message = a2wins ⟩
turn ↻ **1** degrees
hide

TEST

11

TEST: Click 🏳.

SUCCESS: After the countdown, the laser rotates around the emitter, spreading fear and destruction!

ERROR: The laser spins too fast! No one could avoid that!

FIX: Put on your bug-busting boots and check your code. Did you change the number of degrees in your **turn block**?

turn ↻ **1** degrees ✓   turn ↺ **15** degrees ✗

STOP THE SCRIPT! Click 🔴.

Save as **Laser04**.

MISSION OBJECTIVE 4A: AGENT1 ENTERS THE GAME

1 Click ▶ to make a new sprite.
Click the sprite **name field. Rename** the sprite **agent1.**

2 Go to **Costumes**. Make a new costume by clicking 🖌.

Use the paint tools to draw a **bright purple** VALID agent to test their skills against the lasers. Click **OK** when you're done.

Right-click the costume. Rename it **a1**.

Find the three **rotation buttons** at the top of the screen. Click the **middle button** to make sure agent1 doesn't rotate.

3 Find and drag these blocks into the **script space**:

when 🏳 clicked   set size to **100** %
go to x: **0** y: **0**   show

In the **set size block**, click the **text field**. Type **30%**.

EXPERIMENT

4 Click the **set size block** to test. You want **agent1** to be about 0.4–0.8 in (1–2 cm) tall.

Bigger numbers will make **agent1** bigger; smaller numbers will make it smaller.

Experiment until you get it right.

EXPERIMENT

5 In the **go to block**, click the **text fields**. Change it to **go to x: –200 y: 130.**

6 Click the **go to block** to test the position. **Agent1** should sit in the top left corner of the stage without going off the screen.

The **x:** **text field** will move **agent1** left and right; the **y:** **text field** will move it up and down.

Experiment until you get it right.

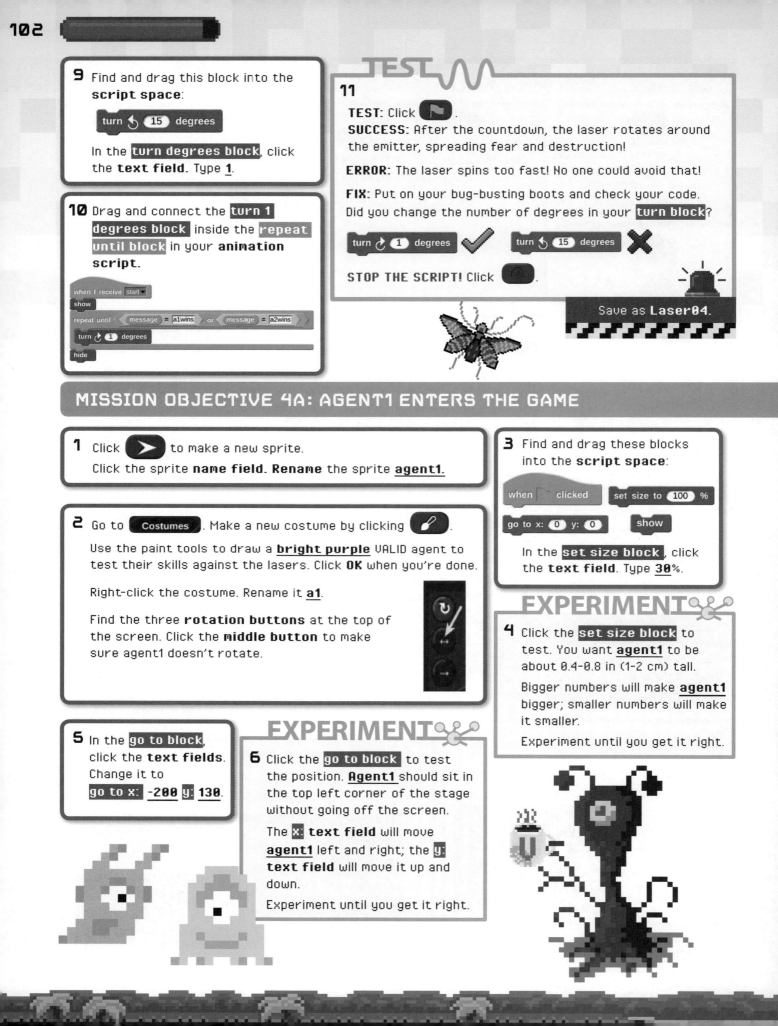

7 Connect the blocks together to make a **setup script**:

```
when green flag clicked
set size to 30%
go to x: -200 y: 130
show
```

or

```
when   clicked
set size to 30 %
go to x: -200 y: 130
show
```

COPY THE CODE

8 Find and drag these blocks into the **script space**:

```
when space ▼ key pressed      hide    show

wait 1 secs      play sound ▼
```

In the **when key pressed block**, click the drop-down arrow. Choose **a**.

9 Click [icon]. Choose **sounds** to open the **sound importer**. Double-click **Finger Snap** to import it. Click **Cancel** to close the **sound importer**.

0:01	0:02	0:00	0:00
Play	Play	Play	Play
Cat	Chord	Dog 1	Dog 2
0:00	0:01	0:01	0:01
Play	Play	Play	Play
Finger Snap	Kitten	Laugh Female	Laugh Male 1
0:03	0:02	0:01	0:00

Import   Cancel

10 Go to the **script space**. In the **play sound block**, click the drop-down arrow. Choose **Finger Snap**.

Connect the blocks to make an **event script**:

```
when a key pressed
hide
play sound Finger Snap
wait 1 secs
show
```

or

```
when a ▼ key pressed
hide
play sound Finger Snap ▼
wait 1 secs
show
```

COPY THE CODE

SNAP!

Save as **laser05**.

TEST

11
TEST: Click [flag]. Press the **a** key to hide agent1.
SUCCESS: Agent1 disappears for a second with a snap and then reappears!
ERROR: Something doesn't look right. Reread the instructions with your bug-hunting visor activated.

STOP THE SCRIPT! Click [icon].

EXPERIMENT

12 **agent1** must disappear long enough to avoid the laser passing by. Adjust how long the sprite hides by increasing or decreasing the number in the wait block. Bigger numbers make it easier; lower numbers make it harder.

> This part is the hardest. It must be challenging enough that trainees improve, but not impossible. Impossible is no fun for anyone. It's a delicate balance.

MISSION OBJECTIVE 4B: AGENT2 ENTERS THE GAME

1 Right-click the **agent1 sprite**. Choose **duplicate** to make a copy.
Click the sprite **name field**. Rename it **agent2**.
Go to **Costumes**. Drag the **a1 costume** into the **code menu area** to delete it.

2 Make a new costume by clicking [brush icon].
Use the tools to paint a **bright green** agent for **agent2**. Make it roughly the same size as the old costume. Click **OK** when you're done.
Right-click the **new costume. Rename** it **a2**.
Click the **a2** costume so it shows on the stage.
Go to the **script space**.

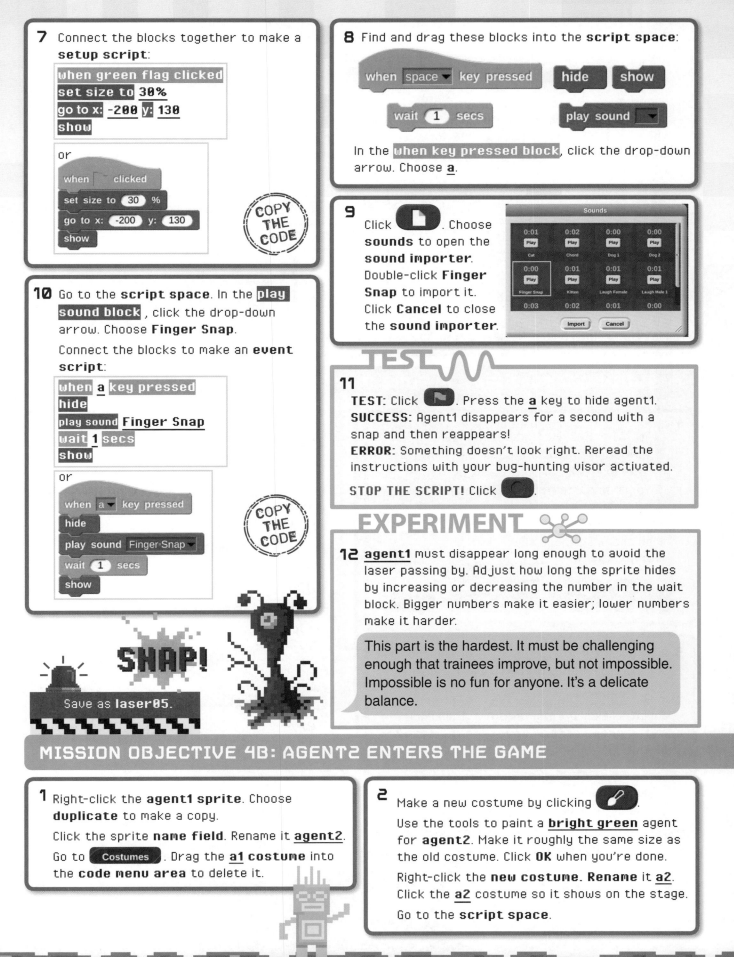

EXPERIMENT

3

For this to work, we'll need to reverse the polarity.

agent2 should start in the opposite corner to **agent1**. In the setup script for **agent2**, change the numbers to their opposites. If you had **x: -200** for agent1, then for **agent2** you will have **x: 200**. If you had **y: 140**, then you will have **y: -140**. Click the script to test it looks right. You might need to adjust if your **agent2** is a different size or shape.

TEST

5

TEST: Click 🏁. Press **l**.
SUCCESS: Agent2 hides with a "pop", then reappears! Woohoo!

STOP THE SCRIPT! Click ⬤.

4 In the **animation script**, click the drop-down arrow in the **when key pressed block**. Choose **l**.

Click ⬤. Choose **sounds** to open the **sound importer**.

Double-click **Pop** to import it. Click **Cancel** to close the **sound importer**.

Drag **Finger Snap** into the **code menu area** to delete it.

Go to the **script space**. In the **play sound block**, click the drop-down arrow. Choose **Pop**.

Save as **Laser06**.

MISSION OBJECTIVE 5: FIGURE OUT WHO IS BETTER AT LASER DODGE

1

It's time, Pax. Remember when we started listening for messages? Now it's time to shout our broadcasts from the rooftops! Or from the laser sprite.

Click the **laser sprite button**.

Find and drag these blocks into the **script space**:

touching ▢ ?

when ⬡

broadcast ▾

hide

2

We need to match up the **touching color block** with the main color of the agent.

In the **touching color block**, click the **color square**. Then click on the **purple** part of **agent1** in the **stage area**.

In the **broadcast block**, click the drop-down arrow. Choose **new** to make a new broadcast message. Call it **a2wins**.

Connect the blocks to make an **endgame script**:

when ⟨ touching ▢ ?
broadcast a2wins ▾
hide

COPY THE CODE

3 Right-click the **starter block** of the endgame script. Choose **duplicate** to make a copy.

In the **touching color block** of the copied script, click the **color square**. Then click on the **green** part of **agent2** in the **stage area**.

In the **broadcast block**, click the drop-down arrow. Choose **new** to make a new broadcast message. Call it **a1wins**.

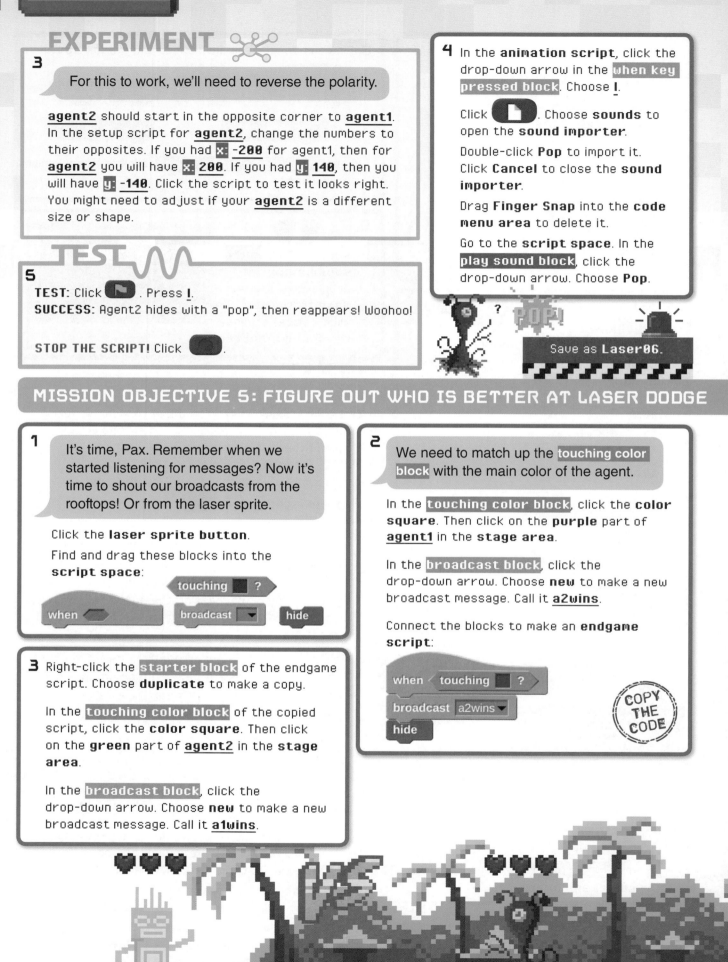

4 Click the **agent1** sprite button.

agent1

Find and drag these blocks into the **script space**:

`when I receive ▼`   `hide`

5 Change the blocks and connect them to make an **endgame script** to match:

`when I receive a2wins` `hide`

or

`when I receive a2wins` `hide`

COPY THE CODE

6 Click the **agent2** sprite button.

agent2

Find and drag these blocks into the **script space**:

`when I receive ▼`   `hide`

7 Change the blocks and connect them to make an **endgame script** to match:

`when I receive a1wins` `hide`

or

`when I receive a1wins ▼` `hide`

COPY THE CODE

TEST

8

TEST 1: Click 🏁. Let the laser hit **agent1**.
SUCCESS: Agent1 is defeated! Agent2 stays on screen in victorious victory!
TEST 2: Click 🏁. Let the laser hit **agent2**.
SUCCESS: Agent2 is defeated and flees! Agent1 stays on screen.
ERROR: The losing agent stays on screen! The winning agent hides! Travesty!
FIX: Get out your bug-hunting brush and comb through your code to find the bugs.

STOP THE SCRIPT! Click 🔴.

9

Stage

Click `Stage`.

Click `Backgrounds`.
Create two new backgrounds by clicking 🖌.

10 In the first background, write **Agent 2 wins!** in big letters. Click **OK**.

Right-click the new background.
Rename it a2wins!.

In the second background, write **Agent 1 wins!** in big letters. Click **OK**.

Right-click the new background.
Rename it a1wins!

sector3.1415

AGENT 2 WINS

a2wins

AGENT 1 WINS

a1wins

11 Go to the **script space**. Find and drag these blocks into the **script space**:

`when I receive ▼` ×2

`switch to costume ▼` ×2

In the **when I receive blocks**, click the drop-down arrows. Change them to **a1wins** and **a2wins**.
In the **switch to costume blocks**, click the drop-down arrows. Change them to **a1wins** and **a2wins**.

12 Connect the blocks to make two **endgame scripts**:

```
when I receive a1wins
switch to costume a1wins!
```
and
```
when I receive a2wins
switch to costume a2wins!
```

or

```
when I receive a1wins ▾
switch to costume a1wins ▾
```
and
```
when I receive a2wins ▾
switch to costume a2wins ▾
```

COPY THE CODE

TEST 〰

13

TEST: Click 🏁. Let the laser hit agent 2!
(He has an exo-skeleton.)
SUCCESS: The laser stops! The emitter disappears!
The background says agent 1 is the superior agent!

Save as **Laser07**.

CHALLENGE ⛺

14 Find someone to play with. Challenge them to see who lasts the longest against the little gray box of doom. What happens when the laser hits agent 1?

Pax, a message just came in from ETAMI. Our agents have made it safely inside the facility.

Is everything ok? Have they found the missing coders?

Not yet but so far, so good. I couldn't have done it without you Pax! You've looped the loop like a BOSS. I need to go over our plan with Natterninja and Glitchbane, but ETAMI will take you to meet the Echo Agents.

The clones?

They're harmless! Well, until the day they decide to build a clone army to take over the galaxy and rule it with an iron fist . . .

Riiiight . . .

But seriously, they will be coordinating the search from their lab. They could use some help. Are you up to it?

NEW MESSAGE ✖

Go with ETAMI to meet the mysterious Echo Agents and help them search the enemy base?

Y/N

CLONING AND DUPLICATION

with the Echo Agents

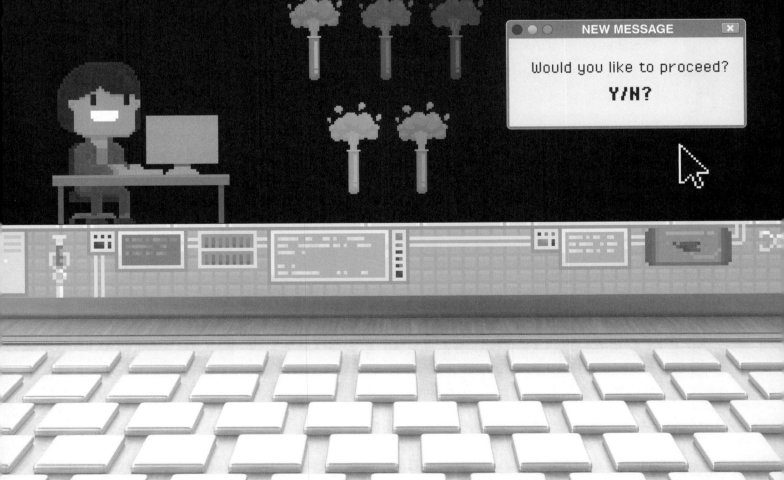

It's your fifth training session as a coder recruit at VALID. You worked with Agent Finity to help her field team infiltrate a secret CORUPT base on a remote island and search for signs of kidnapped VALID coders. To find their way around the base, the field team is going to need clones, so ETAMI is taking you to see EchoOne and EchoZero.

I've heard the Echo Agents are a little odd.

EchoOne and EchoZero are highly valued scientific experts and VALID supercoders.

You're right. I'm sure they're coolbeans.

And it has been three whole Earth days since something exploded!

ETAMI! Great news! The field team has found a hidden message in the base, left by one of the kidnapped coders. We think it's the key to their security systems.

If we can decrypt it, we might be able to hack into their security systems and get access to the inner sanctum!

Using clones! Hundreds of beautiful CLONES! Mwa-ha-ha-ha-ha!

Umm . . . hi . . .

This is the new recruit, Potential Agent X.

Nice to meet you. Don't worry about EchoOne: she can be a little "evil-genius-y" sometimes.

I'd say more "mad-scientist-y."

Potential Agent X requires clone training.

You've come to the right lab!

We'll teach you everything you ever wanted to know about cloning, Pax!

And some things you NEVER wanted to know!

NEW MESSAGE   ✕

Follow the Echo Agents to the science lab and help them crack the coded message?

Y/N

MISSION DOSSIER

>> USE CLONES TO HACK THE SECURITY SYSTEM

The field team reports the missing coders have been moved deeper into the base. The field team must crack the highly advanced security systems protecting the lower levels. Only the Echo Agents and their specialist cloning knowledge can help!

LEVEL: 5

INSTRUCTORS: Agent EchoZero and Agent EchoOne

BACKGROUND: The Echo Agents run VALID's cutting-edge science lab. As twins, they're fascinated by cloning and duplication. They could triple a Telvian Titch-Trooper in two seconds, and EchoOne probably would. Luckily, EchoZero is the voice of reason when his sister gets a bit clone-happy.

ECHO AGENTS

MISSION OBJECTIVE 1: WRITING ON THE WALL (USING CLONES!)

PROJECT OUTLINE

NAME: SECRET MESSAGES

GOAL: FIGURE OUT HOW THE MISSING CODERS LEFT A SECRET MESSAGE USING CLONES

REQUIREMENTS: 1. WRITE A MESSAGE ON A WHITEBOARD USING CLONES
2. HIDE THE MESSAGE FROM THE ENEMY

One of the missing coders is a cloner, like us. He's used clones to leave a secret message. What do you know about clones, Pax?

It's a way of making copies?

Right. When you're coding, you often need many copies of something.

Say you're writing code with a sprite who is juggling elephants. You can make two elephant sprites with the same code.

You could duplicate them!

Yep! But what if you wanted to juggle four elephants?

Or 933 elephants?

Hmm. ETAMI would say duplicating that many elephants is inefficient.

Instead we make **one** elephant sprite; the **master** elephant sprite. We give that elephant a costume, some scripts to make it walk, trumpet, and dance, THEN we write some code to make clones. Each clone has its own copy of the elephant scripts and costumes!

When the juggling is over, the clones are deleted. Everyone lives happily ever after!

Our kidnapped coders knew about clones and left us a secret VALID message. I'll show you how.

1 Open a web browser on your computer. Type **snap.berkeley.edu/run** into your browser bar and hit enter. If you have a Snap! account, log in. Otherwise, acquire a human adult to help you make an account.

2 Click [Stage]. Go to [Backgrounds]. Make a new background by clicking to open the **paint editor**. Draw a concrete wall in the CORUPT base. Add a whiteboard over the top of it.

Click [OK] when you're done. Right-click the new background. **Rename it whiteboard**.

3 Right-click the **whiteboard** background. Choose **duplicate** to make a copy.

Right-click the **whiteboard(2)** background. Choose **edit** to make changes.

Write the mission instructions on the whiteboard.

> **MISSION INSTRUCTIONS**
> **Hold down the space key and use the mouse to draw. Click V to reveal the secret message.**

Click [OK] when you're done.

Right-click the new background. **Rename it missioninstructions**.

missioninstruction

4 Click [Scripts]. to go to the **script space**. Find and drag these blocks into the **script space**:

when [ ] clicked   when space ▾ key pressed

switch to costume [▾] × 2

5 In the **switch to costume blocks**, click the drop-down arrows. Change them to **missioninstructions** and **whiteboard**.

6 Connect the blocks to make a **setup script** and a **keypress script** matching:

when green flag clicked
switch to costume **missioninstructions**

and

when space key pressed
switch to costume **whiteboard**

or

when [ ] clicked
switch to costume missioninstructions ▾

or

when space ▾ key pressed
switch to costume whiteboard ▾

COPY THE CODE

TEST

7

TEST: Click [🏳] to run your code.
SUCCESS: The background has instructions. Much help. Many knowledge.
TEST: Press the space key.
SUCCESS: A blank whiteboard appears.

STOP THE SCRIPT!
After each test, click [ ] to stop all the scripts running. Otherwise, things get funky real fast. . .

Save as **Secret01**.

8 This is where it gets fun. We use a dot to draw the message. This is the master dot: the dot we clone to make more dots.

Click [>] Sprite. Go to [Costumes].

Click [🖊] to make a new costume.

Use [⬤] to draw a giant colored dot in the middle of the screen. Click [OK] when you're done.

masterdot

Right-click the costume. **Rename it masterdot**.

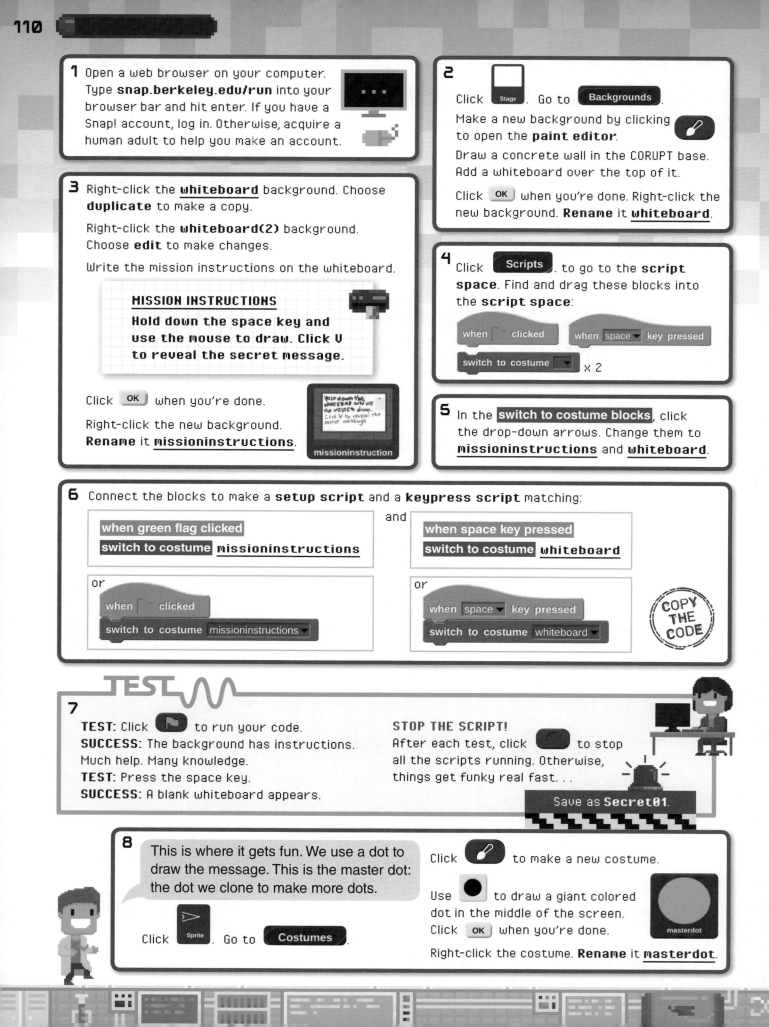

9 Click **Scripts**.
Find and drag these blocks into the **script space**:

when [ ] clicked

go to x: (0) y: (0)

set size to (100) %

broadcast [▼]

10 Mostly you don't use the master sprite itself. You just use its clones, so you set the master sprite to start off-stage.

In the **go to block**, click the **text fields**.
Change them to **x: 500 y: 500**.   go to x: (500) y: (500)

So I don't need a setup script like usual?

You need TWO!

EchoZero is right. You write one setup script for your master sprite and one setup script for your clones! The master sprite setup script runs when you click the green flag: the clone setup script starts when you make a new clone. It's so you can make each clone a bit different. You'll see!

11 In the **broadcast block**, click the drop-down arrow. Choose **new** to make a new **broadcast** message. Call it **start**. Click **OK**.

In the **set size block**, click the **text field**. Type **10**.

EXPERIMENT

12 Click the **set size block** to run it by itself. The master dot should be the same size as your mouse-pointer. Change the **set size number** to make it bigger or smaller.

13 Connect the blocks to make a **setup script** matching:

> **when green flag clicked**
> **go to x: 500 go to y: 500**
> **set size to 10%**
> **broadcast start**

or

when [ ] clicked
go to x: (500) y: (500)
set size to (10) %
broadcast start ▼

COPY THE CODE

14 Let's make some clones!

When we want unlimited clones, we make them in a **forever** loop.

If I only wanted 10 clones, would I use a **repeat 10** loop?

Exactly! These scripts are called clone-maker scripts.

Use create a clone of [▼] to create them.

Find and drag these blocks into the **script space**:

when I receive [▼]

forever   if [⬡]

key space ▼ pressed?

create a clone of [▼]

15 In the **when I receive block**, click the drop-down arrow. Choose **start**.

Click and drag the **key pressed block** into the blank hexagon of the **if block**.

if ⟨ key space ▼ pressed? ⟩

16 We'll clone the master dot when spacebar is pressed down.

In the **create a clone block**, click the drop-down arrow. Choose **myself**.

Connect the blocks to make a **clone-maker script** to match:

> **when I receive start**
> **forever**
>   **if key space pressed**
>   **create a clone of myself**

or

when I receive start ▼
forever
  if ⟨ key space ▼ pressed? ⟩
    create a clone of myself ▼

COPY THE CODE

17 We must write a **setup script** for the clones.

Don't the clones use the **masterdot** setup script?

They use both! The **masterdot** setup script sets up everything that is the SAME in all the clones.

The clone setup script uses its own starter block and it sets up things that might be different for each clone, like XY coordinates. Each of these clones will start wherever the mouse-pointer is, so each one will have a different set of XY coordinates.

I'm so confused right now.

It's VERY confusing, but we'll show you what to do and help you understand.

Find and drag these blocks into the **script space**:

    when I start as a clone   go to [▼]

20 See, every clone gets its own coordinates when it's made, so we get dots all over the stage!

Awesomebeans. Can we change other things too?

Find and drag these blocks into the **script space**:

    change ghost ▼ effect by 25   mouse y

21 In the **change effect by block**, choose **color**.

    change color ▼ effect by 25

Click and drag the **mouse y** block into the empty text field of the **change color effect block**.

    change color ▼ effect by mouse y

Click and drag the **change color effect by mouse y block**. Insert it at the top of the **clone setup script**.

    when I start as a clone
    change color ▼ effect by mouse y
    go to mouse-pointer ▼

18 In the **go to block**, click the drop-down arrow. Choose **mouse-pointer**.

Connect the blocks to make a **clone setup script** to match:

    when I start as a clone
    go to mouse-pointer

or

    when I start as a clone
    go to mouse-pointer ▼

COPY THE CODE

TEST

19
TEST: Click [⚑]. Hold down the **spacebar** to write a message on the whiteboard.
SUCCESS: The dotty message follows the mouse-pointer!
ERROR: Nothing happens! Disaster!
FIX: Check your **go to block** is set to **mouse-pointer**.

    go to mouse-pointer ▼ ✓   go to ▼ ✗

ERROR: If your tests don't pass or your code does something unexpected, it's time to go bug-hunting. Strap on your bug-hunting goggles and read your code aloud. What is each block doing and why?

STOP THE SCRIPT! Click [⬤].

When you're making clones, make sure you click [⬤] when you've finished with the script.

Right! Otherwise you end up with leftover clones from your last message.

Too many clones means a bad time for everyone.

TEST

22
TEST: Click [⚑]. Try writing secret messages.
SUCCESS: Rainbow messages!

STOP THE SCRIPT! Click [⬤].

Save as **Secret02**.

ACHIEVEMENT UNLOCKED!
CLONER
2 LEVEL

MISSION OBJECTIVE 2: HIDE THE MESSAGE FROM PRYING EYES

1 Find and drag these blocks into the **script space**:

forever · if · else · show · hide · key space pressed?

2 In the `key pressed block`, click the drop-down arrow. Choose **v**.

Click and drag the `key v pressed?` block into the blank hexagon of the `if else block`.

3 Connect the blocks at the end of the **clone setup script** to match:

```
when I start as a clone
change color effect by mouse y
go to mouse-pointer
forever
    if key v pressed?
        show
    else
        hide
```

or

```
when I start as a clone
change color ▼ effect by (mouse y)
go to mouse-pointer ▼
forever
    if < key v ▼ pressed? >
        show
    else
        hide
```

COPY THE CODE

TEST

4

TEST: Click 🚩. Hold down the **spacebar** to write a message.
SUCCESS: Nothing happens! The screen stays the same! What?!
TEST: Press the **v** key. Then let it go!
SUCCESS: The message appears! And disappears!
ERROR: Something strange is happening. Go back to the end of the last test, then read the instructions again. Does your code match Pax's?

STOP THE SCRIPT! Click 🛑.

EXPERIMENT

5 Experiment with the color effect for your clones. Instead of using `mouse y`, try these:

`mouse x`

`pick random 10 to 200`   `mouse x + mouse y`

The field team have cracked the code and found the message! They've given us a back door into the security system.

We might be able to transmit some junk data to overload the system and open the doors. Up for that, Pax?

Remotely hacking into a CORUPT security system? Yes!

Save as **Secret03**.

MISSION DOSSIER

➤➤ OVERLOAD THE SYSTEM! WITH JUNK!

The missing coders have left the key to hacking into the CORUPT security. The Echo Agents think they can transmit enough junk data to force an overload. That will shut down the system long enough to get our team inside before CORUPT catches on. Here goes nothing...

LEVEL: 5

INSTRUCTORS: Agent EchoZero and Agent EchoOne

MISSION OBJECTIVE 1: DESIGN A SINGLE BIT

PROJECT OUTLINE
NAME: TRANSMISSION
GOAL: TRANSMIT THE CLONED CODE AND REMOVE AS MANY VALID BITS AS POSSIBLE.
REQUIREMENTS:
1. DESIGN A SINGLE BIT TO TEST THE TRANSMISSION PROTOCOL
2. USE CLONES TO FLOOD THE CORUPT BASE-CONTROL WITH LOGIC ERRORS
3. USE MOUSE-CLICK EVENTS TO REMOVE THE VALID SYMBOL IN THE TRANSMISSION
4. USE VARIABLES TO COUNT THE DELETED BITS

1 Open a web browser on your computer. Type **snap.berkeley.edu/run** into your browser bar and hit **enter**.

Start a new project by clicking [ ]. Choose **new**.

Click **Stage**. Go to **Backgrounds**. Make a new background by clicking [ ] to open the **paint editor**.

Paint a cyberspace transmission background. Click **OK** when you're done.
Pax's looks like this:

Yours can be
however you like!

2 Right-click the new background. **Rename** it **sending**.

Right-click **sending**. Choose **duplicate** to make a copy.

Right-click **sending(2)**. Choose **edit** to make changes.

3 Use [ ] and [ ] to make a sign on top of the background that says **V-bit sent**. Click the **undo button** if you make a mistake. Click **OK**.

Right click **sending(2)**. Rename it **sent**.

4 Click **Scripts**. Find and drag these blocks into the **script space**:

when [ ] clicked   when I receive [▼]

switch to costume [▼] x 2   stop all [▼]

5 In the first **switch to costume block**, click the drop-down arrow. Choose **sending**.

Connect **switch to costume sending** underneath the **when green flag clicked block** to make a **setup script**.

6 In the **when I receive block**, click the drop-down arrow. Choose **new** to make a new **broadcast** message. Call it **missed**. Click **OK**.

In the second **switch to costume block**, click the drop-down menu. Choose **sent**.

7 What does the **stop all block** do?

It stops all scripts in all sprites, including the forever loops, which are what we use to make our clones.

If we don't stop them, they make clones forever.

Connect the blocks to make an **endgame script** to match:

COPY THE CODE

when I receive **missed**
switch to costume **sent**
stop all

or

when I receive missed [▼]
switch to costume sent [▼]
stop all [▼]

TEST

8
TEST: Click **Control**. Find a **broadcast block**. Click the drop-down arrow. Choose **missed**. Click the **broadcast missed block** to run it by itself.
SUCCESS: The background says V-bit sent!
TEST: Click [⚑].
SUCCESS: The background is sending. . .
ERROR: A wild bug appears! Check your code matches the examples.

STOP THE SCRIPT!
Click [ ].

9

Click 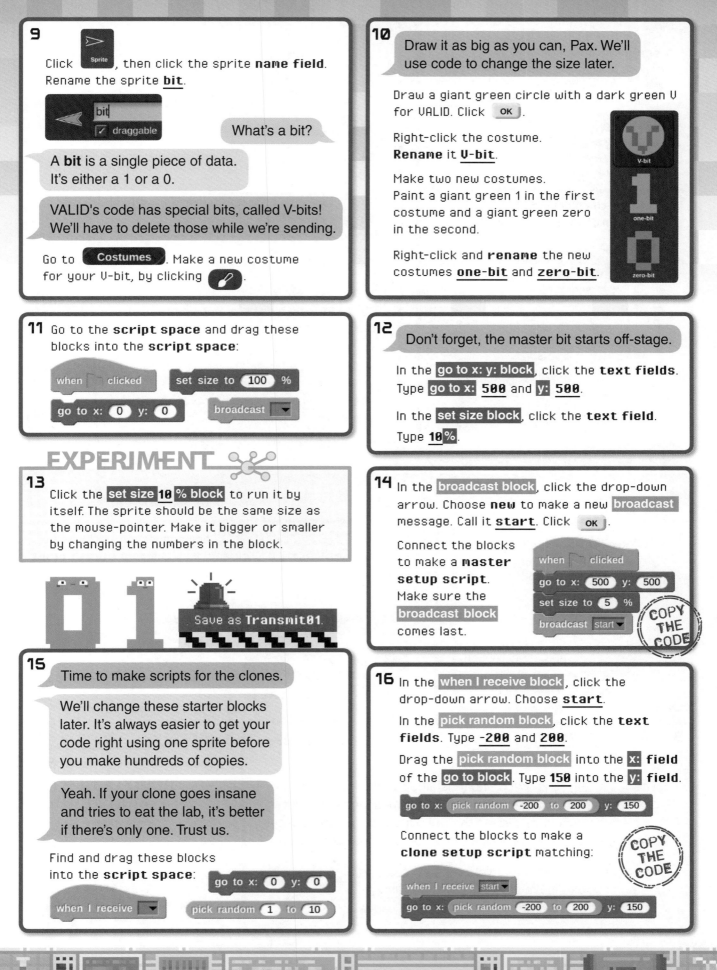 **Sprite**, then click the sprite **name field**. Rename the sprite **bit**.

bit
☑ draggable

What's a bit?

A **bit** is a single piece of data. It's either a 1 or a 0.

VALID's code has special bits, called V-bits! We'll have to delete those while we're sending.

Go to **Costumes**. Make a new costume for your V-bit, by clicking 🖊.

10

Draw it as big as you can, Pax. We'll use code to change the size later.

Draw a giant green circle with a dark green V for VALID. Click **OK**.

Right-click the costume. **Rename** it **V-bit**.

Make two new costumes. Paint a giant green 1 in the first costume and a giant green zero in the second.

Right-click and **rename** the new costumes **one-bit** and **zero-bit**.

11 Go to the **script space** and drag these blocks into the **script space**:

when ⚑ clicked set size to 100 %
go to x: 0 y: 0 broadcast ▾

12

Don't forget, the master bit starts off-stage.

In the **go to x: y: block**, click the **text fields**. Type **go to x: 500** and **y: 500**.

In the **set size block**, click the **text field**. Type **10**%.

EXPERIMENT

13

Click the **set size 10 % block** to run it by itself. The sprite should be the same size as the mouse-pointer. Make it bigger or smaller by changing the numbers in the block.

Save as **Transmit01**.

14 In the **broadcast block**, click the drop-down arrow. Choose **new** to make a new **broadcast** message. Call it **start**. Click **OK**.

Connect the blocks to make a **master setup script**. Make sure the **broadcast block** comes last.

when ⚑ clicked
go to x: 500 y: 500
set size to 5 %
broadcast start ▾

COPY THE CODE

15

Time to make scripts for the clones.

We'll change these starter blocks later. It's always easier to get your code right using one sprite before you make hundreds of copies.

Yeah. If your clone goes insane and tries to eat the lab, it's better if there's only one. Trust us.

Find and drag these blocks into the **script space**:

go to x: 0 y: 0
when I receive ▾
pick random 1 to 10

16 In the **when I receive block**, click the drop-down arrow. Choose **start**.

In the **pick random block**, click the **text fields**. Type **-200** and **200**.

Drag the **pick random block** into the **x: field** of the **go to block**. Type **150** into the **y: field**.

go to x: pick random -200 to 200 y: 150

Connect the blocks to make a **clone setup script** matching:

when I receive start ▾
go to x: pick random -200 to 200 y: 150

COPY THE CODE

17 Find and drag these blocks into the **script space**:

when I receive ▼

repeat until ◢

y position   ▢ < ▢

change y by 10

18 In the **when I receive block**, click the drop-down arrow. Choose **start**.

Click and drag the **y position block** into the left field of the **less than block**. Type **-300** in the right field.

y position < -300

Drag the **less than block** into the hexagonal field in the **repeat until block**.

In the **change y by block**, click the **text field**. Type **-2**. Drag it inside the **repeat until block**.

19 Connect the blocks to make a **movement script** matching:

when I receive **start**
repeat until **y position** < **–300**
    change y by **–2**

or

when I receive start ▼
repeat until   y position   < -300
change y by -2

COPY THE CODE

TEST

20
TEST: Click 🚩.
SUCCESS: The bit sprite should start at the top of the screen and fall to the bottom.

TEST: Click 🚩 5-10 times.
SUCCESS: The bit sprite will start in different places across the top of the screen.
ERROR: There's something strange in the neighborhood! Who you gonna call? Bug hunters!

STOP THE SCRIPT! Click ⬤ .

Save as **Transmit02**.

MISSION OBJECTIVE 2: OVERLOAD THE SYSTEM

1 Now we know it works . . .

. . . and doesn't explode . . .

. . . we clone!

Drag these blocks into the **script space**:   delete this clone

when I start as a clone   x 2

2 Drag the **delete this clone block** and connect it at the end of the **movement script**. Click and drag the **movement script** and the **clone setup script** and connect them underneath the **when I start as a clone blocks**.

when I receive start ▼   when I start as a clone

repeat until   y position   < -300   when I receive start ▼

change y by -2   when I start as a clone

delete this clone

go to x: pick random -200 to 200   y: 150

3 Drag the **when I receive start blocks** into the **code menu area** to delete them.

The **delete block** is one of the most important blocks for a clone-maker, Pax. When we were writing messages, we just deleted our clones by clicking the red button. But people **always** forget to click the red button. It's safer doing it with code blocks.

There are a few ways that your mission can end. It's up to you to make sure there are no leftover clones when you're done, no matter what happens.

ACHIEVEMENT UNLOCKED!
CLONER

3 LEVEL

4 Click **Variables**, then **Make a variable**.
Name the variable **clone speed**.

5 Find and drag these blocks into the **script space**:

when I receive ▼   wait 1 secs
create a clone of ▼   repeat 10   forever
change ▼ by 1   clone speed
next costume   set ▼ to 0

6 This one needs to happen at the beginning, right? In the master setup script?

In the **set to 0 block**, click the drop-down arrow. Choose **clone speed**. Type **1** in the text field.

Drag the **set clone speed to 1 block** and insert it in the **master setup script**.

COPY THE CODE

when 🏳 clicked
set clone speed ▼ to 1
go to x: 500 y: 500
set size to 5 %
broadcast start ▼

7 In the **when I receive block**, click the drop-down arrow. Choose **start**.

In the **change by 1 block**, click the drop-down arrow. Choose **clone speed**. Click the text field. Type **-0.1**.

change clone speed ▼ by -0.1

In the **repeat 10 block**, click the text field. Type **8**.

Why eight, by the way?

Because there are eight bits in a byte! Transmission gets faster after each byte is sent.

8 In the **create a clone of block**, click the drop-down arrow. Choose **myself**.

Click and drag the **clone speed block** into the text field of the **wait 1 secs block**.

wait clone speed secs

9 Connect the blocks to make a **clone-maker script**:

when I receive **start**
forever
  repeat **8**
    next costume
    create a clone of **myself**
    wait clonespeed secs
    change clonespeed by -0.1

or

when I receive start ▼
forever
  repeat 8
    next costume
    create a clone of myself ▼
    wait clone speed secs
    change clone speed ▼ by -0.1

COPY THE CODE

TEST

10
TEST: Click 🏳.
SUCCESS: It's raining 1s, 0s, and Us!

TEST: Click **Variables**. Click the check box for **clone speed** to make it show on screen. Then click 🏳.
SUCCESS: Clone speed starts at 1. It gets smaller as more bits are made. When it gets below 0, the screen should fill up with bits!
ERROR: Clone production slows, or the screen instantly fills up!
FIX: Check your two **clone speed** blocks. Clone speed should be set to **1** in the **master setup script** and change by **-0.1** in the **clone-maker script**.
STOP THE SCRIPT! Click ⬭.

HINT
If the test passes, uncheck the **clone speed button**.
OK

Save as **Transmit03**.

MISSION OBJECTIVE 3: THE EVIDENCE IN THE TRANSMISSION

1 Find and drag these blocks into the **script space**:

when I am clicked ▼ · if · costume # · play sound ▼ · delete this clone · ☐ = ☐

2 Click and drag the **costume# block** into the left field of the **= block**. Type **1** in the right field.

costume # = 1

3 Click ▬. Choose **sounds** to bring up the **sound importer menu**.

Find a sound. (Pax used **Pop**.) Double-click it to import it. Click **cancel** when you're done. Go back to the **script space**.

In the **play sound block**, click the drop-down arrow. Choose the sound you imported.

Project notes...
New   ^N
Open...   ^O
Save   ^S
Save As...
Import...
Export project...
Export summary...
Import tools
Libraries...
Costumes...
Sounds...

4 Connect the blocks to make an **event script**:

```
when I am clicked
if costume# = 1
    play sound Pop
    delete this clone
```

or

```
when I am clicked ▼
if < costume # = 1 >
play sound Pop ▼
delete this clone
```

5

TEST ∿

TEST: Click ⚑, then click on a falling V-bit.
SUCCESS: The V-bit disappears with a mighty noise!
ERROR: Nothing happens. . .
FIX: Check your costume order. Go to **Costumes**. Click and drag the **V-bit costume** so it's the first costume listed.

STOP THE SCRIPT! Click ▬.

6 Find and drag these blocks into the **script space**:

if · broadcast ▼ · costume # · ☐ = ☐

7 In the **broadcast block**, click the drop-down arrow. Choose **missed**. Connect the blocks:

```
if costume# = 1
    broadcast missed
```

or

```
if < costume # = 1 >
broadcast missed ▼
```

COPY THE CODE

8 Click and drag this script. Insert it into your **movement script** before **delete this clone** but after the **repeat until block**:

```
when I start as a clone
repeat until < y position < -300 >
change y by -2

delete this clone

if < costume # = 1 >
broadcast missed ▼
```

POP!

TEST ∿

9

TEST: Click ⚑. Let a V-bit fall to the bottom.
SUCCESS: The background changes! Code stops falling!
ERROR: An unexpected error has occurred! Grab your bug spray and have a look at your code. Is it the same as Pax's?

STOP THE SCRIPT! Click ▬.

Save as **Transmit04**.

MISSION OBJECTIVE 4: COUNT HOW MANY BITS YOU'VE POPPED!

1 Click **Variables**. Click **Make a variable**.
Name the variable **deleted**.

2 Find and drag these blocks into the **script space**:
set [▼] to [0]   change [▼] by (1)

3 In both blocks, click the drop-down arrow. Choose **deleted**.

Click and drag the set **deleted** to **0** block and insert it in the **setup script** under the when green flag clicked block.

when [ ] clicked
set deleted ▼ to 0
set clone speed ▼ to 1
go to x: (500) y: (500)
set size to (5) %
broadcast start ▼

4 Click and drag the
change **deleted** by **1** block
and insert it in the **event script** under the
play sound **Pop** block.

Make sure the box next to **deleted** in the **code menu area** is clicked.

when I am clicked ▼
if < costume # = 3 >
play sound Pop ▼
change deleted ▼ by (1)
change score ▼ by (1)
delete this clone

TEST ⎍⎍

5
TEST: Click 🏴. Click to delete V-bits.
SUCCESS: When you click a V-bit, **deleted** goes up by 1!
TEST: Click 🏴 to run the test again.
SUCCESS: Deleted resets to 0 when you click 🏴. HUGE SUCCESS!
STOP THE SCRIPT! Click ⬤.

Save as **Transmit05**.

MISSION DOSSIER

≫ GET PAST THE GUARDS

The agents have broken into the base! But nothing is that easy. The coders are held deep in the base. The team must get past the incredibly smelly CORUPT guards!

LEVEL: 5
INSTRUCTORS: Agent EchoZero and Agent EchoOne

MISSION OBJECTIVE 1: MAP OUT THE BASE

Our overload script worked, Pax! The field team is moving into the lower level of the base.

The coders must be near the control room. The field team needs to sneak past the guards.

PROJECT OUTLINE

NAME: BASE SNEAK

GOAL: SNEAK PAST THE GUARDS INTO THE CONTROL ROOM OF THE CORUPT BASE.

REQUIREMENTS:
1. GENERATE A MAP OF THE ENEMY BASE
2. GENERATE SIX ENEMY PATROL GUARDS USING CLONES
3. MAKE THE GUARDS MOVE FASTER WHEN THEY SMELL AGENT Q
4. CREATE A MOVEMENT LOOP FOR AGENT Q USING W, A, S, AND D KEYS.
5. TRIGGER ENDGAME WHEN AGENT Q GETS CAUGHT BY A GUARD

1

Start a new project by clicking 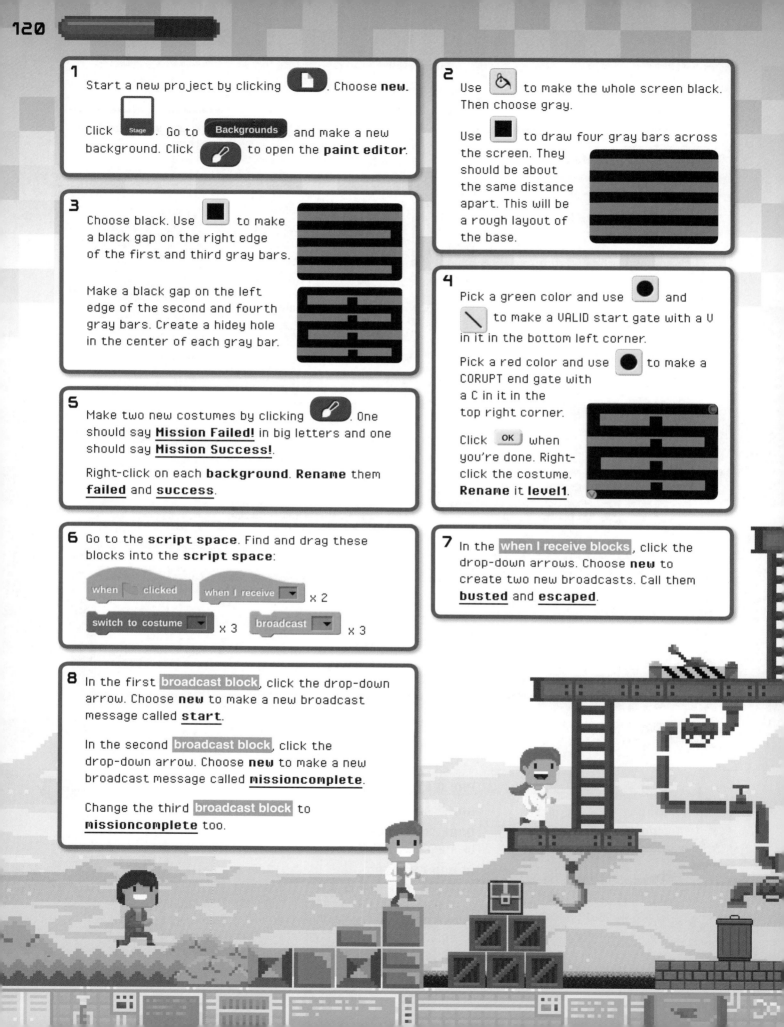. Choose **new**.

Click **Stage**. Go to **Backgrounds** and make a new background. Click 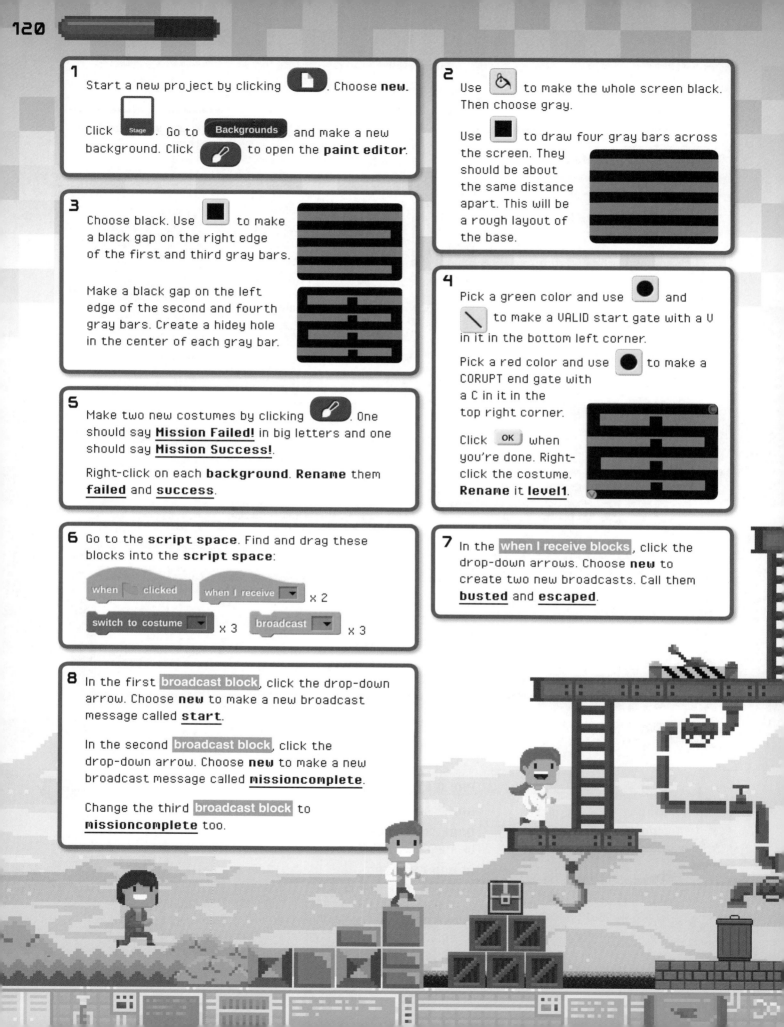 to open the **paint editor**.

2

Use 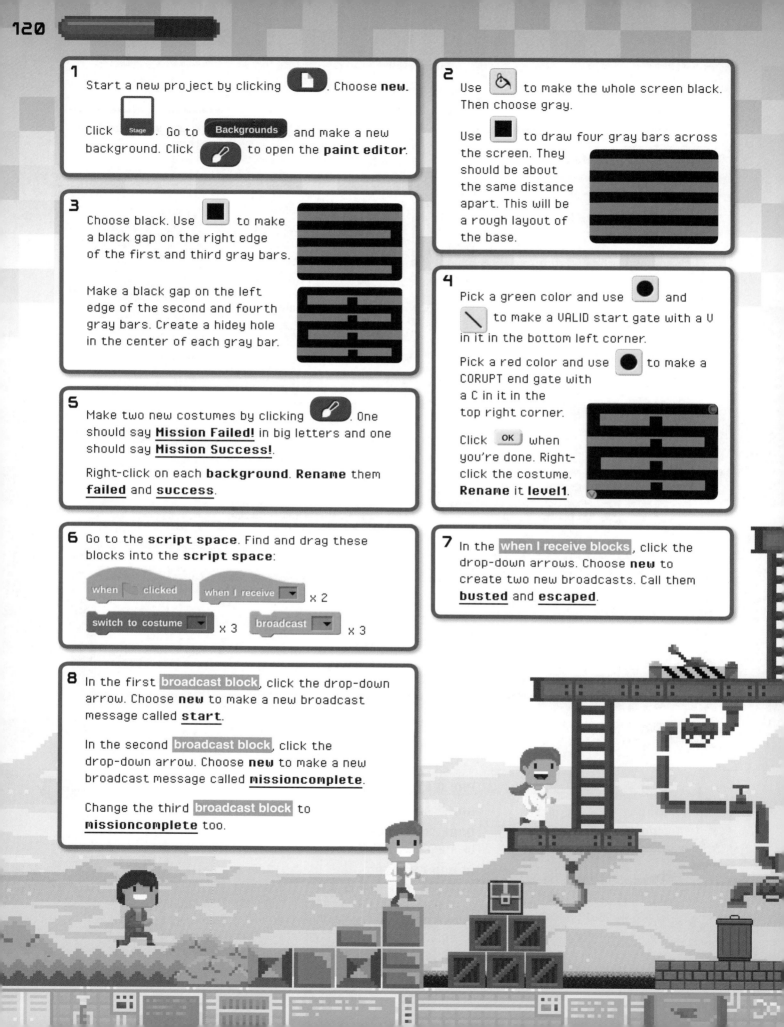 to make the whole screen black. Then choose gray.

Use 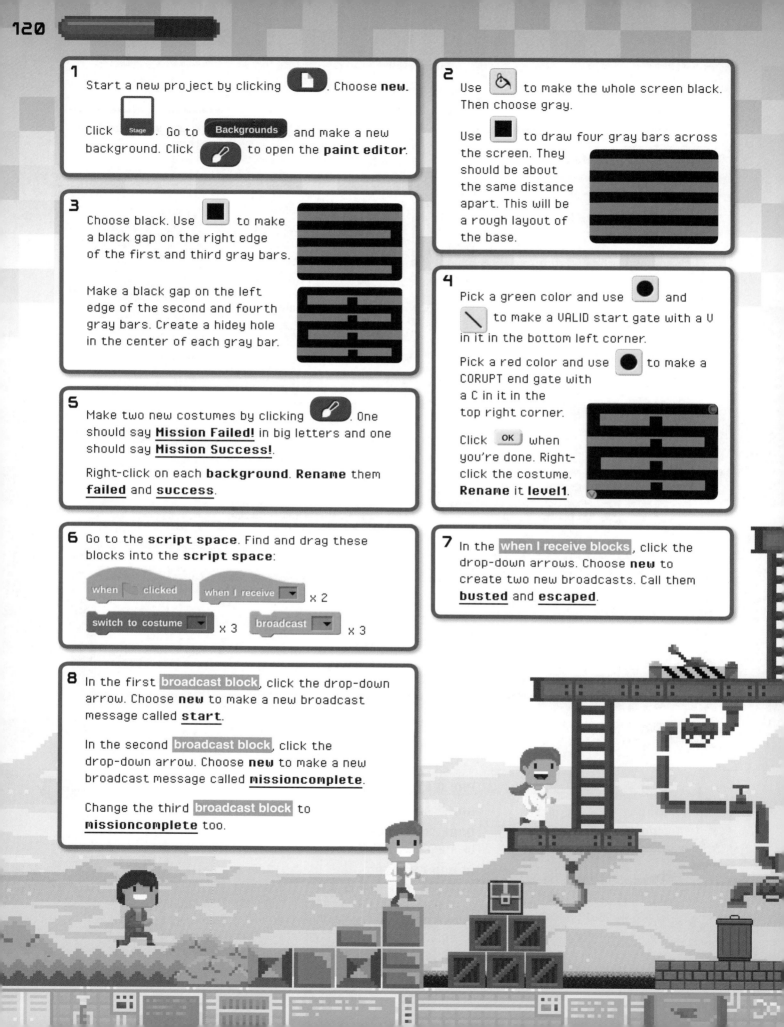 to draw four gray bars across the screen. They should be about the same distance apart. This will be a rough layout of the base.

3

Choose black. Use 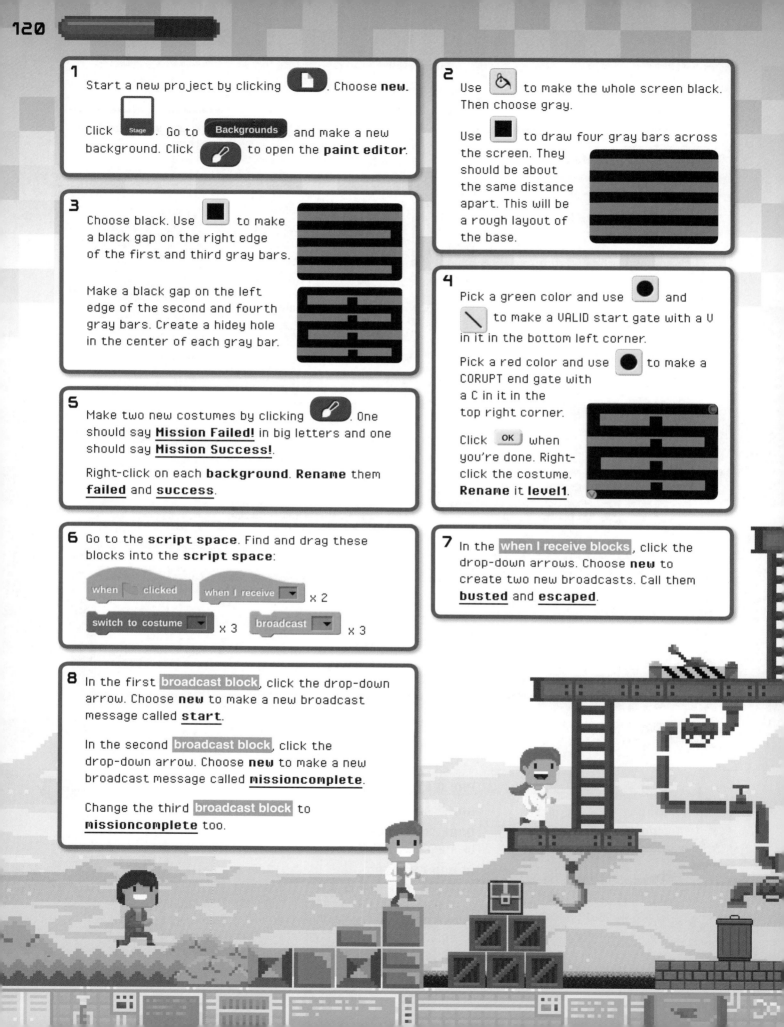 to make a black gap on the right edge of the first and third gray bars.

Make a black gap on the left edge of the second and fourth gray bars. Create a hidey hole in the center of each gray bar.

4

Pick a green color and use 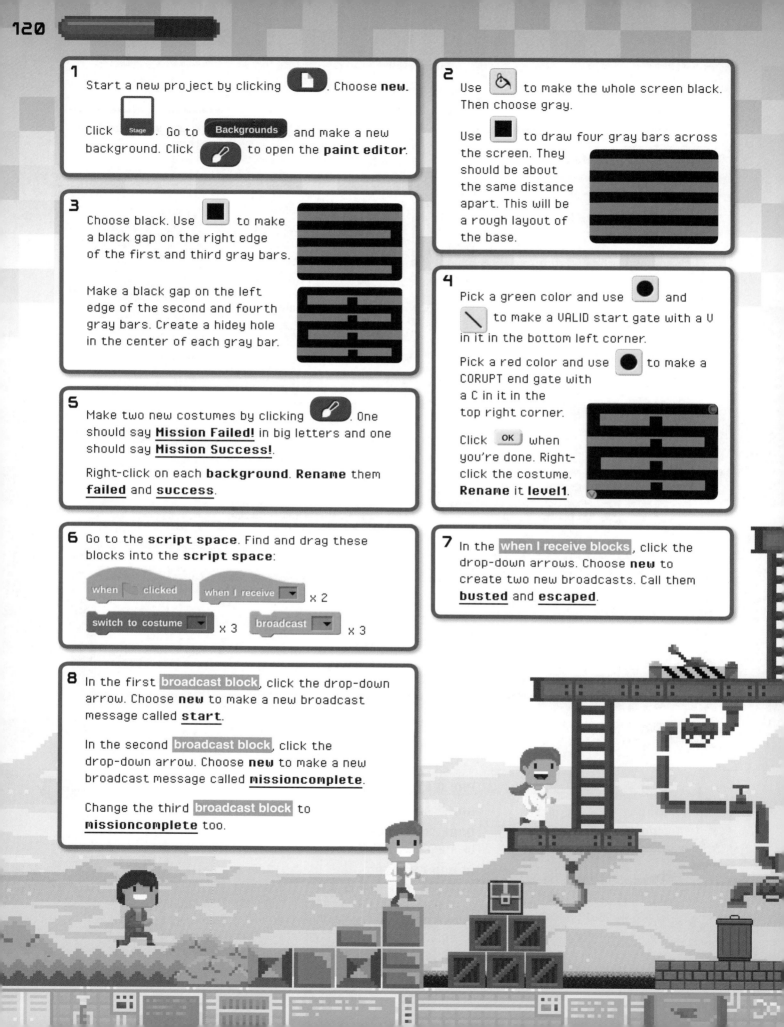 and 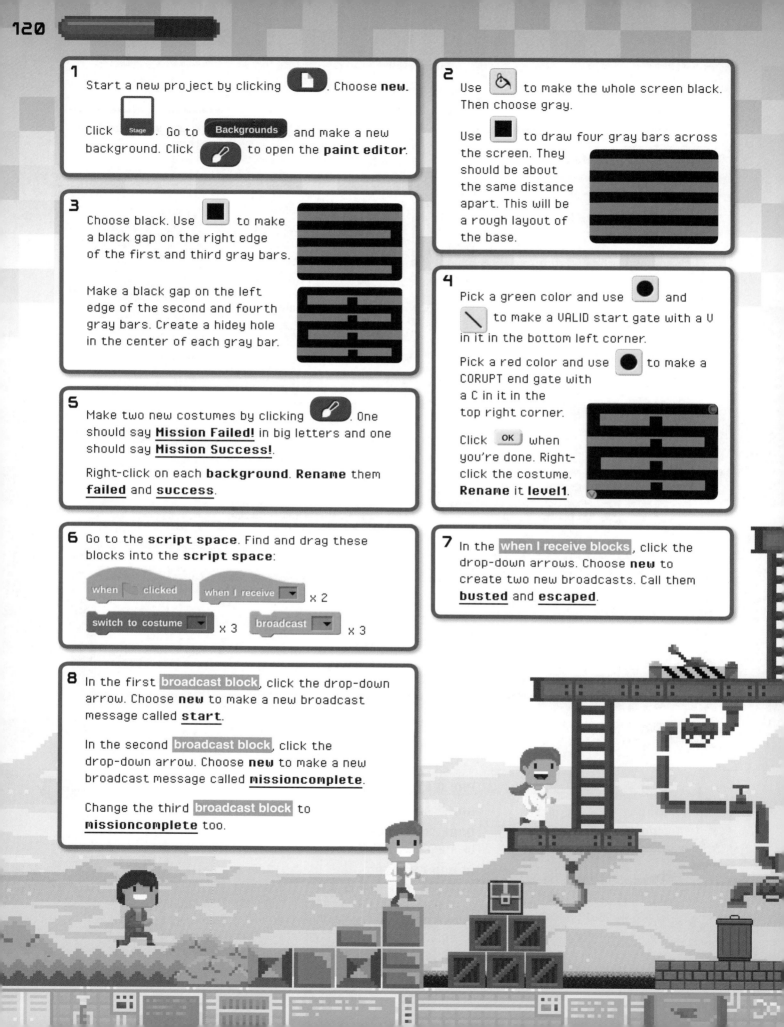 to make a VALID start gate with a V in it in the bottom left corner.

Pick a red color and use 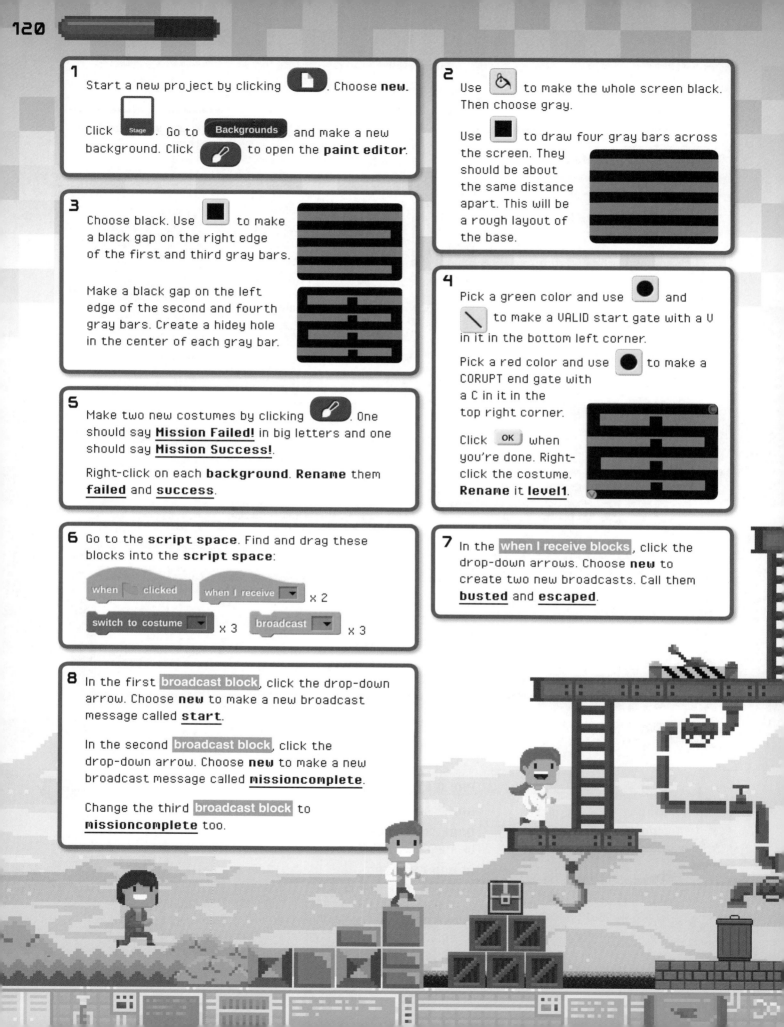 to make a CORUPT end gate with a C in it in the top right corner.

Click **OK** when you're done. Right-click the costume. **Rename** it **level1**.

5

Make two new costumes by clicking 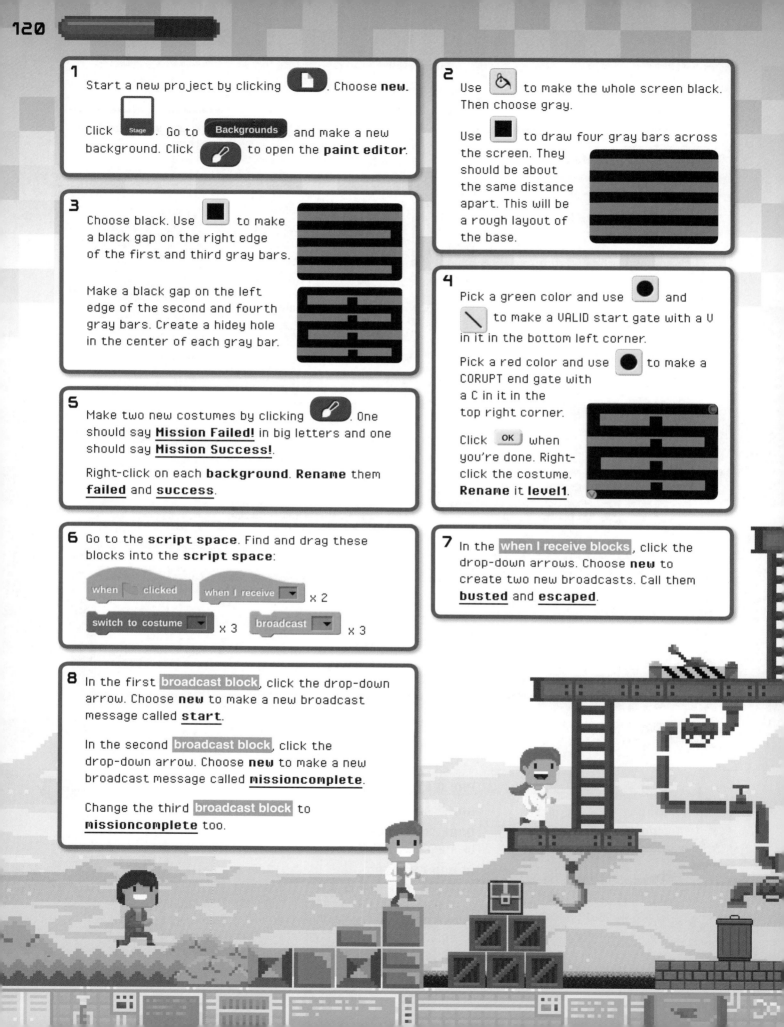. One should say **Mission Failed!** in big letters and one should say **Mission Success!**.

Right-click on each **background**. **Rename** them **failed** and **success**.

6

Go to the **script space**. Find and drag these blocks into the **script space**:

when clicked
when I receive ▼ x 2
switch to costume ▼ x 3
broadcast ▼ x 3

7

In the **when I receive blocks**, click the drop-down arrows. Choose **new** to create two new broadcasts. Call them **busted** and **escaped**.

8

In the first **broadcast block**, click the drop-down arrow. Choose **new** to make a new broadcast message called **start**.

In the second **broadcast block**, click the drop-down arrow. Choose **new** to make a new broadcast message called **missioncomplete**.

Change the third **broadcast block** to **missioncomplete** too.

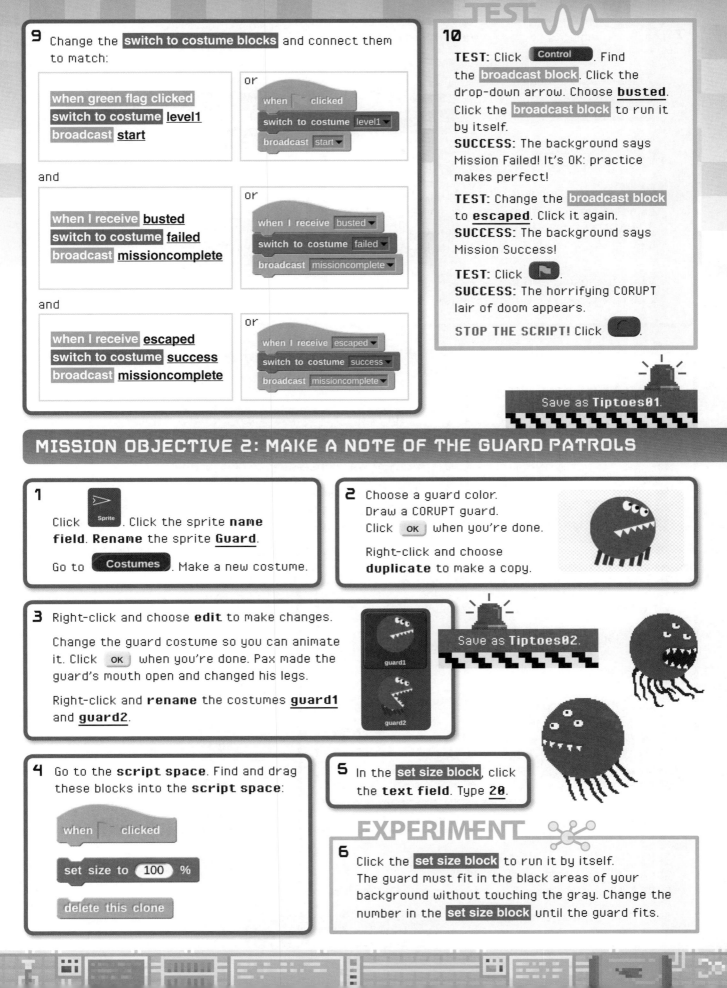

9 Change the **switch to costume blocks** and connect them to match:

when green flag clicked
switch to costume **level1**
broadcast **start**

or
when ⚑ clicked
switch to costume level1 ▾
broadcast start ▾

and

when I receive **busted**
switch to costume **failed**
broadcast **missioncomplete**

or
when I receive busted ▾
switch to costume failed ▾
broadcast missioncomplete ▾

and

when I receive **escaped**
switch to costume **success**
broadcast **missioncomplete**

or
when I receive escaped ▾
switch to costume success ▾
broadcast missioncomplete ▾

10

TEST: Click [Control]. Find the **broadcast block**. Click the drop-down arrow. Choose **busted**. Click the **broadcast block** to run it by itself.
SUCCESS: The background says Mission Failed! It's OK: practice makes perfect!

TEST: Change the **broadcast block** to **escaped**. Click it again.
SUCCESS: The background says Mission Success!

TEST: Click ⚑.
SUCCESS: The horrifying CORUPT lair of doom appears.

STOP THE SCRIPT! Click ⬣.

Save as **Tiptoes01**.

MISSION OBJECTIVE 2: MAKE A NOTE OF THE GUARD PATROLS

1 Click [Sprite]. Click the sprite **name field. Rename** the sprite **Guard**.

Go to [Costumes]. Make a new costume.

2 Choose a guard color. Draw a CORUPT guard. Click [OK] when you're done.

Right-click and choose **duplicate** to make a copy.

3 Right-click and choose **edit** to make changes.

Change the guard costume so you can animate it. Click [OK] when you're done. Pax made the guard's mouth open and changed his legs.

Right-click and **rename** the costumes **guard1** and **guard2**.

Save as **Tiptoes02**.

4 Go to the **script space**. Find and drag these blocks into the **script space**:

when ⚑ clicked

set size to 100 %

delete this clone

5 In the **set size block**, click the **text field**. Type **20**.

EXPERIMENT

6 Click the **set size block** to run it by itself. The guard must fit in the black areas of your background without touching the gray. Change the number in the **set size block** until the guard fits.

7 Connect the blocks to make a **master setup script**:

```
when green flag clicked
set size to 16 %
delete this clone
```

or

```
when ⚑ clicked
set size to 16 %
delete this clone
```

Why are we deleting clones at the start?

When this **master setup script** runs, no clones have been made yet. Any clones that ARE here when this script runs are left over from whoever ran the code last.

We're trying to prevent a CLONEPOCALYPSE here, Pax...

8 Find and drag these blocks into the **script space**:

```
when I start as a clone
```
```
forever
```
```
move 10 steps
```
```
if on edge, bounce
```

What does the **if on edge, bounce block** do?

It stops sprites moving off stage. When the guards hit the edge, they turn around.

Like slightly evil clockwork.

9 In the **move 10 steps block**, click the **text field**. Type **1**.

Connect the blocks to make a **movement script**:

```
when I start as a clone
forever
  move 1 steps
  if on edge, bounce
```

COPY THE CODE

TEST

10 We haven't made any clones yet. We can't test this.

True! But if I click this script, the master guard . . .

. . . will pretend it's a clone, so we can test before we're knee-deep in cloney creeps.

TEST: Click the new script to run the code.
SUCCESS: The guard glides back and forth across the stage. Sinister.

STOP THE SCRIPT! Click ⬤ .

11 He looks a little stilted, wouldn't you say EchoOne?

Yeah, let's let him stretch his... er . . .

Tentacles?

Let him stretch his tentacles a bit!

Find and drag these blocks into the **script space**:

```
forever
```
```
next costume
```
```
wait 1 secs
```
```
when I start as a clone
```

12 In the **wait 1 secs block**, click the text field. Type **0.2**.

Connect the blocks to make an **animation script** to match:

```
when I start as a clone
forever
  next costume
  wait 0.2 secs
```

or

```
when I start as a clone
forever
  next costume
  wait 0.2 secs
```

TEST

13
TEST: Click the new script.
SUCCESS: The guard is animated!
ERROR: Make sure your guard costumes are different!

STOP THE SCRIPT! Click ⬤ .

Save as **Tiptoes03**.

MISSION OBJECTIVE 3: MAKE THE GUARDS SPEED UP!

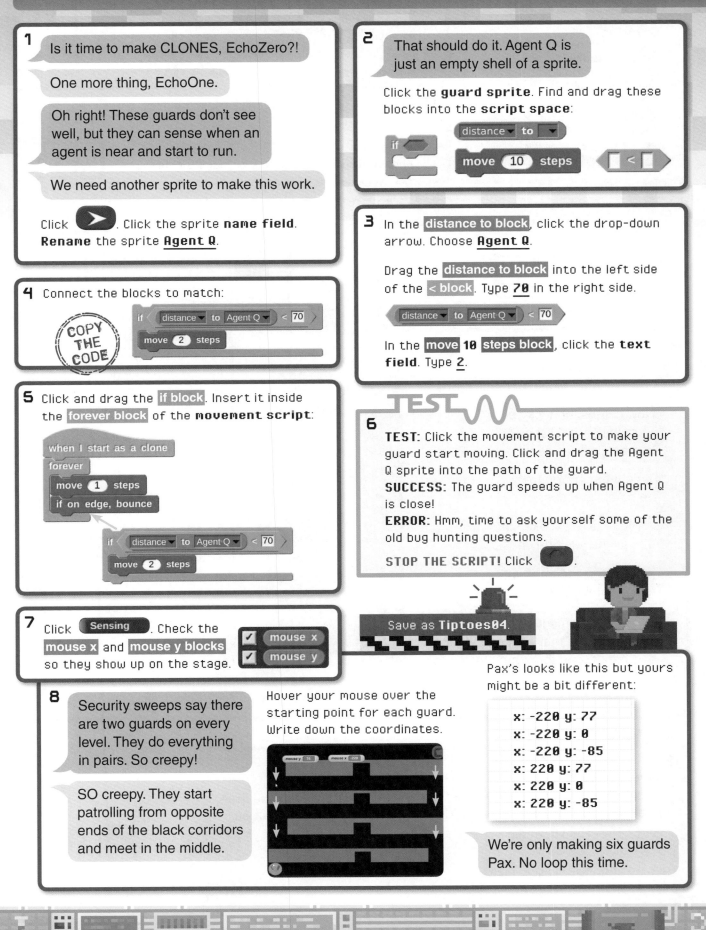

1 Is it time to make CLONES, EchoZero?!

One more thing, EchoOne.

Oh right! These guards don't see well, but they can sense when an agent is near and start to run.

We need another sprite to make this work.

Click **▶**. Click the sprite **name field**. **Rename** the sprite **Agent Q**.

2 That should do it. Agent Q is just an empty shell of a sprite.

Click the **guard sprite**. Find and drag these blocks into the **script space**:

distance ▾ to ▾

if

move 10 steps

☐ < ☐

3 In the **distance to block**, click the drop-down arrow. Choose **Agent Q**.

Drag the **distance to block** into the left side of the **< block**. Type **70** in the right side.

distance ▾ to Agent Q ▾ < 70

In the **move 10 steps block**, click the **text field**. Type **2**.

4 Connect the blocks to match:

COPY THE CODE

if distance ▾ to Agent Q ▾ < 70
move 2 steps

5 Click and drag the **if block**. Insert it inside the **forever block** of the **movement script**:

when I start as a clone
forever
  move 1 steps
  if on edge, bounce

if distance ▾ to Agent Q ▾ < 70
move 2 steps

6 TEST

TEST: Click the movement script to make your guard start moving. Click and drag the Agent Q sprite into the path of the guard.
SUCCESS: The guard speeds up when Agent Q is close!
ERROR: Hmm, time to ask yourself some of the old bug hunting questions.

STOP THE SCRIPT! Click **⬤**.

Save as **Tiptoes04**.

7 Click **Sensing**. Check the **mouse x** and **mouse y blocks** so they show up on the stage.

☑ mouse x
☑ mouse y

8 Security sweeps say there are two guards on every level. They do everything in pairs. So creepy!

SO creepy. They start patrolling from opposite ends of the black corridors and meet in the middle.

Hover your mouse over the starting point for each guard. Write down the coordinates.

Pax's looks like this but yours might be a bit different:

x: -220 y: 77
x: -220 y: 0
x: -220 y: -85
x: 220 y: 77
x: 220 y: 0
x: 220 y: -85

We're only making six guards Pax. No loop this time.

9 Find and drag these blocks into the **script space**:

when I receive ▼

point in direction (90 ▼) x 2

go to x: (0) y: (0) x 7

create a clone of ▼

10 In the `when I receive block`, click the drop-down arrow. Choose **start**.

In the `point in direction blocks`, click the drop-down arrows. Change one to **90** and the other to **-90**.

11 In the `create a clone of block`, click the drop-down arrow. Choose **myself**.

Right-click the `create a clone of myself block`. Choose **duplicate** 6 times to make 6 copies.

12 As usual, the master guard starts off stage.

So underappreciated, EchoOne.

In one of the `go to blocks`, click the **text fields**. Change them to x:**500** y:**500**.

13 Connect the blocks to make a **clone-maker script**:

when I receive start
point in direction **90**
go to x: **0** y: **0**
create a clone of **myself**
go to x: **0** y: **0**
create a clone of **myself**
go to x: **0** y: **0**
create a clone of **myself**
point in direction **-90**
go to x: **0** y: **0**
create a clone of **myself**
go to x: **0** y: **0**
create a clone of **myself**
go to x: **0** y: **0**
create a clone of **myself**
go to x: **500** y: **500**

14 The clones can't all start in the middle of the stage!

Now comes the tricky bit. Remember that list of x and y coordinates you wrote down?

Type them in! You must be careful because . . .

. . . you have to make sure that all the left-side ones . . .

. . . that's all the ones with a minus symbol for x . . .

. . . need to come first. The first three are the clones that start on the left and the second three are the . . .

. . . clones that start on the right!

when I receive start ▼
point in direction (90 ▼)
go to x: (-220) y: (77)
create a clone of myself ▼
go to x: (-220) y: (0)
create a clone of myself ▼
go to x: (-220) y: (-85)
create a clone of myself ▼
point in direction (-90 ▼)
go to x: (220) y: (77)
create a clone of myself ▼
go to x: (220) y: (0)
create a clone of myself ▼
go to x: (220) y: (-85)
create a clone of myself ▼
go to x: (500) y: (500)

Look at the list of starting locations for the cloned sprites. Copy them into the `go to blocks` in your **clone-maker script**. Pax's script looks like this.

TEST

15

TEST: Click 🏳.
SUCCESS: Six clones start their patrols on the three levels of the base.
ERROR: All your guards are facing the wrong way. Go to the costumes, choose edit, and click `flip ↔`.

STOP THE SCRIPT! Click ⬤.

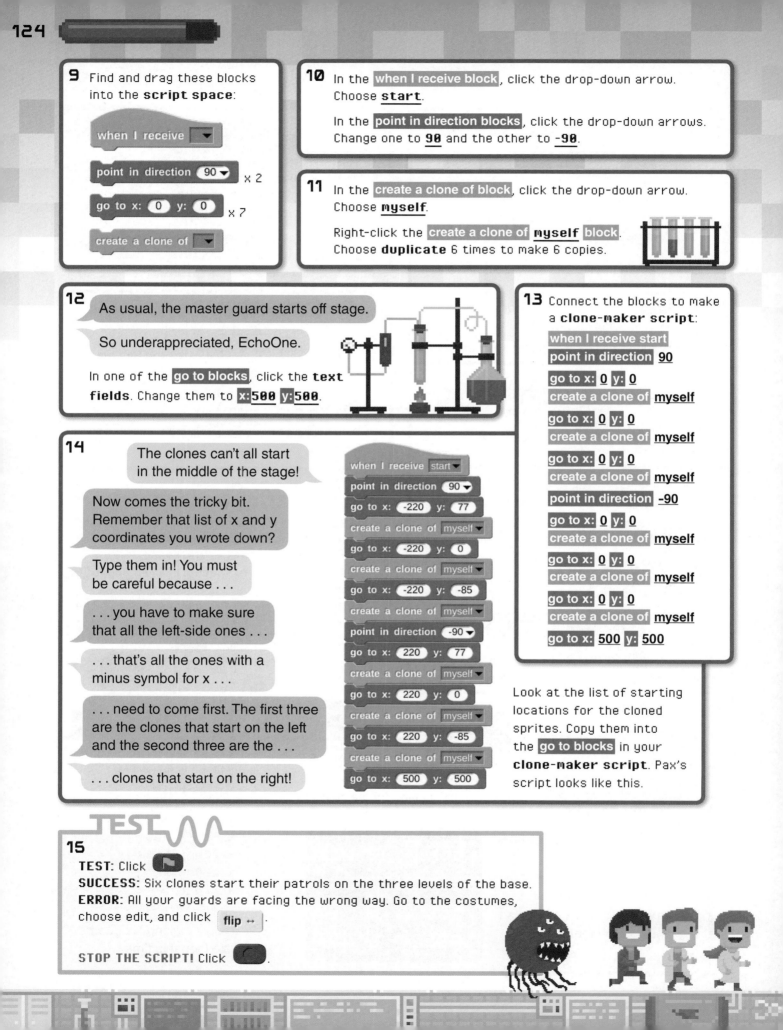

16 What do I always say, EchoZero?

One day you'll accidentally clone your own ear and then you'll be sorry?

Er . . . and "make sure you hide the evidence". Make a clone: delete a clone. The last thing we need is more guards.

Find and drag these blocks into the **script space**:

`when I receive ▼`   `delete this clone`

17 The guards guard, then they're deleted.

And if they go bonkers and take over the planet, no one can trace it back to you!

In the `when I receive block`, click the drop-down arrow. Choose **missioncomplete**. Connect the blocks.

`when I receive missioncomplete ▼`
`delete this clone`

ACHIEVEMENT UNLOCKED!
CLONER

4 LEVEL

Save as **Tiptoes05**.

MISSION OBJECTIVE 4: LEAF ON THE WIND

1 Click the **Agent Q sprite**. Go to `Costumes` and make a new costume.

Draw a costume with a green VALID badge on it. Click `OK` when you're done.

2 Right-click and choose **duplicate** to make a copy of the sprite.

Right-click and **edit** one of the costumes. Move Agent Q's legs or tentacles, ruffle its hair or antennae. Maybe Agent Q is from a species that changes color when it moves? Click `OK` when you're done.

Right-click both costumes. Rename them **walk1** and **walk2**.

walk2

walk1

3 Find the three **rotation buttons** at the top of the screen.

Click the **left-right rotation button** in the middle to make sure Agent Q only faces left or right.

only face left/right · nt Q · ✓ draggab

Save as **Tiptoes06**.

EXPERIMENT

5 Agent Q must be small enough to fit into the hidey-holes in the map. In the `set size block`, change Agent Q's size so the sprite fits. In Pax's script, Agent Q ended up being **9**%!

4 Go to the **script space**. Find and drag these blocks into the **script space**:

`when ⚑ clicked`

`set size to 100 %`   `go to x: 0 y: 0`   `show`

6 We need starting coordinates for Agent Q!

I can figure it out with the mouse coordinates.

Move your **mouse-pointer** over the middle of the green starting gate on the stage. Write down the `mouse x` and `mouse y` values.

7 In the **go to block**, click the **text fields**. Type in the x and y coordinates you wrote down.

> Normally we broadcast at the end of the setup script to tell the other scripts to start.

> We don't need to here. We want Agent Q and the guards to start at the same time. The stage broadcasts when to start and all the other sprites listen for that.

9 In the **when I receive block**, click the drop-down arrow. Choose **start**. In the **key pressed? block**, click the drop-down arrow. Choose **w**. In the **change y by 10 block**, click the text field. Type **5**.

10 Connect the blocks to make a **movement script**:

```
when I receive start
forever
  if key w is pressed
    change y by 5
    if on edge, bounce
```

or

```
when I receive start ▼
forever
  if  key w ▼ pressed?
    change y by 5
    if on edge, bounce
```

8

> The next thing we need is movement. Agent Q can move left or right . . .

> . . . and up and down.

> How are your movement skills, Pax?

> Natterninja showed me how to make four movement scripts using events.

> Good! We'll use keypress events again, but we're going to lump all our movement scripts . . .

> . . . into one giant loop. It's much easier to keep track of one movement script instead of four!

Find and drag these blocks into the **script space**:

```
if < >        forever
```

```
key space ▼ pressed?        when I receive ▼
if on edge, bounce          change y by 10
```

TEST

11 TEST: Click 🏳, then press **w**.
SUCCESS: Agent Q moves up!

STOP THE SCRIPT! Click ⏹.

12

> Hmm, Agent Q can cheat and go up through the wall.

> Echo Zero, can Agent Q walk through walls?

> Let me check the personnel file . . . No, Agent Q is not a cloud of gas.

> OK, let's patch this.

Find and drag these blocks into the **script space**:

```
change y by 10
```
```
touching ■ ?        if < >
```

In the **touching [ ] block**, click the colored square, then click the gray walls on the stage.

In the **change y by 10 block**, click in the text field. Type **5**.

13 Connect the blocks inside the **movement script**:

```
when I receive start
forever
  if key w is pressed
    change y by 5
    if on edge, bounce
      touching [ ]
    change y by -5
```

or

```
when I receive start ▼
forever
  if  key w ▼ pressed?
    change y by 5
    if on edge, bounce
    if < touching ■ ? >
      change y by -5
```

COPY THE CODE

> Now if Agent Q touches the gray area, it moves back the same distance it moved forwards.

> Like the **if on edge, bounce block**?

> Sort of! **if on edge, bounce** is a similar function block. When you make your own blocks, you'll see.

14

TEST: Click 🏳. Press **w**.
SUCCESS: Agent Q stops at the wall.
ERROR: Agent Q zooms through the wall!
Check your numbers match the example.

STOP THE SCRIPT! Click ⟲.

Save as **Tiptoes07**.

HINT
If Agent Q doesn't move at all, it might be because it starts directly underneath the gray wall. Drag the sprite into some black space and press **w** to make sure everything works. **OK**

15

Now that up movement is working, let's duplicate that code to move down.

Right-click the top (outer) **if block**. Choose **duplicate**.

Insert the duplicated code underneath the top **if block**, inside the **forever loop**.

In the new **key pressed block**, click the drop-down arrow. Choose **s**.

```
when I receive start
forever
  if key w pressed?
    change y by 5
    if on edge, bounce
    if touching ?
    change y by -5

  if key s pressed?
    change y by 5
    if on edge, bounce
    if touching ?
    change y by -5
```

16

We're going down instead of up, so reverse the two numbers.

In the **change y by blocks**, click the **text fields**. Reverse them so the top one is **-5** and the next one is **5**.

When you press s, Agent Q's y value goes down. When you need to go backwards, the y value goes up.

```
if key s pressed?
  change y by -5
  if on edge, bounce
  if touching ?
  change y by 5
```

17

Use the **duplicate** feature to make two new movement scripts. Connect them inside the **forever loop**.

Swap the **change y blocks** for **change x blocks**. Use the **a** key for left and the **d** key for right.

18

TEST: Click 🏳.
Use **w**, **a**, **s**, and **d** to move the agent to the red door.
SUCCESS: Agent Q moves left, right, up, **and** down!
ERROR: BUG HUNT! Check your code matches:
STOP THE SCRIPT!
Click ⟲.

```
when I receive start
forever
  if key w pressed?
    change y by 5
    if on edge, bounce
    if touching ?
    change y by -5

  if key s pressed?
    change y by -5
    if on edge, bounce
    if touching ?
    change y by 5

  if key a pressed?
    change x by -5
    if on edge, bounce
    if touching ?
    change x by 5

  if key d pressed?
    change x by 5
    if on edge, bounce
    if touching ?
    change x by -5
```

19

Find and drag these blocks into the **script space**:

point in direction 90 ▼ x 2

In one **point in direction block**, click the drop-down arrow. Choose **(-90) left**.

Click and drag the **point in direction -90 block** and connect it inside the **if a key pressed block**.

Click and drag the other one **point in direction block** and connect it inside the **if d key pressed block**.

```
if key a pressed?
  point in direction -90
  change x by -5
  if on edge, bounce
  if touching ?
  change x by 5

if key d pressed?
  point in direction 90
  change x by 5
  if on edge, bounce
  if touching ?
  change x by -5
```

Save as **Tiptoes08**.

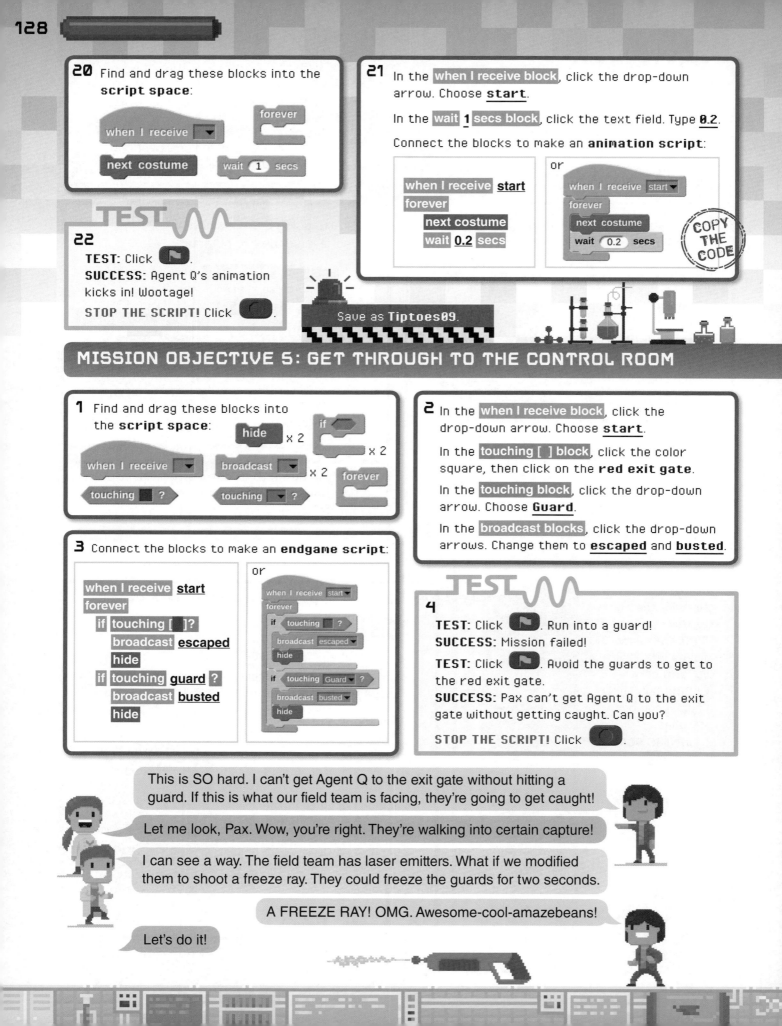

20 Find and drag these blocks into the **script space**:

when I receive ▼   forever

next costume   wait 1 secs

21 In the `when I receive block`, click the drop-down arrow. Choose **start**.

In the `wait 1 secs block`, click the text field. Type **0.2**.

Connect the blocks to make an **animation script**:

```
when I receive start
forever
    next costume
    wait 0.2 secs
```

or

```
when I receive start ▼
forever
    next costume
    wait 0.2 secs
```

COPY THE CODE

TEST

22
TEST: Click 🏁.
SUCCESS: Agent Q's animation kicks in! Wootage!

STOP THE SCRIPT! Click ⬤.

Save as **Tiptoes09**.

MISSION OBJECTIVE 5: GET THROUGH TO THE CONTROL ROOM

1 Find and drag these blocks into the **script space**:

hide x 2   if ◄ x 2

when I receive ▼   broadcast ▼ x 2   forever

touching ■ ?   touching ▼ ?

2 In the `when I receive block`, click the drop-down arrow. Choose **start**.

In the `touching [ ] block`, click the color square, then click on the **red exit gate**.

In the `touching block`, click the drop-down arrow. Choose **Guard**.

In the `broadcast blocks`, click the drop-down arrows. Change them to **escaped** and **busted**.

3 Connect the blocks to make an **endgame script**:

```
when I receive start
forever
    if touching [ ]?
        broadcast escaped
        hide
    if touching guard ?
        broadcast busted
        hide
```

or

```
when I receive start ▼
forever
    if touching ■ ?
        broadcast escaped ▼
        hide
    if touching Guard ▼ ?
        broadcast busted ▼
        hide
```

TEST

4
TEST: Click 🏁. Run into a guard!
SUCCESS: Mission failed!

TEST: Click 🏁. Avoid the guards to get to the red exit gate.
SUCCESS: Pax can't get Agent Q to the exit gate without getting caught. Can you?

STOP THE SCRIPT! Click ⬤.

This is SO hard. I can't get Agent Q to the exit gate without hitting a guard. If this is what our field team is facing, they're going to get caught!

Let me look, Pax. Wow, you're right. They're walking into certain capture!

I can see a way. The field team has laser emitters. What if we modified them to shoot a freeze ray. They could freeze the guards for two seconds.

A FREEZE RAY! OMG. Awesome-cool-amazebeans!

Let's do it!

REVISION:
*** PUT THE GUARDS TO SLEEP USING A FREEZE RAY ***

1 Click ▶ to make a new sprite.
Click the sprite **name field**.
Rename it <u>freezeray</u>.

2 Go to **Costumes**. Make a new costume.
Draw an icy freeze ray from the left side of the screen to the right. Click ⊕ .

Move the crosshairs to the left end of your freeze ray. Click **OK**.

Right-click the new costume. **Rename** it <u>blast</u>.

3 Go to the **script space**. Find and drag these blocks into the **script space**:

when ⚑ clicked
go to x: 0 y: 0
set size to 100 %

EXPERIMENT

4 The freeze ray must fit in the black spaces.
In the **set size block**, change the size to <u>20</u>%.
Click the block to see how big this makes it.
Make it bigger or smaller by changing the number.

5 In the **go to block**, click the **text fields**.
Type **x:500 y:500**.

Connect the blocks to make a **setup script**.

when ⚑ clicked
set size to 15 %
go to x: 500 y: 500

We'll use sprites for the freeze ray, but what do I always say, EchoZero?

One day a clone army will conquer the galaxy and then you'll be sorry?

No! It's "get it working for one sprite before you make the clones"!

Coolbeans!

The freeze ray code is complicated. Think about all the things it needs to do, then do them one by one.

It needs to go to Agent Q when it's fired.

And face the right direction.

And move towards the edge of the stage.

And freeze anything in its way!

Awesomebeans. I've got a list.

6 Find and drag these blocks into the **script space**:

show
when space ▾ key pressed
go to ▾
point in direction 90 ▾
costume # ▾ of ▾

7 We can use this **go to block** to make sure the freeze ray goes to wherever Agent Q is.

In the **go to block**, click the drop-down arrow. Choose **Agent Q**.

8 This **costume# of block** is an attribute block. We'll use it to change the direction of the freeze ray so it's facing the right way.

In the **costume# of block**, click the drop-down arrows. (Click the **right** drop-down arrow first.) Choose **Agent Q**. Then choose **direction** in the **left** text field.

direction ▾ of Agent Q ▾

9 Connect the blocks to make the first part of the **animation script**:

COPY THE CODE

```
when space ▾ key pressed
go to Agent Q ▾
point in direction [direction ▾] of [Agent Q ▾]
```

10

TEST

TEST: Click ▶. Press the spacebar. Try it facing both directions.
SUCCESS: The freeze ray appears at Agent Q. It's facing the right direction!
ERROR: Something weird happens. Get your bug-hunting-est magnifying glass and check your code.

STOP THE SCRIPT! Click ⬤.

11

Now for movement!

Ah! A freeze ray is never still!

The freeze ray only needs to move until it's off the stage, so we don't need a forever loop.

What about a repeat until loop? We can repeat until the x co-ordinate is off the stage?

Find and drag these blocks into the **script space**:

```
repeat until ⬡
```
```
move 10 steps
```
```
x position          × 2
```
```
[ < ]     [ > ]     ⬡ or ⬡
```

12 Click and drag the **x position blocks** into the left sides of the **< and > blocks**.

In the **< block**, click the right text field. Type **-250**.

In the **> block**, click the right text field. Type **250**.

Click and drag the the **<** and **> blocks** into the **or block**.

```
x position < -250   or   x position > 250
```

14

TEST

TEST: Click ▶. Use spacebar to shoot!
SUCCESS: The freeze ray fires off screen!
ERROR: It doesn't move at all. Check that your **<** and **> blocks** are the same as Pax's.

13 Connect the blocks at the end of your **movement script** to match:

```
when space key pressed
go to Agent Q
point in direction direction of Agent Q
repeat until  x position < -250 or x position > 250
    move 10 steps
```

or

```
when space ▾ key pressed
go to Agent Q ▾
point in direction [direction ▾] of [Agent Q ▾]
repeat until  x position < -250  or  x position > 250
    move 10 steps
```

COPY THE CODE

15 Click the **Guard sprite**. Find and drag these blocks into the **script space**.

```
if ⬡
```
```
wait 1 secs
```
```
touching ▾ ?
```

That's number three on the list. Now we need to make the guards freeze.

Yup, we need to mess around in the guards' scripts.

This shouldn't be too hard. We just put a wait block in the guard script if it's touching the freeze ray.

16 In the **touching block**, click the drop-down arrow. Choose **freezeray**.

In the **wait 1 secs block**, click the **text field**. Type **2**.

Connect the blocks and insert them into the guard's **movement script**.

```
when I start as a clone
forever
    move 1 steps
    if on edge, bounce
    if  distance ▾ to Agent Q ▾ < 70
        move 2 steps

        if  touching freezeray ▾ ?
            wait 2 secs
```

17

TEST: Click 🏳. Use the spacebar to freeze some guards!
SUCCESS: When they're hit, the guards stop patrolling for two seconds.
ERROR: They don't stop! We're dooooomed! Check your new guard code is in the right place.

STOP THE SCRIPT! Click 🔴.

Save as **Tiptoes10**.

18

If I press spacebar twice, it acts weird.

Because we're using the master freeze ray sprite.

We need clones!

Click the **freeze ray sprite button**. Find and drag these blocks into the **script space**:

`when I start as a clone`

`delete this clone`

19 Connect the `delete this clone block` at the end of the freeze ray's movement script.

Click and drag the **movement script** and connect it under the `when I start as a clone block`:

`when space ▼ key pressed`

`when I start as a clone`

`go to Agent Q ▼`
`point in direction (direction ▼ of Agent Q ▼)`
`repeat until ⟨ (x position) < -250 ⟩ or ⟨ (x position) > 250 ⟩`
`move 10 steps`
`delete this clone`

20

Agent Q will make the clones.

Don't we need freeze ray clones?

Agent Q has the tentacle on the trigger. Agent Q controls when we make a new freeze ray clone.

Click the **Agent Q sprite button**. Find and drag these blocks into the **script space**:

`when space ▼ key pressed` `create a clone of ▼`

21 In the `create a clone of block`, click the drop-down arrow. Choose **freeze ray**.

Connect the blocks to make a **clone-maker script**.

`when space ▼ key pressed`
`create a clone of freeze ray ▼`

22

TEST: Click 🏳. Press spacebar several times.
SUCCESS: Many freeze ray. Much clone.

STOP THE SCRIPT! Click 🔴.

Save as **Tiptoes11**.

The field team has found the missing coders!

OMG! That's amazing!

Pax, you've deciphered a cryptic message, hacked the enemy mainframe, and kept our team safe from guards.

With CLONES! Mwa-ha-ha-ha-ha!

Is she OK?

Maniacal laughter is inevitable in the mad-scientist business. She'll laugh herself out soon.

Cool...beans...

There's a message from ETAMI. The Introspecter has been called in. He'll extract the team and the coders! Are you ready, Pax?

ACHIEVEMENT UNLOCKED!
CLONER

LEVEL 5

HINT ✖

To make it harder or easier:
• Change the number in the `wait 1 secs block` in the guard movement script.
• Change the number of guards.
• Add more hidey holes.

OK

NEW MESSAGE ✖

Meet the Introspecter and get our people out of the belly of the beast?

Y/N

VARIABLES

with Agent Introspecter

NEW MESSAGE

Would you like to proceed?

Y/N?

You've been recruited by VALID: the supercoder agency defending Earth against intergalactic threats. You've been helping VALID's field team infiltrate the island fortress of CORUPT—an evil organization that has been kidnapping coders for unknown ends. You've found the coders, but they need your help to escape. ETAMI, the leader of VALID, is taking you to meet the Introspecter, the elusive master of variables. With your help, maybe he can come up with a plan to save the day. . .

Is this the Introspecter's hackerspace? It's so dark.

Agent Introspecter prefers the darkness. He claims it helps him interface with cyberspace.

I don't see anyone . . . is he here?

I'm here. But right now, I'm running a security drill on our servers in Madrid, so I guess you could say my body is here . . .

New mission, Agent Introspecter. Agent Finity's team has located the missing coders and they need help with the extraction.

All of them?! Wow! OK, what do they need? An advanced n-dimensional hyperspace expressway?

They have located a submarine launch bay. They need to override the security lockout on the sub.

OK, I'll see if I can find some security holes.

Potential Agent X is going to help you.

Normally I work alone, but I'll need multiple threads going for this to work. An extra pair of eyes might come in handy. Can you handle some variables for me?

Solid MAYBE!

Good enough for me!

NEW MESSAGE ☒

Help the Introspecter hack into an enemy vessel and rescue the team from certain doom?

Y/N

MISSION DOSSIER

>> DISCOVER MORE ABOUT VARIABLES

The field team has located the missing coders inside the CORUPT base. They need to find an escape route, and FAST. There's an old submarine in a launch bay on the lower levels and the VALID team is on board. Help the Introspecter hack into the sub security.

LEVEL: 6

INSTRUCTOR: AGENT INTROSPECTER

BACKGROUND: Agent Introspecter is the son of PrincessHappyKittens, the most notorious cyber thief of all. They say he was born with a keyboard in his hands and his first words were "encryption protocol". Unlike his infamous mother, the Introspecter uses his powers for good, not personal gain. He's VALID's foremost security expert, even if he's sometimes a bit "intense".

INTROSPECTER

We've got a few minutes before we get a link up to the sub. What do you know about variables Pax?

I've used them a bit, but I don't really know what they are or how they work.

Good. Always ask if you don't know about something. Variables are a way of storing information. Data.

What kind of data?

They mainly work with numbers and words, but variables can hold anything: functions, sprites, costumes. The key thing about variables is that the data in them can change while you're running your code. What have you used variables for so far?

Umm, for a score?

Perfect example! At the beginning of the mission, the score starts at 0, right? Every time you defuse a bomb or dodge an enemy, your score goes up.

MISSION OBJECTIVE: USE VARIABLES TO BRAG!

1 Open a web browser on your computer. Type **snap.berkeley.edu/run** into your browser bar. Hit enter. If you have a Snap! account then log in, otherwise acquire an adult to help you make an account.

2

You've used some built-in variables too.

I have?

You used the answer block for the Interrogator 4000. The answer block stores the data typed in, but it changes every time you type something new.

Find these blocks and drag them into the **script space**:

when ⚑ clicked   ask what's your name? and wait

say Hello!   join hello world ◀▶   answer x 3

3 In the first `join block` text field, type **My name is**.

Click and drag an `answer block` into the second `join block` text field.

Connect the blocks to make a **setup script**:

```
when ▢ clicked
ask what's·your·name? and wait
say ( join My·name·is  answer ) ◀▶
```

COPY THE CODE

4

TEST

Run it. The computer will replace the answer block with the data you've typed in.

TEST: Click 🏳. Answer the question. Use your VALID coder name, not your real name!
SUCCESS: The sprite reads out your codename!

STOP THE SCRIPT! After each test, click 🛑 to stop all the scripts running.

5

Coolbeans!

Yup, when you run the code, the computer replaces all your variables. Try some extra ones.

Press the right arrow on the `join block` five times.

```
( join My·name·is  answer ) ◀▶
```

In the third text field, type **the mighty, destroyer of worlds, eater of stars and all around BOSS. Don't be fooled if you meet another**

Click and drag the `answer block` into the fourth **join** field.
In the fifth text field type: **as I am the best**

Click and drag the `answer block` into the sixth **join** field.
In the seventh text field type: **of all time!**.

```
when ▢ clicked
ask what's·your·name? and wait
say
  join
  My·name·is  answer
  the·mighty,·destroyer·of·worlds,·eater·of·stars·and·all·around·BOSS.·Don't·be·fooled·if·you·meet·another
  answer  as·I·am·the·best  answer  of·all·time ◀▶
```

6

TEST

TEST: Click 🏳.
Type in your coder name.
SUCCESS: The sprite brags about you! The greatest and best of all time!

STOP THE SCRIPT!
Click 🛑.

Save as **Bragger01**.

Just in time. Uplink established! We've got a line to the sub. Ready, Pax?

Ready to code!

OK, the first thing I'm going to do is to try and disable the security lockout on the sub. Should be fairly simple but I'm going to have to look through the code and try and make sense of it.

How can I help?

CORUPT are REALLY bad coders so there's a bunch of C-bits in their code. I need you to count them in each script so I can disable them. That should get us into the controls.

MISSION DOSSIER

>> DISABLE THE SECURITY LOCKOUT ON THE SUBMARINE

Help the field team and the kidnapped coders escape. Count the C-bits in the CORUPT security code so the Introspecter can disable them and take control of the sub's security lockout.

LEVEL: 6
INSTRUCTOR: AGENT INTROSPECTER

MISSION OBJECTIVE 1: USE CLONES TO MAKE THE BITS

PROJECT OUTLINE

NAME:
HACKER BIT

GOAL:
USE VARIABLES TO KEEP TRACK OF THE NUMBER OF C-BITS IN EACH BIT OF CORUPT CODE.

REQUIREMENTS:
1. USE CLONES TO MAKE THE BITS
2. USE VARIABLES TO STORE THE NUMBER OF C-BITS AND THE ANSWER
3. USE VARIABLES WITH A LOOP TO CONTROL DIFFICULTY.

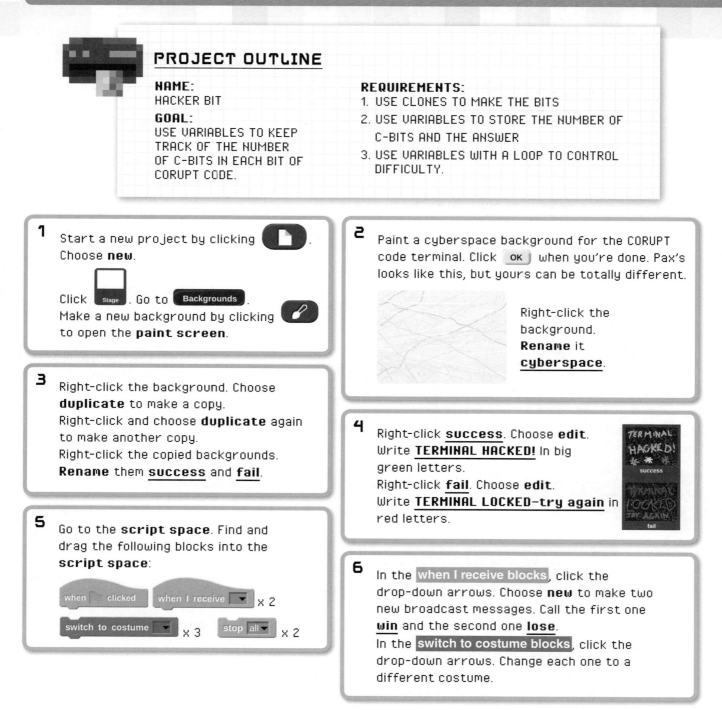

1 Start a new project by clicking [ ]. Choose **new**.

Click **Stage**. Go to **Backgrounds**. Make a new background by clicking to open the **paint screen**.

2 Paint a cyberspace background for the CORUPT code terminal. Click **OK** when you're done. Pax's looks like this, but yours can be totally different.

Right-click the background. **Rename** it **cyberspace**.

3 Right-click the background. Choose **duplicate** to make a copy.
Right-click and choose **duplicate** again to make another copy.
Right-click the copied backgrounds. **Rename** them **success** and **fail**.

4 Right-click **success**. Choose **edit**. Write **TERMINAL HACKED!** In big green letters.
Right-click **fail**. Choose **edit**. Write **TERMINAL LOCKED—try again** in red letters.

TERMINAL HACKED!
* * *
success

TERMINAL LOCKED TRY AGAIN
fail

5 Go to the **script space**. Find and drag the following blocks into the **script space**:

when [ ] clicked   when I receive [▾] x 2
switch to costume [▾] x 3   stop [all ▾] x 2

6 In the **when I receive blocks**, click the drop-down arrows. Choose **new** to make two new broadcast messages. Call the first one **win** and the second one **lose**.
In the **switch to costume blocks**, click the drop-down arrows. Change each one to a different costume.

7 Connect the blocks to make three scripts matching:

when green flag clicked
switch to costume cyberspace

and

when I receive win
switch to costume success
stop all

and

when I receive lose
switch to costume fail
stop all

or

when ⚑ clicked
switch to costume cyberspace ▾

and

when I receive win ▾
switch to costume success ▾
stop all ▾

and

when I receive lose ▾
switch to costume fail ▾
stop all ▾

COPY THE CODE

Save as **Hackerbit01**.

8 Click [Sprite]. Click the sprite **name field**. Name the sprite **hack**.

Go to [Costumes]. Click 🖌 to make a new costume. Draw the Introspecter. Click OK when you're done.

I think my hair is swoopier than that, Pax.

Right-click the costume. **Rename** it **introspecter**.

9

We'll need three costumes for the bits, Pax. The noble 1, the underrated 0, and the horror that is the C-bit.

Click 🖌 to make a new costume.

Draw a BIG, red, oozy, evil "C" symbol for CORUPT. Click OK when you're done. Right-click the new costume to **rename** it **c-bit**.

Make a new costume. Draw a giant 1. Right-click it to **rename** it **1-bit**.

Make a new costume. Draw a giant 0. Right-click it to **rename** it **0-bit**.

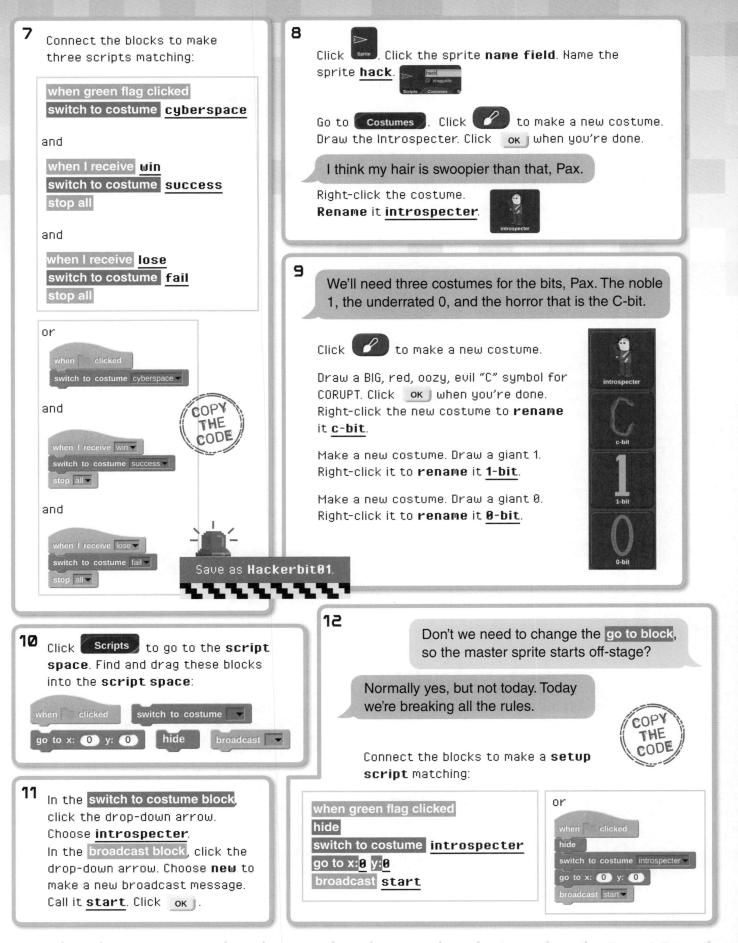

introspecter

c-bit

1-bit

0-bit

10 Click [Scripts] to go to the **script space**. Find and drag these blocks into the **script space**:

when ⚑ clicked   switch to costume ▾
go to x: 0 y: 0   hide   broadcast ▾

11 In the switch to costume block, click the drop-down arrow. Choose **introspecter**. In the broadcast block, click the drop-down arrow. Choose **new** to make a new broadcast message. Call it **start**. Click OK.

12

Don't we need to change the go to block, so the master sprite starts off-stage?

Normally yes, but not today. Today we're breaking all the rules.

COPY THE CODE

Connect the blocks to make a **setup script** matching:

when green flag clicked
hide
switch to costume introspecter
go to x:0 y:0
broadcast start

or

when ⚑ clicked
hide
switch to costume introspecter ▾
go to x: 0 y: 0
broadcast start ▾

13 Find and drag these blocks into the **script space**:

when I receive ▼ × 2

hide × 2

14 In the **when I receive blocks**, click the drop-down arrows. Change the first one to **win** and the second one to **lose**.

15 Connect the **hide blocks** under each starter block to make two **endgame scripts** matching:

when I receive lose ▼
hide

when I receive win ▼
hide

COPY THE CODE

Save as **Hackerbit02**.

16 The submarine code seems to have a maximum of ten bits now, but that might change later.

Find and drag these blocks into the **script space**:

not ⬡

when I receive ▼

if ⬡

repeat 10

message

▯ = ▯

create a clone of ▼

17 In the **when I receive block**, click the drop-down arrow. Choose **start**.

In the **create a clone of block**, click the drop-down arrow. Choose **myself**.

18 Drag the **not block** into the hexagonal space in the **if block**.
Click and drag the **message block** into the left field of the **= block**.
Type **lose** in the right side.
Drag the **message = lose block** into the hexagonal space in the **not block**.

not (message) = lose

19 Connect the blocks to make a **clone-maker script** matching:

when I receive **start**
if not message = **lose**
    repeat **10**
        create a clone of **myself**

or

when I receive start ▼
if ‹ not ‹ message = lose › ›
repeat 10
    create a clone of myself ▼

COPY THE CODE

20 I need to test this, but because I've hidden the master sprite, all the clones are hidden too.

If you want to make a quick clone setup script, I don't mind.

Find and drag these blocks into the **script space**:

go to x: 0 y: 0

when I start as a clone

show

pick random 1 to 10 × 2

21 In the first **pick random block**, click the text fields. Type **-200** to **200**.
Drag the **pick random block** into the **x:** field of the **go to block**.

In the second **pick random block**, click the text fields. Type **-120** to **120**.
Drag the **pick random block** into the **y:** field of the **go to block**.

22 Connect the blocks to make a clone **setup script** matching:

```
when I start as a clone
go to x: pick random -220 to 220 y: pick random -120 to 120
show
```

or

```
when I start as a clone
go to x: pick random -200 to 200 y: pick random -120 to 120
show
```

COPY THE CODE

23

TEST: Click 🏳.
SUCCESS: Introspecter clones as far as the eye can see! Which isn't far, because he's in the way.
ERROR: There's only one Introspecter!
FIX: Glitchbane would say to check the order of your blocks!

STOP THE SCRIPT! Click ⬤.

You know what you're doing with clones, Pax. The Echo Agents have taught you well.

Save as **Hackerbit03**.

24 Find and drag these blocks into the **script space**:

```
set size to 100 %     switch to costume ▼
pick random 1 to 10
```

In the **set size block**, click the text field and type **15%**.

25

CORUPT doesn't want to make it too easy for us, so the bits are random. Let's pick a random costume from the list. How many costumes are there now?

4 in total.

The first costume is the Introspecter costume. We can't use that for a bit costume. When we start a new clone, we want the second, third, or fourth costume.

In the **pick random block**, type **2** in the left text field and **4** in the right text field.

Connect the blocks at the end of your **clone setup script**.

```
when I start as a clone
go to x: pick random -200 to 200 y: pick random -120 to 120
show
set size to 15 %
switch to costume pick random 2 to 4
```

COPY THE CODE

26

TEST: Click 🏳.
SUCCESS: The screen is full of 1s, 0s, and oozy c-bits.
ERROR: I can still see the Introspecter!
FIX: Check the order of the costumes in Costumes.
The Introspecter should be at the top of the list.

STOP THE SCRIPT! Click ⬤.

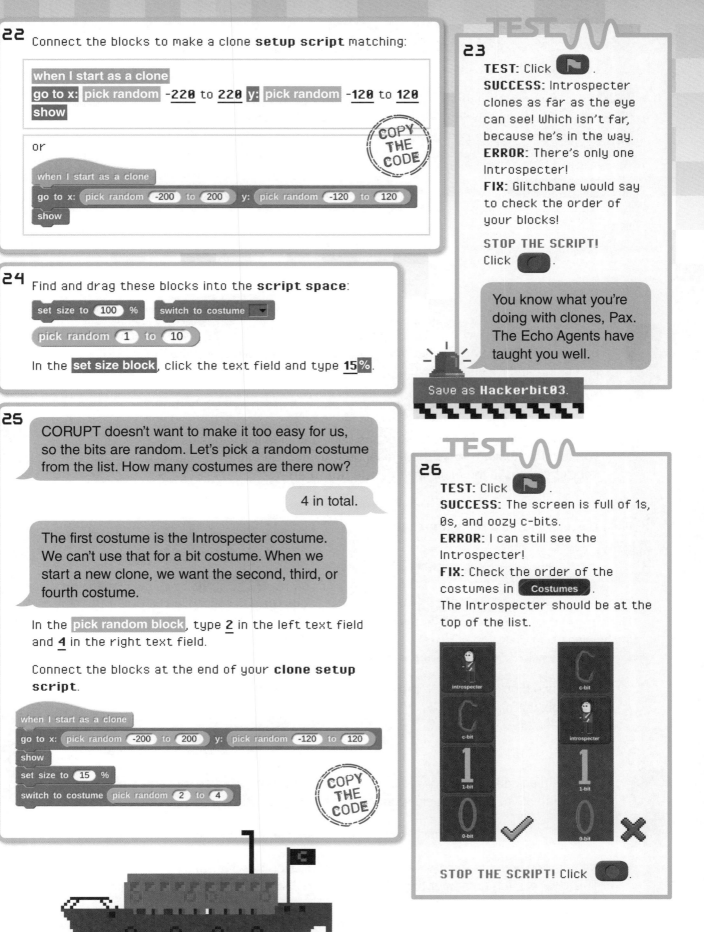

MISSION OBJECTIVE 2: USE VARIABLES TO STORE YOUR DATA

1

We must store the number of c-bits in a variable each time, so we can check you've counted them correctly.

Click **Variables**.

Click **Make a variable**.

2

Always give your **variables** logical names, or you can get confused and create bugs.

That's like with costumes and sprites. It's easier to change or fix them when the names make sense, like a scoring variable called score.

Name the variable **c-bits**.
Click **OK**.

Variable name
c-bits
• for all sprites ○ for this sprite only
OK   Cancel

When you create new variables, they show up on the stage. It's good for testing, because it will tell you exactly what value is in the variable, even when the code is running and it's changing.

Ooh! Glitchbane showed me that. It's a bug-hunter variable.

When you finish your mission code, go back and hide the variables you used for testing. Make them disappear by unclicking the check box next to the block in the **code menu area**.

☐ c-bits

3

Drag these blocks into the **script space**:

if
costume #
[ ] = [ ]   change ▼ by 1

Click and drag the **costume# block** into the left text field of the **= block**. Type **2** in the right text field.

4

Make sure you check the costume numbers there, PAX.

Go to **Costumes**. Make sure the **c-bit costume** is second in the list. If it's not, click and drag it under the **Introspecter costume**. Go back to the **script space** when you're done.

These two blocks are super important for variable work, Pax. Don't mix them up.   set ▼ to 0   change ▼ by 1

What's the difference?

The set block deletes the old value and resets it. You mostly use these at the beginning of your script to clear out old data from your variables . . . mostly.

Right. So, it's not what we want for counting c-bits on the go.

No, the one you see most often in loops or after events is this **change by block**. This one tells the computer to add one to the variable or take one away.

Coolbeans.

5

In our case, we want to add one to the variable.

In the `change by 1 block`, choose `c-bits`. Connect the blocks at the end of your **clone setup script**, matching:

```
when I start as a clone
go to x: pick random -220 to 220 y: pick random -120 to 120
show
set size to 15%
switch to costume pick random 2 to 4
if costume# = 2
    change c-bits by 1
```

or

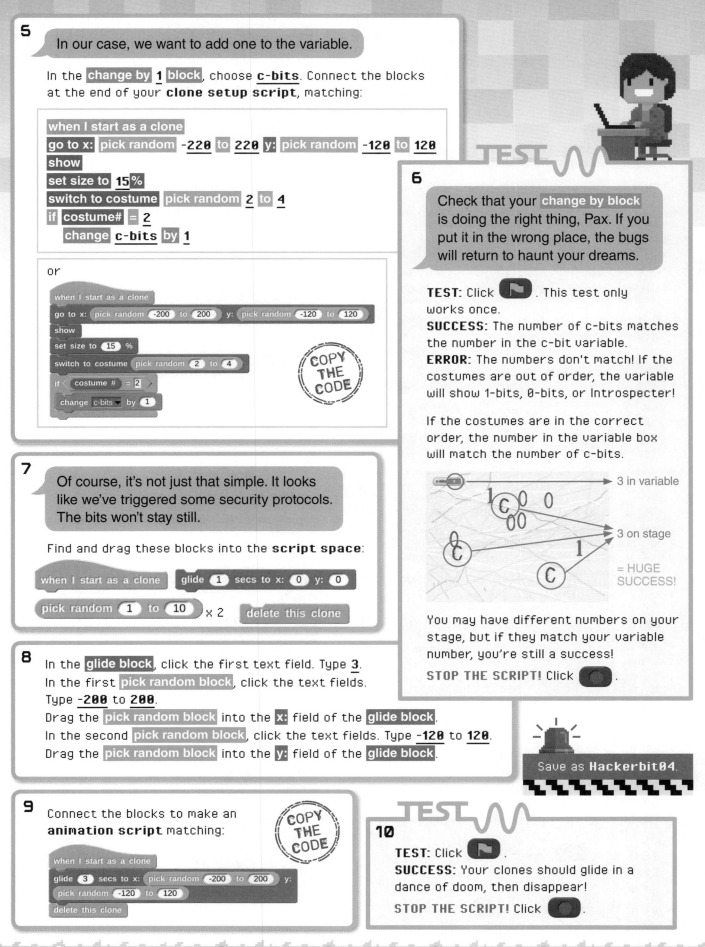

COPY THE CODE

6

Check that your `change by block` is doing the right thing, Pax. If you put it in the wrong place, the bugs will return to haunt your dreams.

TEST: Click 🏳. This test only works once.
SUCCESS: The number of c-bits matches the number in the c-bit variable.
ERROR: The numbers don't match! If the costumes are out of order, the variable will show 1-bits, 0-bits, or Introspecter!

If the costumes are in the correct order, the number in the variable box will match the number of c-bits.

3 in variable

3 on stage

= HUGE SUCCESS!

You may have different numbers on your stage, but if they match your variable number, you're still a success!

STOP THE SCRIPT! Click ⬤.

7

Of course, it's not just that simple. It looks like we've triggered some security protocols. The bits won't stay still.

Find and drag these blocks into the **script space**:

`when I start as a clone`   `glide 1 secs to x: 0 y: 0`

`pick random 1 to 10` x 2   `delete this clone`

8

In the `glide block`, click the first text field. Type **3**.
In the first `pick random block`, click the text fields. Type **-200** to **200**.
Drag the `pick random block` into the `x:` field of the `glide block`.
In the second `pick random block`, click the text fields. Type **-120** to **120**.
Drag the `pick random block` into the `y:` field of the `glide block`.

Save as **Hackerbit04**.

9

Connect the blocks to make an **animation script** matching:

COPY THE CODE

```
when I start as a clone
glide 3 secs to x: pick random -200 to 200 y:
pick random -120 to 120
delete this clone
```

10

TEST: Click 🏳.
SUCCESS: Your clones should glide in a dance of doom, then disappear!
STOP THE SCRIPT! Click ⬤.

11

While this code is gliding around, tell me how many c-bits there are, so I can blast them to dust using the power of VALID logic!

Find and drag these blocks into the **script space**:

`wait 1 secs`   `broadcast ▼ and wait`

In the **wait 1 secs block**, type **3** in the text field.

12

In the **broadcast and wait block**, choose **new** to make a new broadcast. Call it **ask**. Click **OK**.
Connect the blocks at the end of your **clone-maker script**:

```
when I receive start ▼
if  not < message = lose >
    repeat 10
        create a clone of myself ▼

wait 3 secs
broadcast ask ▼ and wait
```

13

Timing is vital. If we mess it up, the team could be stuck, with CORUPT guards closing in. I'll tell you when to count the bits.

Find and drag these blocks into the **script space**:

`if`   `else`

`when I receive ▼`   `show`   `hide`

`ask what's your name? and wait`   `c-bits`

`broadcast ▼` x 2   `< ☐ = ☐ >`   `answer`

14

Now we'll use the master sprite!

And he's already wearing the right costume and he's in the right place!

In the **when I receive block**, choose **ask**.

In the **ask block**, click the text field. Type:
How many c-bits are there?

15

This is going to get pretty hairy. If even one c-bit gets through, we've lost forever . . . Or until someone hits the green flag . . .

In the **broadcast blocks**, click the drop-down arrows. Choose **win** in one and **lose** in the other.

Drag the **answer block** into the left text field of the **equals block**. Drag the **c-bits block** into the other text field.

Drag `< answer = c-bits >` into the hexagonal space in the **if else block**.

16

Connect the blocks to make an **ask script**:

```
when I receive ask
show
ask How many c-bits are there? and wait
if answer = c-bits
    broadcast win
else
    broadcast lose
hide
```

or

```
when I receive ask ▼
show
ask How many c-bits are there? and wait
if < answer = c-bits >
    broadcast win ▼
else
    broadcast lose ▼
hide
```

COPY THE CODE

TEST

17

TEST: Click 🏴.
SUCCESS: When the bits disappear, the Introspecter asks you a question!

TEST: Click 🏴 to run it again!
ERROR: It says you're wrong when you're not!

STOP THE SCRIPT! Click 🛑.

Hmm, there's something wrong. How many c-bits were on the stage?

3 the first time and 2 the second time! I'm SO sure!

What does it say in the variable readout on stage?

It says . . . 5?

At the end of the first run, the value in the `c-bits variable` was 3. We didn't reset it, so it was still 3 when you clicked the **green flag**.

And then in the second run it added 2 new clones to make 5!

Yeah. We need to use the `set to block` to make sure the variable always starts at 0.

18 Find and drag this block into the **script space**:

`set [ ▼ ] to 0`

In the `set to block`, choose **c-bits**.

19

Where do I put it? In the setup script?

You just need to make sure it's set to 0 before you try to use it or change it. We'll put this one in the clone-maker script for now. I'll show you why after this test.

Click and drag the `set` **c-bits** `to` **0** `block`. Insert it **above** the `repeat 10 block` in the clone-maker script.

`set c-bits ▼ to 0`

```
when I receive start ▼
if ⟨ not ⟨ message = lose ⟩ ⟩
    repeat 10
        create a clone of myself ▼
    wait 3 secs
    broadcast ask ▼ and wait
```

TEST

20

TEST: Run the tests again! Click ⚑ twice.
SUCCESS: Both answers are correct!

STOP THE SCRIPT!
Click ⬤.

Save as **Hackerbit05**.

ACHIEVEMENT UNLOCKED!

VARIATOR

LEVEL 2

MISSION OBJECTIVE 3: USE VARIABLES TO CONTROL THE DIFFICULTY

1 Click **Variables**, then **Make a variable**. Name the variable **maximum**.

Find and drag these blocks into the **script space**:

`set [ ▼ ] to 0`   `change [ ▼ ] by 1`   `repeat 10`

`maximum`

2

We have ten scripts to run, so the clone-maker script must run ten times.

Click and drag the `if block` from the **clone-maker script**. Connect it inside the new `repeat 10 block`.

COPY THE CODE

```
repeat 10
    if ⟨ not ⟨ message = lose ⟩ ⟩
        set c-bits ▼ to 0
        repeat 10
            create a clone of myself ▼
```

3 Drag the `repeat 10` block back under the `when I receive start` block. Reconnect the `wait 3 secs` and `broadcast ask` blocks inside the `repeat 10` block.

```
when I receive start ▾
repeat 10
  if not ( message = lose )
    set c-bits ▾ to 0
    repeat 10
      create a clone of myself ▾
  wait 3 secs
  broadcast ask ▾ and wait
```

COPY THE CODE

4 On the upside, if we make it through those ten scripts, we're safe. After 10 loops, we're good!

Click and drag the `broadcast win` block from the **ask script**. Connect it at the end of the **clone-maker script**.

```
when I receive ask ▾
show
ask How many c-bits are there? and wait
if ( answer = c-bits )
  broadcast win ▾
else
  broadcast lose ▾
hide
```

```
when I receive start ▾
repeat 10
  if not ( message = lose )
    set c-bits ▾ to 0
    repeat 10
      create a clone of myself ▾
  wait 3 secs
  broadcast ask ▾ and wait
```

TEST ∿

5 Bad news. Each script gets harder.

Aww . . .

TEST: Click 🚩.
SUCCESS: When you count the c-bits correctly, you get a new set of bits.
STOP THE SCRIPT! Click ⏹.

6 Use variables to increase the difficulty. Every time we look at a new script, there are more and more bits, so you must count faster and faster.

Hmm, I don't get that . . .

The maximum number of bits in the first script is 10.

In the `set to 0 block`, choose **maximum**. Type **10** in the text field.

Insert the `set maximum to 10 block` in the **setup script**.

```
when  clicked
set maximum ▾ to 10
hide
switch to costume introspectre ▾
go to x: 0 y: 0
broadcast start ▾
```

COPY THE CODE

7 Now instead of `repeat 10`, we use it to `repeat maximum`.

Click and drag the `maximum block` into the text field of the inner `repeat loop` in the **clone-maker script**.

```
when I receive start ▾
repeat 10
  if not ( message = lose )
    set c-bits ▾ to 0
    repeat 10  ← maximum
      create a clone of myself ▾
  wait 3 secs
  broadcast ask ▾ and wait
broadcast win ▾
```

8 Now we use the `change by block` to add to the maximum each time.

In the `change by block`, choose **maximum**.

Click and drag the `change maximum by 1 block`. Connect it inside the `if block` in the **ask script**.

```
when I receive ask ▾
show
ask How many c-bits are there? and wait
if ( answer = c-bits )
  change maximum ▾ by 1
else
  broadcast lose ▾
hide
```

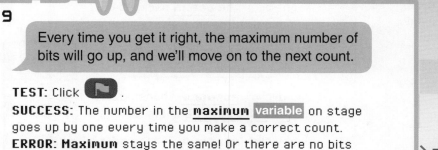

TEST

9

Every time you get it right, the maximum number of bits will go up, and we'll move on to the next count.

TEST: Click 🏳.

SUCCESS: The number in the **maximum** **variable** on stage goes up by one every time you make a correct count.

ERROR: **Maximum** stays the same! Or there are no bits any more.

FIX: Read through your code. Say what each line does out loud.

STOP THE SCRIPT! Click ⬡.

ACHIEVEMENT UNLOCKED!

VARIATOR

LEVEL 3

Save as **Hackerbit06**.

Are you ready for the count Pax? Mentally, physically, emotionally...

You hack in, I count the bits. Easybeans.

And the coders escape from the den of evil!

MISSION DOSSIER

>> HELP THE VALID TEAM ESCAPE IN THE SUBMARINE

Help the Introspecter override the security controls on the sub and escape before the guards notice the coders they're supposed to be guarding have disappeared.

LEVEL: 6

INSTRUCTOR: AGENT INTROSPECTER

MISSION OBJECTIVE 1: I LIKE TO BE CODING THE SEA

PROJECT OUTLINE

NAME:
LAIR ESCAPE

GOAL:
HELP THE CODERS AND THE FIELD TEAM PILOT THE SUB TO THE EXTRACTION POINT.

REQUIREMENTS:
1. USE CLONES TO MAKE A SCROLLING SEA BACKGROUND
2. USE VARIABLES TO MONITOR THE DISTANCE THE SUB'S TRAVELED.
3. ATTACH THE PROPELLER SPRITE TO THE SUBMARINE.
4. USE THE X-POSITION TO TRACK THE SUB'S POSITION.
5. USE CLONES TO TRY AND STOP THE ESCAPEES.
6. RECORD DAMAGE TO THE SUB USING VARIABLES.

1
Open a web browser and go to **snap.berkeley.edu/run**. Start a new project by clicking ⬜. Choose **new**.

2
Click [Stage]. Go to [Backgrounds]. Make a new background by clicking 🖌 to open the **paint screen**.

3

Use 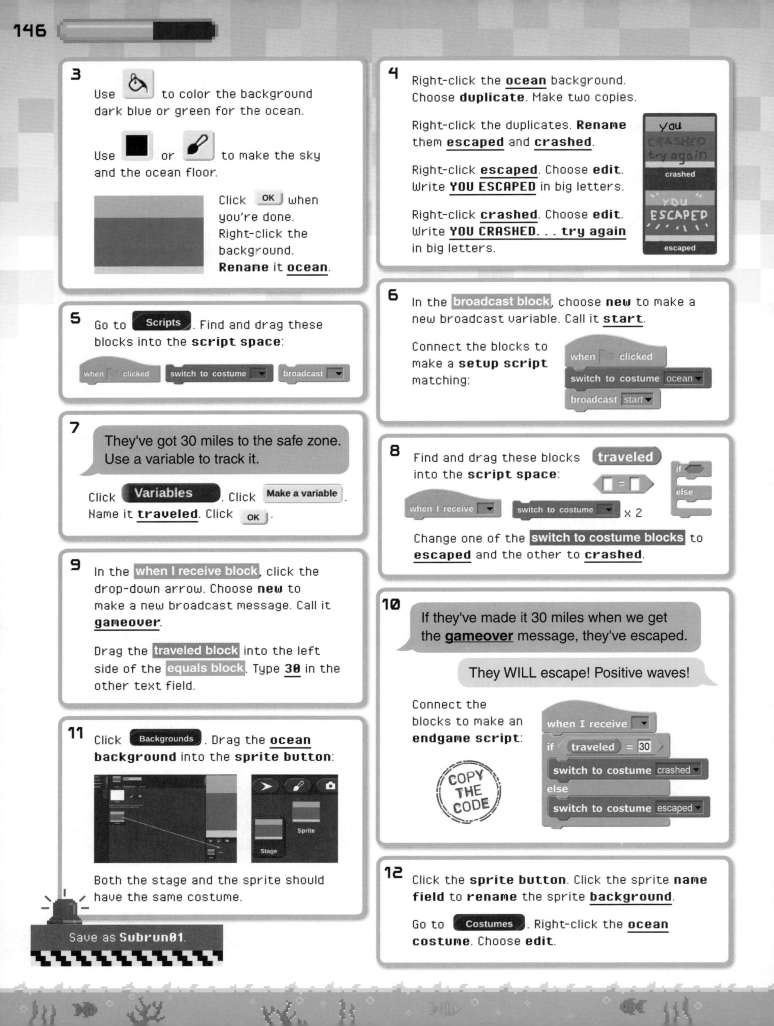 to color the background dark blue or green for the ocean.

Use ■ or ✦ to make the sky and the ocean floor.

Click OK when you're done. Right-click the background. **Rename** it **ocean**.

4

Right-click the **ocean** background. Choose **duplicate**. Make two copies.

Right-click the duplicates. **Rename** them **escaped** and **crashed**.

Right-click **escaped**. Choose **edit**. Write **YOU ESCAPED** in big letters.

Right-click **crashed**. Choose **edit**. Write **YOU CRASHED. . . try again** in big letters.

YOU
CRASHED
try again
crashed

YOU
ESCAPED
escaped

5

Go to Scripts . Find and drag these blocks into the **script space**:

when clicked   switch to costume ▼   broadcast ▼

6

In the broadcast block, choose **new** to make a new broadcast variable. Call it **start**.

Connect the blocks to make a **setup script** matching:

when clicked
switch to costume ocean ▼
broadcast start ▼

7

They've got 30 miles to the safe zone. Use a variable to track it.

Click Variables . Click Make a variable . Name it **traveled**. Click OK .

8

Find and drag these blocks into the **script space**:

traveled

when I receive ▼   switch to costume ▼ x 2   □ = □   if / else

Change one of the switch to costume blocks to **escaped** and the other to **crashed**.

9

In the when I receive block, click the drop-down arrow. Choose **new** to make a new broadcast message. Call it **gameover**.

Drag the traveled block into the left side of the equals block. Type **30** in the other text field.

10

If they've made it 30 miles when we get the **gameover** message, they've escaped.

They WILL escape! Positive waves!

Connect the blocks to make an **endgame script**:

COPY THE CODE

when I receive ▼
if ⟨ traveled = 30 ⟩
switch to costume crashed ▼
else
switch to costume escaped ▼

11

Click Backgrounds . Drag the **ocean background** into the **sprite button**:

Sprite
Stage

Both the stage and the sprite should have the same costume.

Save as **Subrun01**.

12

Click the **sprite button**. Click the sprite **name field** to **rename** the sprite **background**.

Go to Costumes . Right-click the **ocean costume**. Choose **edit**.

13 Draw items for the background of your mission. These will make it look like everything is moving, so keep them simple. Pax drew clouds, fish in the sea, and rocks and seaweed at the bottom.

14 When you're done, click the **checkered area** on [image] and use [brush] to make the blue sky, ocean, and the yellow sand disappear. Click OK.

Right-click the **ocean** costume. **Rename** it **floaties**.

floaties

15 Find and drag these blocks into the **script space**:

when clicked
go to x: 0 y: 0
create a clone of ▼

HINT

The stage should show the **ocean background** and the **floaties** should show on top! If it doesn't, click [flag]. Check the **background sprite** is selected. OK

16 In the **go to block**, type **x:500 y:500**.

In the **create a clone block**, choose **myself**.

17 Connect the blocks to make a **master setup** script:

when clicked
go to x: 500 y: 500
create a clone of myself ▼

COPY THE CODE

18 Find and drag these blocks into the **script space**:

when I start as a clone   delete this clone
go to x: 0 y: 0   create a clone of ▼
glide 1 secs to x: 0 y: 0   x 2

19 In the **go to block**, click the **x:** text field. Type **480**.

In both **glide blocks**, click the text fields. Change them to **glide 10 secs to x:-480 y:0**.

20 We'll use clones to move the floaties. They start off-stage to the right and slowly glide across the stage.

Connect the blocks to make the beginning of the **clone animation** script:

when I start as a clone
go to x: 480 y: 0
glide 10 secs to x: -480 y: 0

21 **TEST:** Click [flag].
SUCCESS: The floaties drift majestically across the screen.
STOP THE SCRIPT! Click [stop].

22 Ooh, I see what you're doing. When it gets to the end, do we make another one that does the same thing?

That's the idea!

In the **create a clone block**, choose **myself**.

Connect it at the end of the **clone animation** script.

when I start as a clone
go to x: 480 y: 0
glide 10 secs to x: -480 y: 0
create a clone of myself ▼

23 **TEST:** Click [flag].
SUCCESS: The floaties drift across, but there's a strange gap between one clone and the next.
STOP THE SCRIPT! Click [stop].

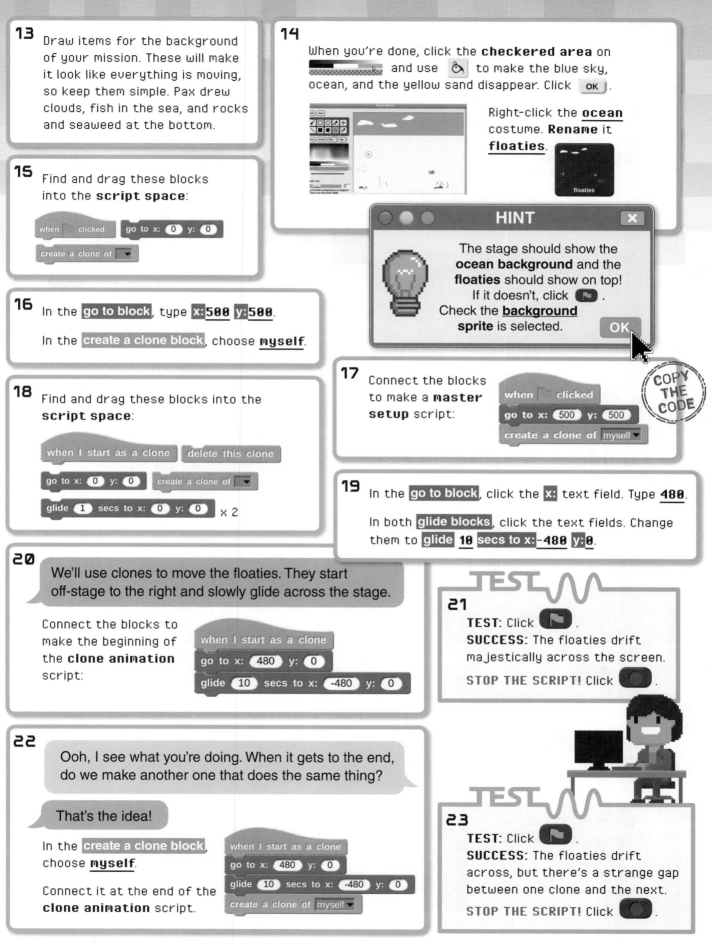

24

If I don't make a clone until the first one has finished gliding, there's a weird gap in the scrolling.

That's why we have two glide blocks. Let's break it up and clone it when the floaties get to the middle of the stage.

In the first glide to x:-480 y:0 block in the **clone animation** script, change the x:-480 to x:0.

Connect the remaining blocks to make a **clone animation** script matching:

```
when I start as a clone
go to x: 480 y: 0
glide 10 secs to x: 0 y: 0
create a clone of myself ▾
glide 10 secs to x: -480 y: 0
delete this clone
```

COPY THE CODE

ACHIEVEMENT UNLOCKED!

CLONER

6 LEVEL

25

TEST

TEST: Click 🏴.
SUCCESS: Continuous floaties! The weird gaps are gone!
STOP THE SCRIPT!
Click ⬤.

26 Find and drag these blocks into the **script space**:

when ◇   ▢ = ▢   message   delete this clone

27 Click and drag the message block into the left text field of the = block. Type **gameover** in the right field.

Connect the blocks to make an **endgame script**:

```
when  message = gameover
delete this clone
```

Save as Subrun02.

MISSION OBJECTIVE 2: MARK THE MILES TO SAFETY

1 Click ▶ to make a new sprite. Click the sprite **name field**. Rename the sprite **sub**.

Go to Costumes. Click 🖌 to make a new costume.

2 Draw a giant submarine. It can have portholes (windows), a periscope, and anything else it needs to transport the coders to escape the wrath of CORUPT. Leave room for a propeller to power it, but don't draw it in yet.

Click OK when you're done.

Right-click the costume. **Rename** it **sub1**.

3 Looks like this sub can only go forwards.

Click the **don't rotate button** in the rotation buttons.

4 Go to `Scripts`. Find and drag these blocks into the **script space**:

`when clicked`
`go to x: 0 y: 0`
`set ▼ to 0`
`point in direction 90 ▼`
`show`
`set size to 100 %`

EXPERIMENT

5 In the **set size block**, change the number. Test it by clicking the block to run it by itself. The sub should be 0.4-0.8 in (1-2 cm) long.

8 In the **when I receive block**, choose **gameover**.

Connect the two blocks to make an **endgame script**.

Save as `Subrun03`.

10 In the **when I receive block**, choose **start**.

Click and drag the **message block** into the left field of the **= block**. Type **gameover** in the right field.

Connect the blocks to make an empty **movement script**:

`when I receive start ▼`
`repeat until < message = gameover >`

13 Connect the blocks together and drag them into the **movement script**:

`when I receive start ▼`
`repeat until < message = gameover >`

`if < key space ▼ pressed? > and < x position < 200 > >`
`change x by 10`

6 In the **set to 0 block**, choose **traveled**.

In the **go to block**, click the **y:** field. Type **-80**. Click the **go to block** and change the **y coordinate** if your sub is traveling along the sand.

Connect the blocks to make a **setup script**.

COPY THE CODE

`when clicked`
`show`
`set size to 18 %`
`point in direction 90 ▼`
`go to x: 0 y: -80`
`set traveled ▼ to 0`

7 We need to track them until they hit the safety mark.

Find and drag these blocks into the **script space**:

`when I receive ▼`
`hide`

9 Find and drag these blocks into the **script space**:

`repeat until < >`
`when I receive ▼`
`message`
`< = >`

11 Looks like movement in subs is too hard for CORUPT coders. This sub ONLY moves forwards.

Find and drag these blocks into the **script space**:

`< and >`
`key space ▼ pressed?`
`if < >`
`< < >`
`change x by 10`
`x position`

12 Drag the **x position block** into the left field of the **< block**. Type **200** in the right field.

Drag the **key space pressed block** into the left field of the **and block**.

Drag the **x position < 200 block** into the right field of the **and block**.

`< key space ▼ pressed? > and < x position < 200 >`

14

TEST: Click 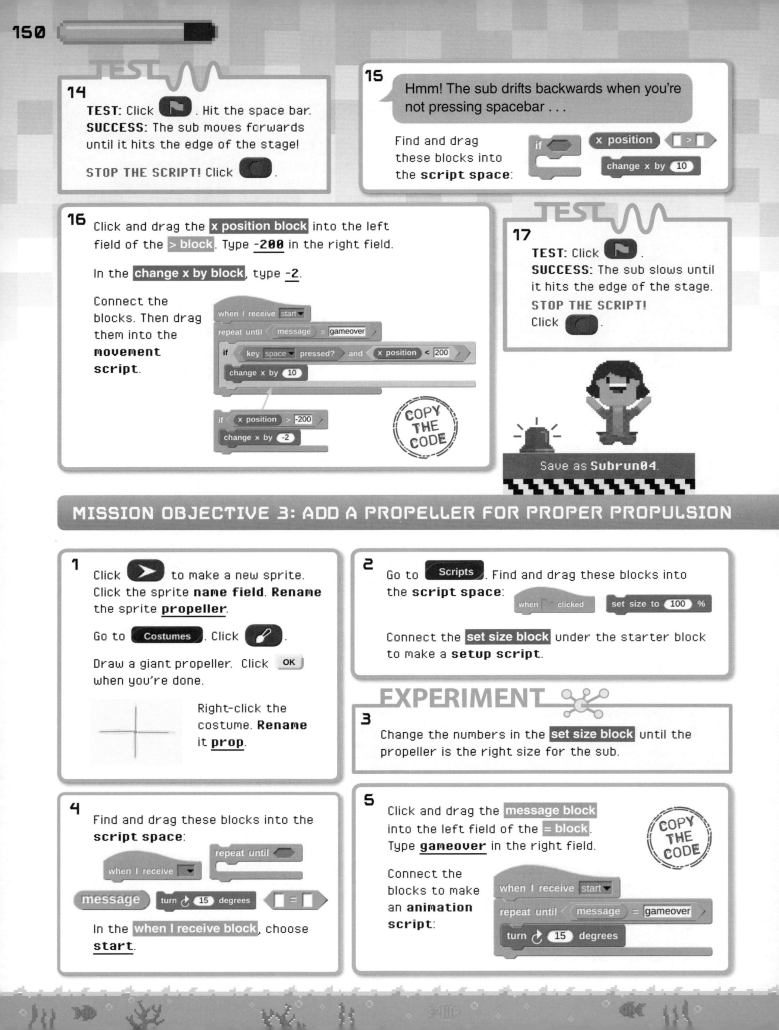. Hit the space bar.
SUCCESS: The sub moves forwards until it hits the edge of the stage!

STOP THE SCRIPT! Click .

15

Hmm! The sub drifts backwards when you're not pressing spacebar . . .

Find and drag these blocks into the **script space**:

if
x position
>
change x by 10

16

Click and drag the **x position block** into the left field of the **> block**. Type **-200** in the right field.

In the **change x by block**, type **-2**.

Connect the blocks. Then drag them into the **movement script**.

```
when I receive start ▼
repeat until < message = gameover >
    if < key space ▼ pressed? > and < x position < 200 >
        change x by 10
```

```
if < x position > -200 >
    change x by -2
```

COPY THE CODE

17

TEST: Click .
SUCCESS: The sub slows until it hits the edge of the stage.
STOP THE SCRIPT! Click .

Save as **Subrun04**.

MISSION OBJECTIVE 3: ADD A PROPELLER FOR PROPER PROPULSION

1

Click to make a new sprite. Click the sprite **name field**. **Rename** the sprite **propeller**.

Go to **Costumes**. Click .

Draw a giant propeller. Click **OK** when you're done.

Right-click the costume. **Rename** it **prop**.

2

Go to **Scripts**. Find and drag these blocks into the **script space**:

when clicked
set size to 100 %

Connect the **set size block** under the starter block to make a **setup script**.

EXPERIMENT

3

Change the numbers in the **set size block** until the propeller is the right size for the sub.

4

Find and drag these blocks into the **script space**:

repeat until
when I receive ▼
message
turn ↻ 15 degrees
=

In the **when I receive block**, choose **start**.

5

Click and drag the **message block** into the left field of the **= block**. Type **gameover** in the right field.

Connect the blocks to make an **animation script**:

```
when I receive start ▼
repeat until < message = gameover >
    turn ↻ 15 degrees
```

COPY THE CODE

6

TEST: Click 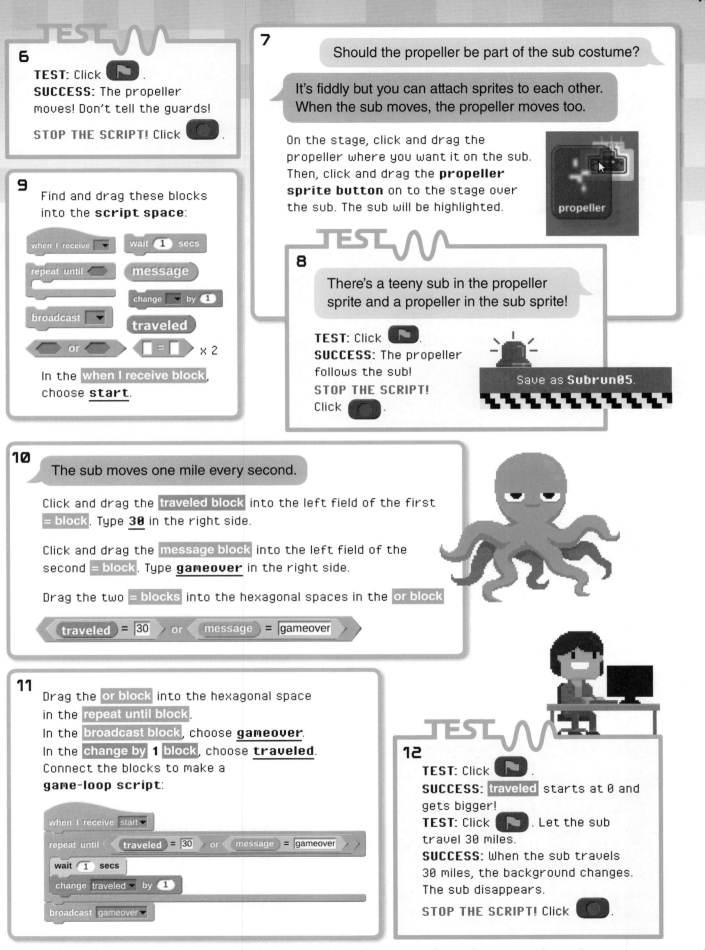.
SUCCESS: The propeller moves! Don't tell the guards!

STOP THE SCRIPT! Click .

7

Should the propeller be part of the sub costume?

It's fiddly but you can attach sprites to each other. When the sub moves, the propeller moves too.

On the stage, click and drag the propeller where you want it on the sub. Then, click and drag the **propeller sprite button** on to the stage over the sub. The sub will be highlighted.

propeller

TEST

8

There's a teeny sub in the propeller sprite and a propeller in the sub sprite!

TEST: Click .
SUCCESS: The propeller follows the sub!
STOP THE SCRIPT!
Click .

Save as Subrun05.

9

Find and drag these blocks into the **script space**:

when I receive ▼   wait ① secs
repeat until ◇
                   message
                   change ▼ by ①
broadcast ▼
                   traveled
◇ or ◇   ☐ = ☐   x 2

In the when I receive block, choose **start**.

10

The sub moves one mile every second.

Click and drag the traveled block into the left field of the first = block. Type **30** in the right side.

Click and drag the message block into the left field of the second = block. Type **gameover** in the right side.

Drag the two = blocks into the hexagonal spaces in the or block

traveled = 30 or message = gameover

11

Drag the or block into the hexagonal space in the repeat until block.
In the broadcast block, choose **gameover**.
In the change by 1 block, choose **traveled**.
Connect the blocks to make a **game-loop script**:

when I receive start ▼
repeat until ⟨ traveled = 30 or message = gameover ⟩
  wait ① secs
  change traveled ▼ by ①
broadcast gameover ▼

12

TEST: Click .
SUCCESS: traveled starts at 0 and gets bigger!
TEST: Click . Let the sub travel 30 miles.
SUCCESS: When the sub travels 30 miles, the background changes. The sub disappears.

STOP THE SCRIPT! Click .

MISSION OBJECTIVE 4: A CORUPT PURSUIT

1

CORUPT have launched a pursuit vessel!

Click ▶ to make a new sprite. Click the sprite **name field**. **Rename** the sprite **C-boat**.

Go to **Costumes**. Draw a scary boat.

Click **OK** when you're done.

Right-click the costume. Rename it **guardboat**.

2

Find and drag these blocks into the **script space**:

when ▢ clicked   go to x: 0 y: 0

set size to 100 %   point in direction 90 ▾   show

EXPERIMENT

3

The boat is a similar size to the sub. Change the number in the **set size block**. Click the block to run it. Try different numbers until it looks right. Pax ended up with **15%**.

The boat must sit on the water line. Change the number in the **y:** field of the **go to block**. Click the block to run it. Try different numbers until it's in the right place. Pax's boat ended up at **y:92**.

4

Connect the blocks to make a **setup script**:

when ▢ clicked
set size to 15 %
go to x: 0 y: 92
point in direction 90 ▾
show

COPY THE CODE

5

TEST: Click 🚩.
SUCCESS: The boat is the right size, in the right place.
STOP THE SCRIPT! Click ⬤.

Save as **Subrun06**.

6

Find and drag these blocks into the **script space**:

▢ = ▢

when I receive ▾   message   repeat until ⬡

glide 1 secs to x: 0 y: 0   costume # ▾ of ▾

In the **when I receive block**, choose **start**.

Click and drag the **message block** into the left field of the **= block**. Type **gameover** in the right field.

7

In the **glide block**, click the first text field. Type **0.5 secs**.

In the **costume# of block**, click the **right** drop-down arrow. Choose **sub**. Click the left drop-down arrow. Choose **x position**.   x position ▾ of sub ▾

8

Click and drag the **x position of sub block** into the **x:** field of the **glide block**. Type the boat's **y** coordinate (you can find it in the boat **setup script**) in the **y:** field. Connect the blocks to make a **movement script**:

when I receive start ▾
repeat until < message = gameover >
glide 0.5 secs to x: x position ▾ of sub ▾ y: 92

COPY THE CODE

9

TEST: Click 🚩. Move the sub with the spacebar.
SUCCESS: The boat is worryingly close behind the sub...
STOP THE SCRIPT! Click ⬤.

Save as **Subrun07**.

MISSION OBJECTIVE 5: USE CLONES TO STOP ESCAPEES

1

They're dropping depth charges to overload the sub's electrical systems!

Click ▶ to make a new sprite. Click the sprite **name field**. **Rename** the sprite **charge**.

Go to **Costumes** to paint a new costume.

Draw a giant explosive charge.

Click **OK** when you're done.

Right-click the costume. **Rename** it **explosion**.

2

Find and drag these blocks into the **script space**:

`when ⚑ clicked`
`go to x: 0 y: 0`

In the **go to block**, type **x:500 y:500**.

Connect the two blocks to make a **master setup script**.

3

Find and drag these blocks into the **script space**:

`when I start as a clone`
`go to ▼`
`repeat 10`
`set size to 100 %`
`turn ↻ 15 degrees`
`delete this clone`
`change y by 10`
`pick random 1 to 10`

In the **go to block**, choose **C-boat**.

EXPERIMENT

4

When they start, the charges are about 0.2 in (5 mm) in size. Change the number in the **set size block**. Click the block to run it by itself. Try different numbers until they look right. Pax ended up at **3**%.

5

In the **change y by block**, type **-1**.

In the **pick random block**, type **50** in the left text field and **200** in the right field.

Drag the **pick random block** into the text field of the **repeat block**.

6

Connect the blocks to make an **animation script**:

COPY THE CODE

`when I start as a clone`
`set size to 3 %`
`go to C-boat ▼`
`repeat pick random 50 to 200`
`change y by -1`
`turn ↻ 15 degrees`
`delete this clone`

TEST

7

TEST: Click ⚑, then click the new animation script to run by itself.
SUCCESS: The charge starts at the boat and spins down.
TEST: Click the animation script. Wait until the charge stops, then retry it a few times.
SUCCESS: The charges stop at different heights each time.
STOP THE SCRIPT! Click ⬤.

Save as **Subrun08**.

8

OMG! The charges randomly explode!

Find and drag these blocks into the **script space**:

`repeat 10`
`change size by 10`

In the **change size by block**, type **3**.

Connect the two blocks together. Then connect them above the **delete this clone block**.

`when I start as a clone`
`set size to 3 %`
`go to C-boat ▼`
`repeat pick random 50 to 200`
`change y by -1`
`turn ↻ 15 degrees`
`delete this clone`
`repeat 10`
`change size by 3`

9

TEST: Click 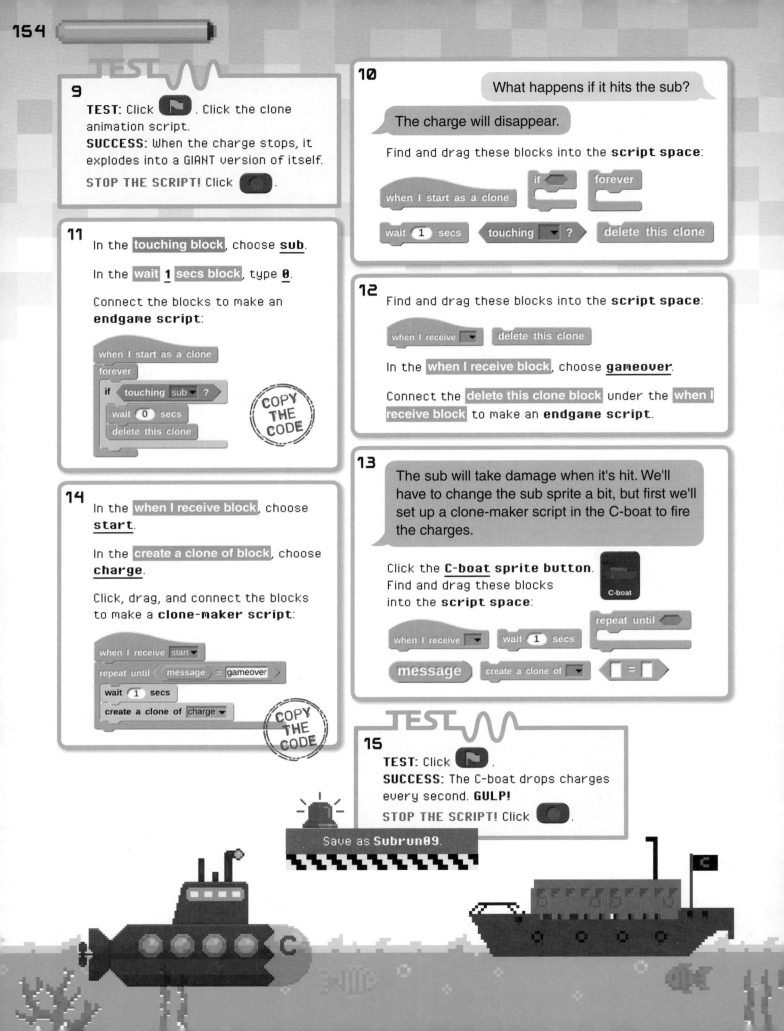. Click the clone animation script.

SUCCESS: When the charge stops, it explodes into a GIANT version of itself.

STOP THE SCRIPT! Click ⬤.

10

What happens if it hits the sub?

The charge will disappear.

Find and drag these blocks into the **script space**:

```
when I start as a clone

if < >

forever

wait 1 secs

touching ▼ ?

delete this clone
```

11

In the **touching block**, choose **sub**.

In the **wait 1 secs block**, type **0**.

Connect the blocks to make an **endgame script**:

```
when I start as a clone
forever
  if < touching sub ▼ ? >
    wait 0 secs
    delete this clone
```

COPY THE CODE

12

Find and drag these blocks into the **script space**:

```
when I receive ▼      delete this clone
```

In the **when I receive block**, choose **gameover**.

Connect the **delete this clone block** under the **when I receive block** to make an **endgame script**.

13

The sub will take damage when it's hit. We'll have to change the sub sprite a bit, but first we'll set up a clone-maker script in the C-boat to fire the charges.

Click the **C-boat sprite button**. Find and drag these blocks into the **script space**:

C-boat

```
when I receive ▼      wait 1 secs

repeat until < >

message      create a clone of ▼      < = >
```

14

In the **when I receive block**, choose **start**.

In the **create a clone of block**, choose **charge**.

Click, drag, and connect the blocks to make a **clone-maker script**:

```
when I receive start ▼
repeat until < message = gameover >
  wait 1 secs
  create a clone of charge ▼
```

COPY THE CODE

15

TEST: Click 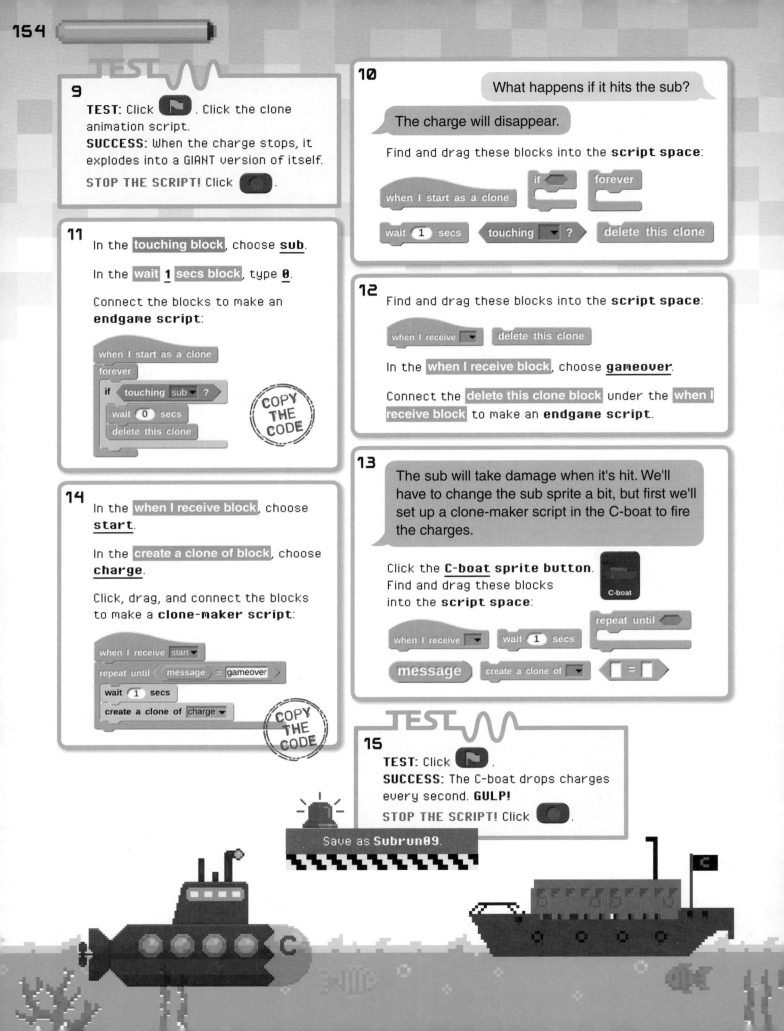.

SUCCESS: The C-boat drops charges every second. GULP!

STOP THE SCRIPT! Click ⬤.

Save as **Subrun09**.

MISSION OBJECTIVE 6: SET UP A VARIABLE TO COUNT YOUR HITS

1

It takes three hits to disable the sub.

We'll use sensing blocks to count the hits and store them in a variable. When the variable gets to three, the sub goes down.

Click **Variables** and **Make a variable**. Call the new variable **lives**.

2

Click the **sub sprite button**. Find and drag these blocks into the **script space**:

when I receive ▼   wait 1 secs   set ▼ to 0   if
touching ▼ ?   broadcast ▼   repeat until
□ = □   change ▼ by 1   lives

3

In the **set to 0 block**, choose **lives**. Click the text field. Type **3**.

Click and drag the **set lives to 3 block**. Connect it at the end of the **setup script**.

when ▢ clicked
show
set size to 18 %
point in direction 90 ▼
go to x: 0 y: -80
set traveled ▼ to 0
set lives ▼ to 3

4

In the **when I receive block** choose **start**.

Click and drag the **lives block** into the left field of the **= block**. Type **0** in the right side.

Connect the blocks to make an empty **game-loop script**:

when I receive start ▼
repeat until ⟨ lives = 0 ⟩

5

In the **touching block**, choose **charge**.

In the **change by block**, choose **lives**. Click the text field. Type **-1**.

In the **broadcast block**, choose **gameover**.

Connect the blocks to match: COPY THE CODE

if ⟨ touching charge ▼ ? ⟩
change lives ▼ by -1
wait 1 secs

6

Connect the **if block** inside the **repeat until block** in the **game-loop** script.

when I receive start ▼
repeat until ⟨ lives = 0 ⟩

if ⟨ touching charge ▼ ? ⟩
change lives ▼ by -1
wait 1 secs

Click and drag the **broadcast block** and connect it at the end of the **game-loop script**.

7

TEST: Click ▢. Let the sub get hit.
SUCCESS: When the sub is hit, the **lives** variable goes down.

STOP THE SCRIPT!
Click ⬤.

Save as **Subrun10**.

8

Go to **Costumes** in the **sub** sprite.

Right-click the **sub1 costume**. Choose **duplicate** to make a copy.

Right-click the copy. **Rename** it **sub2**.

Edit sub2. Add some minor damage from the explosion.

9

Right-click **sub2**. Choose **duplicate** to make a copy.

Right click the copy. **Rename** it **sub3**.

Edit sub3. Draw MORE damage to the sub.

sub3

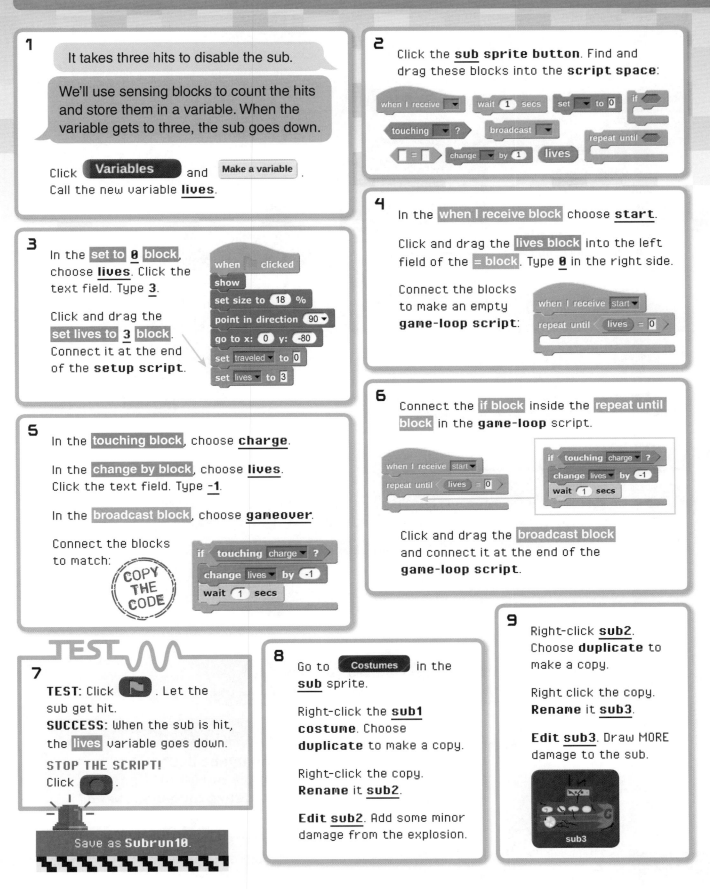

10 Find and drag these blocks into the **script space**:

`next costume`   `switch to costume ▼`

In the **switch to costume block**, choose **sub1**.

11 Click and drag the **switch to costume block** to connect at the end of the setup script.

```
when     clicked
show
set size to 18 %
point in direction 90 ▼
go to x: 0 y: -80
set traveled ▼ to 0
set lives ▼ to 3
switch to costume sub1 ▼
```

12 Click and drag the **next costume block** into the game-loop script underneath **change lives** by **-1**.

Play the game to make sure your new code works!

```
when I receive start ▼
repeat until   lives = 0
  if   touching charge ▼ ?
    change lives ▼ by -1
    next costume  ←
    wait 1 secs

broadcast gameover ▼
```

Save as **Subrun11**.

CHALLENGE 🚩

Add controls to move your sub up and down. Use the y coordinates. Think of a way to use **if blocks** and predicates to stop it going into the sand or sky.

ACHIEVEMENT UNLOCKED!

VARIATOR

LEVEL 4

They made it? Everyone's OK?

Yes! The VALID chopper is bringing them here... hmm. There's an urgent message from Gartz, one of the rescued coders. They've been forced to build something for CORUPT.

Build what?

It's garbled. Something about a space ... base ... robot?

That does NOT sound good!

I'll clean up this message to get more info. Go to Doubleshot. If there's a giant space robot, we need him! ETAMI will take you.

NEW MESSAGE ✕

Find Agent Doubleshot and figure out what's got the Introspecter so spooked?

Y/N

BLOCK-MAKING AND FUNCTIONS

with Agent Doubleshot

NEW MESSAGE ✖

Would you like to proceed?

Y/N?

Coders have been mysteriously disappearing from their beds, their schools, their recharge pods. With your help, the VALID supercoders have tracked down and rescued the kidnapped coders from the island lair of notorious criminal organization CORUPT. The rescue team is en route to VALID HQ, but a garbled message about space robots suggests that the real trouble is still to come. . .

Agent Doubleshot reporting for duty!

Oh good! Agent Doubleshot, this is Potential Agent X.

The recruit! Doubleshot has heard about you!

I'm confused. Aren't you Agent Doubleshot?

You can't tell from Doubleshot's good looks and deep, thoughtful hairstyle?

You are correct Potential Agent X. Despite his . . .

EXTREMELY charming. . .

. . .insistence of referring to himself in the third person, Agent Doubleshot is our foremost block-maker and field agent. Doubleshot, our satellites have just alerted us to a hidden missile system on the island. Now it has been activated.

Hmm, they're not giving up without a fight . . . The coders must be more important to them than we thought.

Preliminary reports suggest the coders have vital information for us.

Do we know where the attack will be?

Current trajectory suggests VALID HQ.

Wait, that's where we are! They're attacking HERE?!

Stay strong Pax, my little friend. Doubleshot, block-maker extraordinaire, is here. You and I can build the blocks to get us out of this mess.

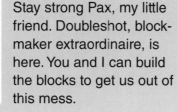

NEW MESSAGE

Go with Doubleshot and build a missile defense system to save VALID HQ and your new friends?

Y/N

MISSION DOSSIER

>> PROTECT VALID FROM CORUPT'S ATTACK!

The rescued coders have secrets to tell and CORUPT will stop at nothing to prevent them from reaching VALID HQ and the supercoders. ETAMI's satellite network has detected missile launches from the island base. The countdown is on to get the defense system online to protect VALID HQ from the wrath of CORUPT.

LEVEL: 7

INSTRUCTOR: Agent Doubleshot

BACKGROUND: Agent Doubleshot is the last line of defense, with his photographic memory giving him the ultimate edge. People assume he's all brawn and no brain, but Agent Doubleshot is an expert strategist both in the field and behind a keyboard. His quick-thinking block-maker skills have saved the day more than once.

DOUBLESHOT

All right Pax, I need to get you up to speed on block making, FAST. Ready?

So ready.

When you go to the code menu, the blocks in there are all shortcuts that you can use. Some of them tell your sprites and costumes to DO things: those are **command blocks**. Like `wait 1 secs` or `go to x: 0 y: 0`. Others let you build statements that can either be true or false, so you can make decisions. We call those **predicate blocks**.

Like `and`, `= `, or `> `?

Yes. Then we have these little rounded blocks, like `x position`, `answer`, or `+`. These are **reporter blocks**, because they report information to us. We use these to tell us what's in a variable, like the Introspecter showed you.

So, **command blocks** give orders, **predicate blocks** tell you what's true or not, and **reporter blocks** report information.

Good. Behind every single block in the code menu is more code.

Behind the code, there's . . . just more code?

It's code all the way down, Pax. Until you get to ETAMI's 1s and 0s. So, when there's no block to do exactly what you want, you can code your own.

I can write Snap! blocks? Coolbeans!

OK, before we get started with missile defense, we must ensure we can track the missiles as they leave the island.

MISSION OBJECTIVE: TRACK THE TARGET!

PROJECT OUTLINE
NAME: TARGET TRACKER
GOAL: CREATE A BASIC TRACKING SYSTEM FOR OFF-STAGE TARGETS.
REQUIREMENTS: 1. MAKE A COMMAND BLOCK TO CONTROL THE TRACKER MOTION
2. MAKE A PREDICATE TO DETECT WHEN THE TARGET IS OFF STAGE

1 Open a web browser on your computer. Type **snap.berkeley.edu/run** in your browser bar. Hit **enter**. If you have a Snap! account, log in, otherwise acquire an adult to help make an account.

2 Click **Stage**. Go to **Backgrounds**.
Click. Choose **Backgrounds** to open the **backgrounds selector**.

3 Scroll down and double-click the **XY Grid** to import it.
Click **cancel** to close the background selector.

XY Grid

4 Click **Sprite**. Click the sprite **name field**. Name the sprite **Tracker**.

tracker
☑ draggable

Go to **Costumes**. Create a new costume by clicking.

5 Draw a giant arrow pointing to the right.
Click **OK** when you're done.
Right-click the costume. **Rename** it **arrow**.

arrow

6 Click **Scripts**. Find these blocks and drag them into the **script space**:

when [ ] clicked   go to x: 0 y: 0

set size to 100 %   broadcast ▼

In the **set size block**, click the **text field**. Type **25**.

EXPERIMENT

7 The arrow should be about 1.5 in (4 cm) wide. Click the **set size block** and see how big the arrow ends up. You might need to make numbers bigger or smaller.

8 In the **broadcast block**, click the drop-down arrow. Choose **new** to make a new broadcast message. Name it **start**.

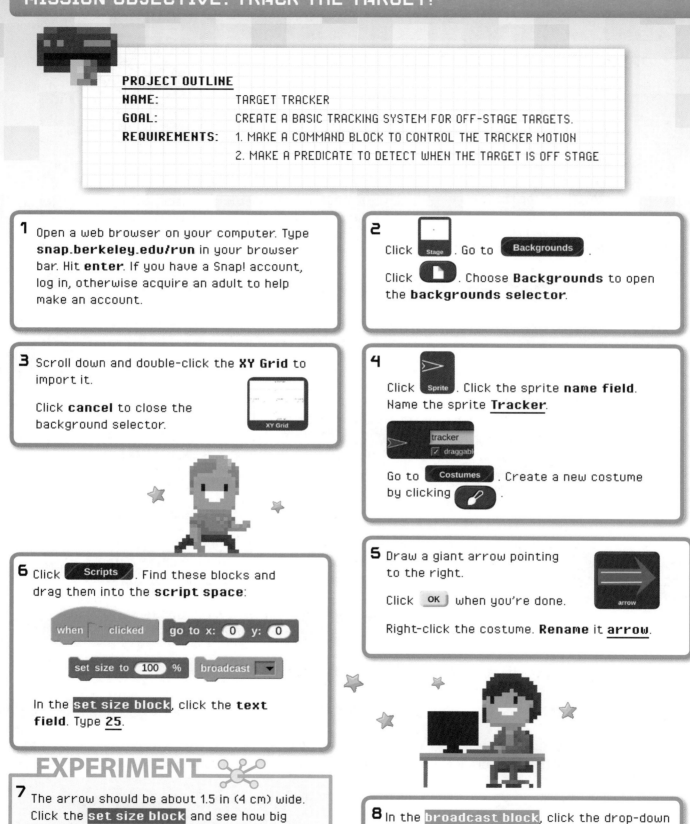

9 Connect the blocks to make a **setup script**:

```
when green flag clicked
go to x: 0 y:0
set size to 25%
broadcast start
```

or

```
when [flag] clicked
go to x: 0 y: 0
set size to 25 %
broadcast start ▾
```

COPY THE CODE

10 Find and drag these blocks into the script space:

```
when I receive ▾

forever

point towards ▾

move 10 steps
```

11 In the **when I receive block**, click the drop-down arrow. Choose **start**.

In the **point towards block**, click the drop-down arrow. Choose **mouse-pointer**.

In the **move 10 steps block**, click the text field. Type **1**.

12 Put the blocks together to make an **event script**:

```
when I receive start ▾
forever
    point towards mouse-pointer ▾
    move 1 steps
```

13

TEST

TEST: Click [flag] to run your script.
SUCCESS: The tracker points to the mouse-pointer and moves slowly towards it!
ERROR: The tracker is super quick, then jitters like a Floopian space beetle!
FIX: Put on your best bug-hunting glasses! Read through your code out loud. Which block controls the speed?

STOP THE SCRIPT! After each test, click ⬤ to stop all the scripts running.

14

Doubleshot will show you how to make this into a new block. Why, you ask? Good question, Pax!

Um, thanks?

You remember when you arrived on Finity's doorstep to learn about the joy of loops? Of course you do. Finity showed you how to write some code without a loop first.

Sure. It was 7 million lines long and didn't work very well.

Classic Finity! Making blocks is a bit like that. Making a block makes it neater than a long script: it's easier to read and to debug. This bit of our code works perfectly, so we can put it in a block without worrying. This is the Make a block box! Doubleshot's favorite dialog box!

In the **code menu area**, click [Make a block] to open the **Make a block** dialog box.

```
Make a block

Motion       Control
Looks        Sensing
Sound        Operators
Pen          Variables
Lists        Other

[                    ]

Command   Reporter   Predicate
● for all sprites   ○ for this sprite only

OK       Cancel
```

15

So, what do all these do?

First! The categories panel. Look familiar?! You bet! This is how we choose where our block shows up in the **code menu**. For now, motion should be highlighted.

Click the motion button to make sure it's highlighted.

16

Is that important?

It's logical. This block will put the sprite in motion. If we want to reuse it later, it's so annoying to hunt through all the categories!

Is this text field for the name of the block?

It certainly is. Choose a nice, describe-y, logical name.

In the text field, type **move towards mouse-pointer**.

17

The three different kinds of blocks you can make are **commands**, **reporters**, and **predicates**.

Our block is moving towards the mouse-pointer. I guess that means it's a **command block**?

Doubleshot agrees!

Click the **Command button** to make sure it's highlighted.

18

These checkboxes control if this block shows up for other sprites or just for this sprite. Doubleshot is a sharing kinda guy, so let's leave it as "for all sprites".

Coolbeans! So, choose the category, choose a name, choose a type, then share it. Easybeans!

Check you've done everything Pax listed, then click OK .

19

Oh! Another box! Aren't we finished?

No! This is the **Block Editor**. It works like a second **script space**. You can drag and drop blocks in here. The big difference is that you can only make **one** script in each Block Editor box, so make it a good one!

What happens if I just drag another starter block in here?

Click and drag when clicked from the **code menu area** into the **Block Editor**.

It won't work Paxeypax. You can only connect blocks underneath the built-in starter block. We're going to use this block to point towards the mouse-pointer and then move.

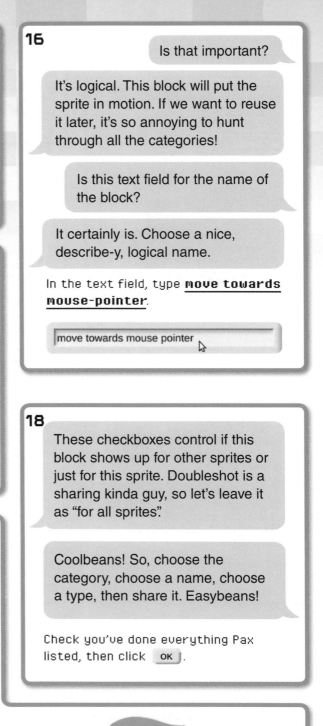

20 Find and drag these blocks into the **Block Editor**:

point towards ▢   move 10 steps

21 In the **point towards block**, choose **mouse-pointer**.

In the **move 10 steps block**, click the text field and type **1**.

Connect the blocks underneath the **starter block** to match:

move towards mouse-pointer
point towards mouse-pointer
move 1 steps

or

+ move + towards + mouse + pointer +

point towards mouse-pointer ▼

move 1 steps

COPY THE CODE

TEST

25

TEST: Click 🏴 to run your script.
SUCCESS: It works the exact same way! The tracker points to the mouse-pointer and slowly moves.

STOP THE SCRIPT!
Click ⬤ .

Save as **Tracker01**.

26

This tracker needs something else, though. We don't need to track when the target is on the stage. We only want to track when the target goes out of sight.

Find and drag these blocks into the **script space**:

if
else   show   hide

22

That should be all you need for now.

Click **OK** to close the **Block Editor** and save your new **command** block.

move towards mouse pointer

23 Click **Motion** in the **categories panel**.

Your block will be at the bottom of the **code menu area**.

OMG! There it is! I wrote a BLOCK!

Find your **event script**. Click and drag the two **motion blocks** into the **code menu area** to delete them.

24 Click and drag your new **move towards mouse-pointer block** and connect it inside the forever loop.

when I receive start ▼
forever

move towards mouse pointer

ACHIEVEMENT UNLOCKED!
BLOCKBUSTER

LEVEL 1

27 Connect the blocks inside the **forever loop** of the **event script**:

when I receive start ▼
forever
move towards mouse pointer
if
show
else
hide

28

What are we going to put in the blank bit?

Doubleshot is going to show you how to make a predicate!

Click `Make a block` to make a new block.

29

This block will tell us if the mouse-pointer is on stage or not. Which category from the make-a-block menu do you think it should go in?

Maybe it's `sensing` whether the mouse-pointer is on-stage or not?

`Sensing` is a good choice!

Click `Sensing`, so your new block will show up in the `sensing` category.

Click the text field. Name the block **mouse is off stage**.

30

Now, this one is not a command. We're not telling sprites to do anything.

It's a reporter?

That's not a bad guess. Reporters and predicates both give us information, so even Doubleshot can get confused. Reporters can tell us numbers or names or lists, but predicates can only be true or false, yes or no, correct or incorrect.

The mouse is either on-screen or it's not. It's true or false, so this is a predicate?

TRUE!

Click **predicate** to make sure the new block is a TRUE/FALSE predicate.

mouse is off stage
Command   Reporter   Predicate

31

OK, it's set to `sensing` category, called **mouse is off stage**, **predicate, for all sprites**.

Make that block, Paxo!

Check that your **Make a block** options are the same as Pax's. Click `OK` to open the **Block Editor**.

HINT ✕

If you are running out of room in the **Block Editor**, click and drag the bottom right corner of the dialog box to make it bigger.

32

What's this report block?

The report block is the important part that tells the script true or false. When you're making a predicate, you must always have one report block, but often you need two or three.

Find and drag these blocks into the **Block Editor**:

33 Click and drag the `mouse x blocks` into the left fields of the `> block` and `< block`.

Check the **XY grid** for the maximum and minimum x coordinates of the stage.

OK, the right edge of the screen is 240.

In the `> block`, type **240** in the right field.

And the left side of the screen is -240.

In the `< block`, type **-240** in the left field.

34 Click and drag the **> block** and **< block** into the blank hexagons of the **or block**.

> ⟨ mouse x ⟩ > 240 ⟩ or ⟨ mouse x ⟩ < -240 ⟩

Click and drag the **or block** into the blank hexagon of the **if block**.

Click and drag the **true block** into the text field of the **report block**.

> report ⟨ true ◯ ⟩

35 Click and drag the **report block** and connect it inside the **if block**.

Connect the **if block** underneath the **mouse is off stage** starter block.

> + mouse + is + off + stage +
>
> if ⟨ mouse x > 240 ⟩ or ⟨ mouse x < -240 ⟩
>
> report ⟨ true ◯ ⟩

36

> This chunk of code will report **true** if the mouse-pointer is off to the left or right of the screen. What happens if that's not true?

> Umm, nothing?

> Hmm, predicates can't be nothing. They MUST be true or false! We need another report block!

Right-click the **report block**. Choose **duplicate** to make a copy. Click to connect it underneath the **if block**.

> + mouse + is + off + stage +
>
> if ⟨ mouse x > 240 ⟩ or ⟨ mouse x < -240 ⟩
>
> report ⟨ true ◯ ⟩
>
> report ⟨ true ◯ ⟩

Click the **true** field to change it to **false**.

> + mouse + is + off + stage +
>
> if ⟨ mouse x > 240 ⟩ or ⟨ mouse x < -240 ⟩
>
> report ⟨ true ◯ ⟩
>
> report ⟨ ◯ false ⟩

COPY THE CODE

37

> That's better. Now if it's true, the block will yell **true**. Otherwise it'll tell us **false**. Good work Paxxy. Let's make sure it works, then we can work out the y coordinates.

Click **OK** to close the **Block Editor** and save your new **predicate** block.

> mouse is off stage

38

> Is it OK to close it even though it's not finished?

> Have I ever lead you wrong, Paxiota? You can come back and edit your blocks later if you need to. Blocks are like any sort of code. They must be tested, as they might contain a sneaky bug or two.

Click and drag the new **mouse is off stage block** into the blank hexagon of the **if else block**.

> when I receive start ▼
>
> forever
>
>   move towards mouse pointer
>
>   if ⟨ ⟩ ← mouse is off stage
>
>   show
>
>   else
>
>   hide

TEST

39

TEST: Click 🏴. Move your mouse off stage left.
SUCCESS: The tracker hides when the mouse-pointer is on the stage (or above or below it) but reappears when you move it to the left.
ERROR: The tracker is always visible. Or NEVER!
FIX: Right-click the new block. Choose **edit** to open the **Block Editor** dialog box. Check that each line of your code matches Pax's.

STOP THE SCRIPT! Click 🔘.

Save as **Tracker02**.

40

We haven't done the y axis though.

Doubleshot thinks it's time, Pax ol' buddy.

Right-click the mouse is off stage block in the script or in the **code menu area**. Choose **edit** to open the **Block Editor** again.

41

The code for the next bit is almost the same, so I'll copy it instead of using new blocks.

Doubleshot is a fan of anything that saves time and effort!

Right-click and duplicate the if block in the **Block Editor**.

42 Drag these blocks into the **Block Editor**:

mouse y x 2

Replace the bottom two mouse x blocks with mouse y blocks.

In the > block and < block, change the text fields to **180** and **-180**.

if < mouse y > 180 or mouse y < -180 >
report true

43 Insert the new if block under the first if block, above the report false block.

+ mouse + is + off + stage +
if < mouse x > 240 or mouse x < -240 >
report true
if < mouse y > 180 or mouse y < -180 >
report true
report false

COPY THE CODE

Drag the unused report false block and the two mouse x blocks into the **code menu area** to delete them. Click **OK** to save your changes.

44 TEST

TEST: Click ⚑. Move the mouse-pointer off the stage to the bottom.
SUCCESS: The tracker hides when the pointer is on stage. If you move off stage, it follows!

STOP THE SCRIPT! Click ⬛.

Save as **Tracker03**.

ACHIEVEMENT UNLOCKED!

BLOCKBUSTER

LEVEL 2

MISSION DOSSIER

>> PROTECT VALID FROM CORUPT'S ATTACK!

CORUPT's missiles are being tracked. Now the race is on to get the VALID HQ defense system up and running!

LEVEL: 7
INSTRUCTOR: Agent Doubleshot

PROJECT OUTLINE

NAME:
DEFENDER
GOAL:
MAKE A MISSILE DEFENSE SYSTEM TO DEFEND VALID HQ.
REQUIREMENTS:
1. USE VARIABLES TO CONTROL A TIMER.
2. MAKE A BLOCK TO CONTROL THE GAME LOOP.
3. USE VARIABLES TO CONTROL THE BASE LIGHTS.
4. USE A REPORTER BLOCK TO PICK A RANDOM MISSILE TARGET.
5. USE A REPORTER BLOCK TO DETERMINE THE FIRING BASE FOR THE VALID GROUND DEFENSE.
6. MAKE A PREDICATE TO DETECT A BASE HIT.

MISSION OBJECTIVE 1: COUNTDOWN TO RESCUE

1 Time is running out. We need to get moving on the missile defense system.

Open a web browser and go to **snap.berkeley.edu/run** or start a new project by clicking the page menu and choosing **new**.

2 Click `Stage`. Go to `Backgrounds`. Click 🖌 to make a new background.

3 Draw the sky and a thin layer of ground. Click `OK` when you're done.

Right-click the background. **Rename** it **sky**.

4 Right-click **sky**. Choose **duplicate** twice to make two copies.

Right-click and **rename** the new backgrounds **win** and **lose**.

Right-click **lose**. Choose **edit**. Write **BASE DESTROYED** in big, sad letters.

Right-click **win**. Choose **edit**. Write **YOU SAVED THE BASE** in gigantic, triumphant letters.

Save as **Defend01**.

5 Click `Scripts` and drag these blocks into the **script space**:

when [ ] clicked

switch to costume [▼]

broadcast [▼]

6 In the **switch to costume block**, click the drop-down arrow. Choose **sky**.

In the **broadcast block**, click the drop-down arrow and make a new **broadcast message** called **start**.

7 Connect the blocks to make a setup script:

```
when green flag clicked
switch to costume sky
broadcast start
```

or

```
when [ ] clicked
switch to costume sky ▼
broadcast start ▼
```

COPY THE CODE

We must protect our base from the CORUPT missiles for 30 minutes. After that, air support will arrive and can take over.

8 Click `Variables` to go to the **variables category**.

Click `Make a variable`. Make a variable called **timer**.

9 To make the **timer** variable work, we must set up a timer to tell us how long to go until help arrives.

Find and drag these blocks into the **script space**:

when I receive [▼]

set [▼] to `0`

repeat until < >

wait `1` secs

change [▼] by `1`

timer

< [ ] = [ ] >

broadcast [▼]

switch to costume [▼]

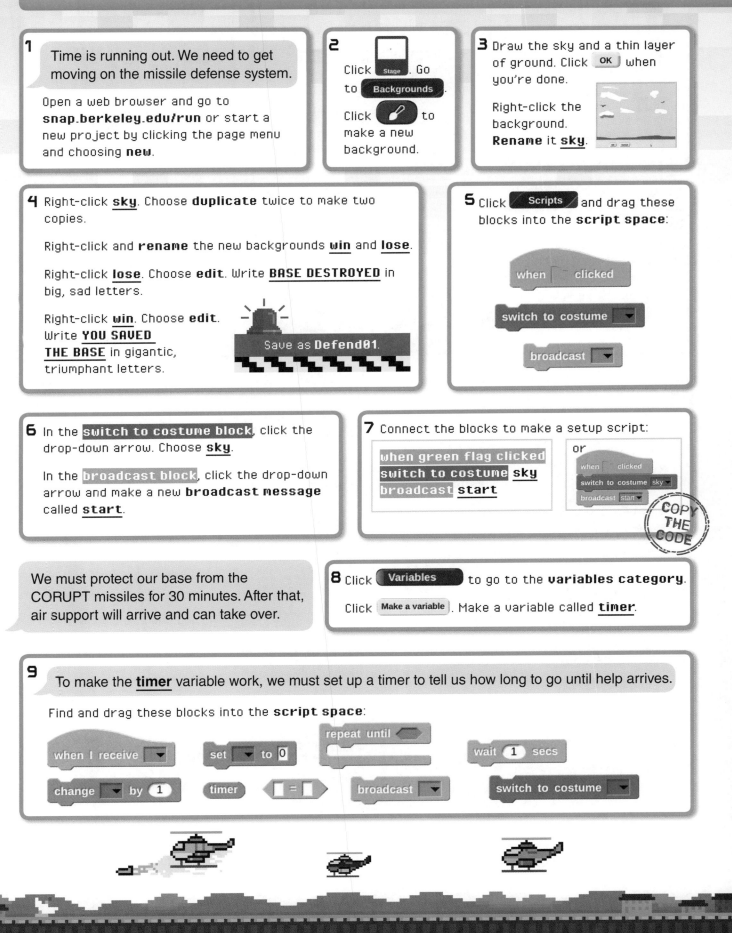

10 In the **when I receive block**, click the drop-down arrow. Choose **start**.

In the **set to 0 block**, and **change by 1 block**, click the drop-down arrows and choose **timer**.

11 Click and drag the **timer block** into the left side of the **=** block. Type **30** in the right side.

In the **switch to costume block**, click the drop-down arrow. Choose **win**.

In the **broadcast block**, click the drop-down arrow and make a new broadcast message called **gameover**.

12 Connect the blocks to make a **timing loop script**:

```
when I receive start
set timer to 0
repeat until timer = 30
    wait 1 secs
    change timer by 1
switch to costume win
broadcast gameover
```

or

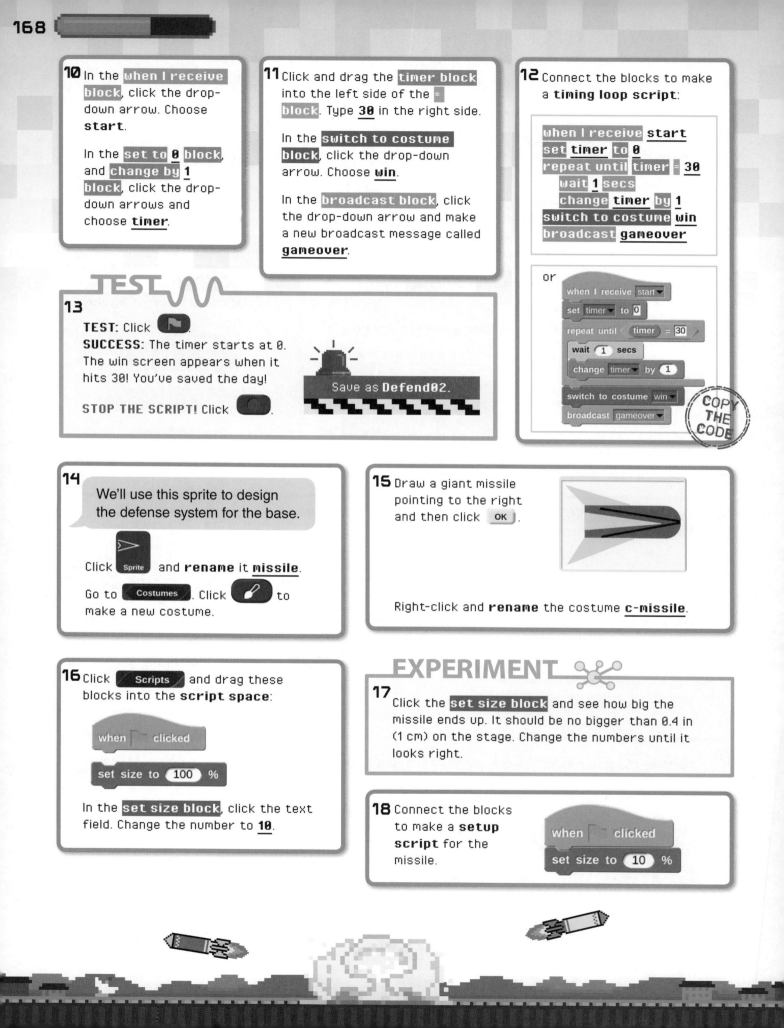

COPY THE CODE

13

TEST

TEST: Click 🏳.
SUCCESS: The timer starts at 0. The win screen appears when it hits 30! You've saved the day!

STOP THE SCRIPT! Click ⬤.

Save as **Defend02**.

14

We'll use this sprite to design the defense system for the base.

Click **Sprite** and **rename it missile**.

Go to **Costumes**. Click 🖌 to make a new costume.

15 Draw a giant missile pointing to the right and then click **OK**.

Right-click and **rename** the costume **c-missile**.

16 Click **Scripts** and drag these blocks into the **script space**:

```
when 🏳 clicked

set size to 100 %
```

In the **set size block**, click the text field. Change the number to **10**.

EXPERIMENT

17 Click the **set size block** and see how big the missile ends up. It should be no bigger than 0.4 in (1 cm) on the stage. Change the numbers until it looks right.

18 Connect the blocks to make a **setup script** for the missile.

```
when 🏳 clicked
set size to 10 %
```

MISSION OBJECTIVE 2: CONTROL THE GAME LOOP

1

Pax my friend, we'll be using the message = **gameover block** a lot.

Can we make a predicate block so we don't have to repeat ourselves?

By gads, Paxater! You might be right!

Click **Make a block** to make a new code block.

2

The new predicate will be "sensing" if the **gameover** message has been sent...

Ha, nice hint Doubleshot!

Click **Sensing** so the new block will appear in the **sensing** category.

Make a block

- Motion
- Looks
- Sound
- Pen
- Lists
- Control
- Sensing
- Operators
- Variables
- Other

Click the text field. Name the new block **gameover**.

3

This will be true or false, right? Either the **gameover** message has been sent or it hasn't.

Correct!

Click the **predicate** button, then click **OK** to open the **Block Editor**.

4

We must set it up so it reports true if the **gameover** message has been sent and **false** otherwise.

Drag these blocks into the **script space**:

if
else

You mean with an if else block?

Genius!

[ ] = [ ]   report [ ]   true ○ × 2   message

5

That's more blocks than if we'd put this straight into the script space. Is this really more efficient?

We do this once, then we can use it any time we make a game loop for a sprite.

More work now means less work later.

Exactly. Being a coder is all about finding shortcuts to avoid doing boring things!

Click and drag (message) into the left field of [ ] = [ ]. Type **gameover** in the right field.

Click one true ○ to change it to ○ false. You should have one **true** and one **false**.

Stunning work, Paxer. This'll save so much time later. Let's take it for a test run!

6 Connect the blocks under the **gameover** starter block to make a **predicate script**:

+ gameover +
if (message = gameover)
report (true ○)
else
report (○ false)

Click **OK** to save the new block.

COPY THE CODE

7

There are three bases to defend from missiles. We must find a way to track how many are still undamaged.

Like . . . a variable?

Yes!

Click **Variables**.

Click **Make a variable** to make a new variable. Call it **bases**.

✓ timer
✓ bases

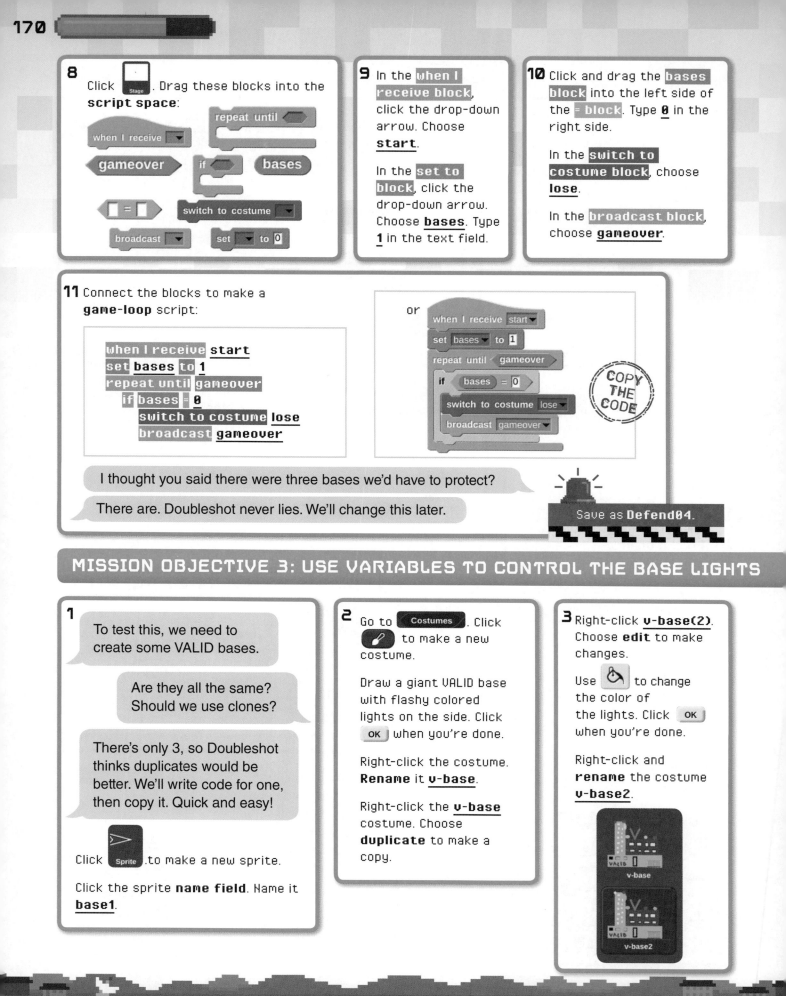

8 Click [Stage]. Drag these blocks into the **script space**:

when I receive ▾ repeat until ⬡ gameover if ⬡ bases ⬡ = ⬡ switch to costume ▾ broadcast ▾ set ▾ to 0

9 In the **when I receive block**, click the drop-down arrow. Choose **start**.

In the **set to block**, click the drop-down arrow. Choose **bases**. Type **1** in the text field.

10 Click and drag the **bases block** into the left side of the **= block**. Type **0** in the right side.

In the **switch to costume block**, choose **lose**.

In the **broadcast block**, choose **gameover**.

11 Connect the blocks to make a **game-loop** script:

```
when I receive start
set bases to 1
repeat until gameover
    if bases = 0
        switch to costume lose
        broadcast gameover
```

or

```
when I receive start ▾
set bases ▾ to 1
repeat until gameover
    if  bases = 0
        switch to costume lose ▾
        broadcast gameover ▾
```

COPY THE CODE

> I thought you said there were three bases we'd have to protect?

> There are. Doubleshot never lies. We'll change this later.

Save as **Defend04**.

MISSION OBJECTIVE 3: USE VARIABLES TO CONTROL THE BASE LIGHTS

1

> To test this, we need to create some VALID bases.

> Are they all the same? Should we use clones?

> There's only 3, so Doubleshot thinks duplicates would be better. We'll write code for one, then copy it. Quick and easy!

Click [Sprite] to make a new sprite.

Click the sprite **name field**. Name it **base1**.

2 Go to [Costumes]. Click [🖌] to make a new costume.

Draw a giant VALID base with flashy colored lights on the side. Click [OK] when you're done.

Right-click the costume. **Rename** it **v-base**.

Right-click the **v-base** costume. Choose **duplicate** to make a copy.

3 Right-click **v-base(2)**. Choose **edit** to make changes.

Use [🪣] to change the color of the lights. Click [OK] when you're done.

Right-click and **rename** the costume **v-base2**.

v-base

v-base2

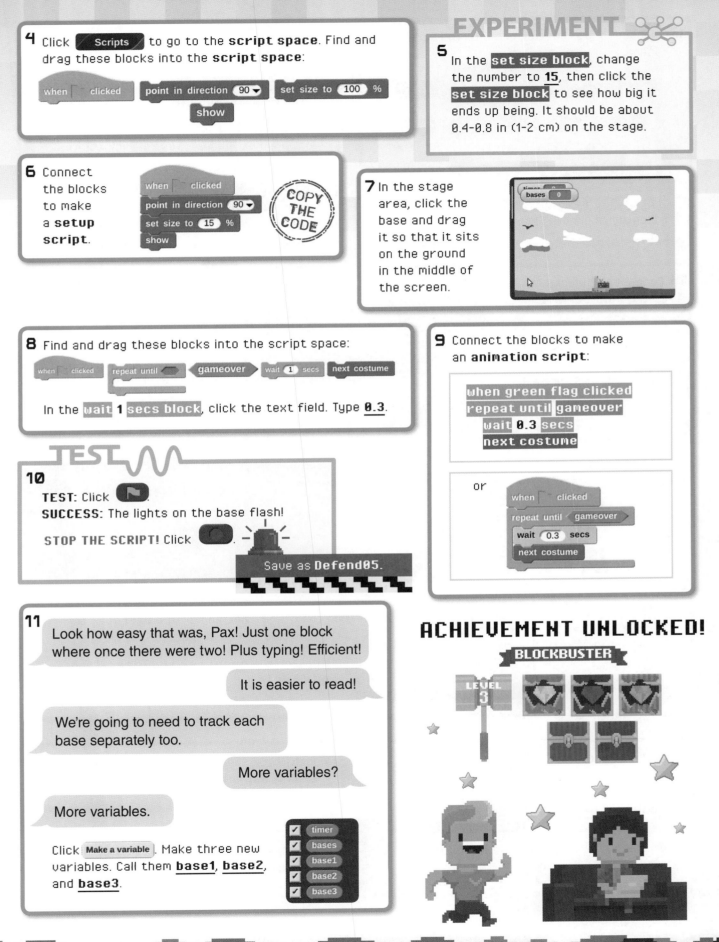

4 Click **Scripts** to go to the **script space**. Find and drag these blocks into the **script space**:

when ◻ clicked   point in direction 90 ▾   set size to 100 %   show

EXPERIMENT

5 In the **set size block**, change the number to **15**, then click the **set size block** to see how big it ends up being. It should be about 0.4-0.8 in (1-2 cm) on the stage.

6 Connect the blocks to make a **setup script**.

when ◻ clicked
point in direction 90 ▾
set size to 15 %
show

COPY THE CODE

7 In the stage area, click the base and drag it so that it sits on the ground in the middle of the screen.

timer 0
bases 0

8 Find and drag these blocks into the script space:

when ◻ clicked   repeat until ◻   gameover   wait 1 secs   next costume

In the **wait 1 secs block**, click the text field. Type **0.3**.

9 Connect the blocks to make an **animation script**:

when green flag clicked
repeat until gameover
    wait 0.3 secs
    next costume

or

when ◻ clicked
repeat until gameover
    wait 0.3 secs
    next costume

TEST

10

TEST: Click 🏴.
SUCCESS: The lights on the base flash!

STOP THE SCRIPT! Click 🔴.

Save as **Defend05**.

11

Look how easy that was, Pax! Just one block where once there were two! Plus typing! Efficient!

It is easier to read!

We're going to need to track each base separately too.

More variables?

More variables.

Click **Make a variable**. Make three new variables. Call them **base1**, **base2**, and **base3**.

✓ timer
✓ bases
✓ base1
✓ base2
✓ base3

ACHIEVEMENT UNLOCKED!

BLOCKBUSTER

LEVEL 3

12 Find and drag these blocks into the script space:

- when I receive ▼
- repeat until ⬡
- base1
- ▢ = ▢
- if ⬡
- touching ▼ ?
- hide
- change ▼ by 1
- set ▼ to 0 x 2

In the **when I receive block**, click the drop-down arrow. Choose **start**.

13 Click and drag the **base1 block** into the left field of the **= block**. Type **0** in the right field.

In the **touching block**, click the drop-down arrow. Choose **missile**.

In the **change by 1 block**, click the drop-down arrow. Choose **bases**. Click the text field. Type **-1**.

In both **set to 0 blocks**, click the drop-down arrows. Choose **base1**. Change one of the text fields to **1** and leave the other at **0**.

14 Connect the blocks to make a **game-loop script**:

or

COPY THE CODE

```
when I receive start
set base1 to 1
repeat until base1 = 0
    if touching missile?
        hide
        change bases by -1
        set base1 to 0
```

```
when I receive start
set base1 to 1
repeat until base1 = 0
    if touching missile ?
        hide
        change bases by -1
    set base1 to 0
```

15

TEST

TEST: Click 🏁. Click and drag the missile on the stage until it touches the base.
SUCCESS: So many things happen! Check that:
1. The base disappears when the missile touches it.
2. Bases and base1 are both set to 0!
3. The lose screen appears!

STOP THE SCRIPT! Click ⬜.

Save as **Defend06**.

16

Now the base code is done, let's make the duplicates, Pax-Pax.

On the stage, click and drag **base1** over to the left side of the stage.

Right-click the **base1 sprite button**. Choose **duplicate** to make a copy.

17 Click **base1(2)**. Click the sprite **name field**. Rename it **base2**.

On the stage, click and drag **base2** into the middle of the screen.

18 Right-click the **base1 sprite button**. Choose **duplicate** to make another copy.

Click **base1(2)**. Click the name field. **Rename it base3**.

On the stage, click and drag **base3** into the right side of the stage.

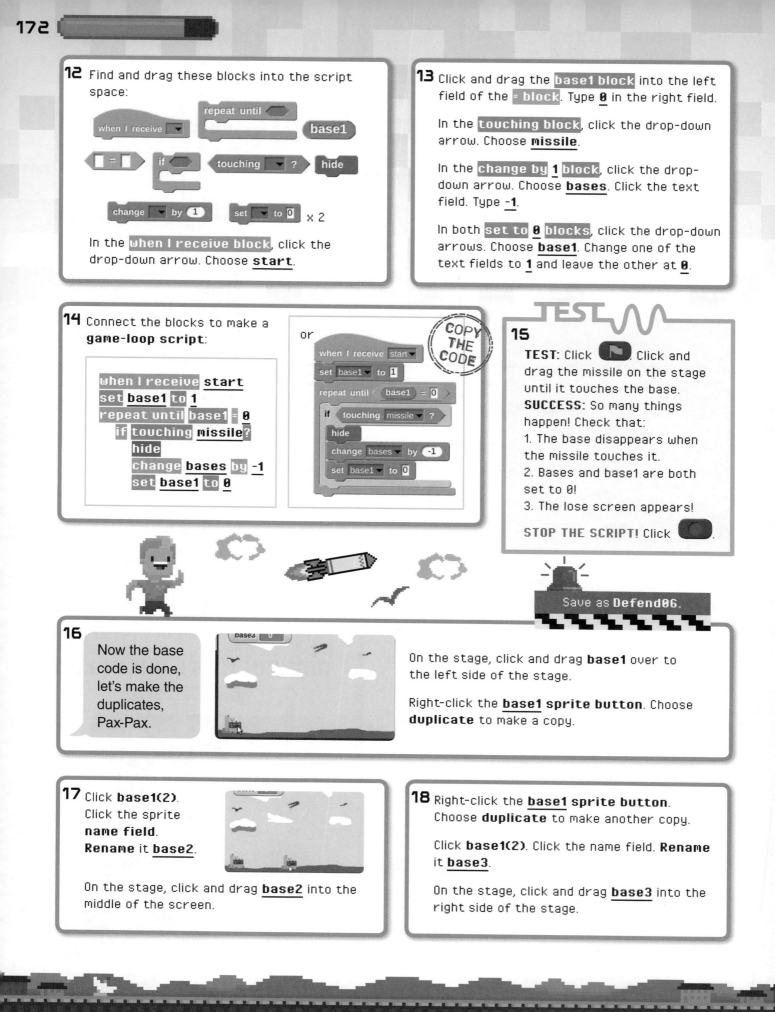

19

Doubleshot thinks you need to change the variables in the game loop too.

Oh yeah! They're all set to base1!

Click the **base2 sprite button**. Find and drag `base2` into the **script space**.

Click and drag `base1` into the **code menu** area to delete it.

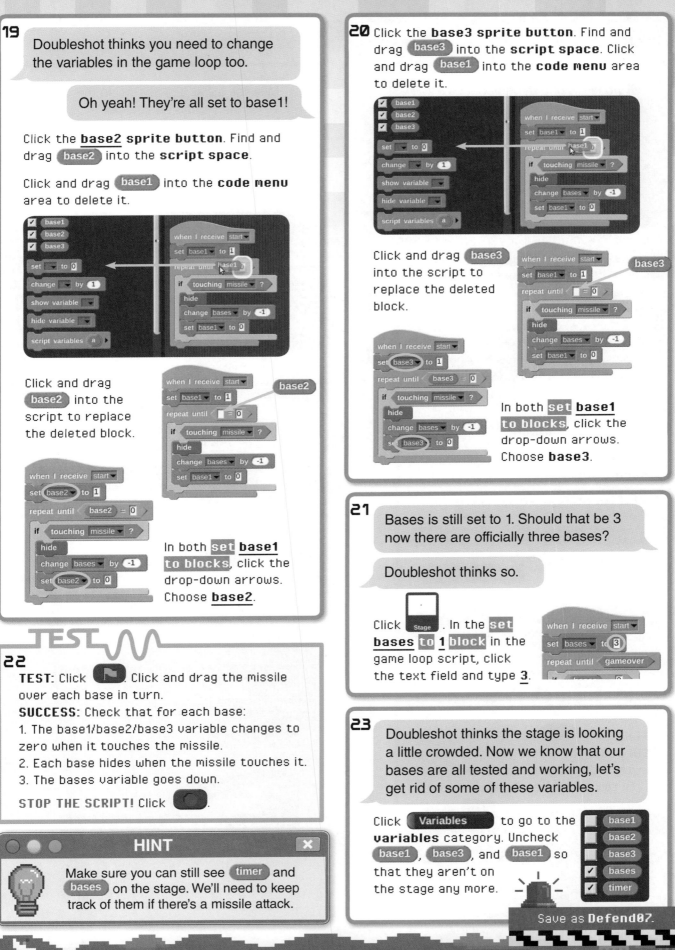

Click and drag `base2` into the script to replace the deleted block.

In both **set base1 to blocks**, click the drop-down arrows. Choose **base2**.

20 Click the **base3 sprite button**. Find and drag `base3` into the **script space**. Click and drag `base1` into the **code menu** area to delete it.

Click and drag `base3` into the script to replace the deleted block.

In both **set base1 to blocks**, click the drop-down arrows. Choose **base3**.

21

Bases is still set to 1. Should that be 3 now there are officially three bases?

Doubleshot thinks so.

Click Stage. In the **set bases to 1 block** in the game loop script, click the text field and type **3**.

22

TEST: Click [flag]. Click and drag the missile over each base in turn.

SUCCESS: Check that for each base:

1. The base1/base2/base3 variable changes to zero when it touches the missile.
2. Each base hides when the missile touches it.
3. The bases variable goes down.

STOP THE SCRIPT! Click [stop].

HINT ✕

Make sure you can still see `timer` and `bases` on the stage. We'll need to keep track of them if there's a missile attack.

23

Doubleshot thinks the stage is looking a little crowded. Now we know that our bases are all tested and working, let's get rid of some of these variables.

Click Variables to go to the **variables** category. Uncheck `base1`, `base3`, and `base1` so that they aren't on the stage any more.

Save as **Defend07**.

MISSION OBJECTIVE 4: TARGET-SETTING

1

If we know one thing about CORUPT systems, Paxiotta, it's that they're not that well written. Their missiles choose random targets, so we're going to use a custom reporter block.

Click the **missile sprite button**.

2

Missiles leave a nasty trail in the sky. We'll need some pen blocks.

Find and drag these blocks into the script space:

set pen color to ■   go to x: 0 y: 0   clear

3 In the `go to block`, type x:**500** and y:**500**. In the `set pen color to block`, click the colored square. Choose bright red.

4 Connect the blocks to the **setup script**:

```
when green flag clicked
set size to 8%
go to x:500 y:500
clear
set pen color to [ ]
```
or
```
when ⚑ clicked
set size to 8 %
go to x: 500 y: 500
clear
set pen color to ■
```

COPY THE CODE

5

We're going to use clones for the missiles, right? The Echo Agents say to get it right for one and then worry about the clones.

Good plan, Paxatron.

Find and drag these blocks into the **script space**:

when I receive ▼   pen down

move 10 steps   go to x: 0 y: 0

repeat until ⬡

pick random 1 to 10   pen up

point towards ▼

In the `when I receive block`, choose **start**.

6 In the `pick random block`, type **-150** to **150**.

Drag the `pick random block` into the `x:` field of the `go to block`. Type **180** in the `y:` field.

go to x: pick random -150 to 150 y: 180

7 In the `point towards block`, choose **base1**.

In the `move 10 steps block`, type **2**.

8 Connect the blocks to make an **animation script**:

```
when I receive start
pen up
go to x:pick random -150 to 150 y:180
pen down
point towards base1
repeat until (BLANK)
    move 2 steps
```

or
```
when I receive start ▼
pen up
go to x: pick random -150 to 150 y: 180
pen down
point towards base1 ▼
repeat until ⬡
    move 2 steps
```

COPY THE CODE

TEST

9

TEST: Click ⚑.
SUCCESS: The missile starts at the top of the stage and draws a creepy red trail towards base1. Duck and cover!

STOP THE SCRIPT! Click ⬤.

Make sure you stop the test, because there's no telling when the movement loop will finish.

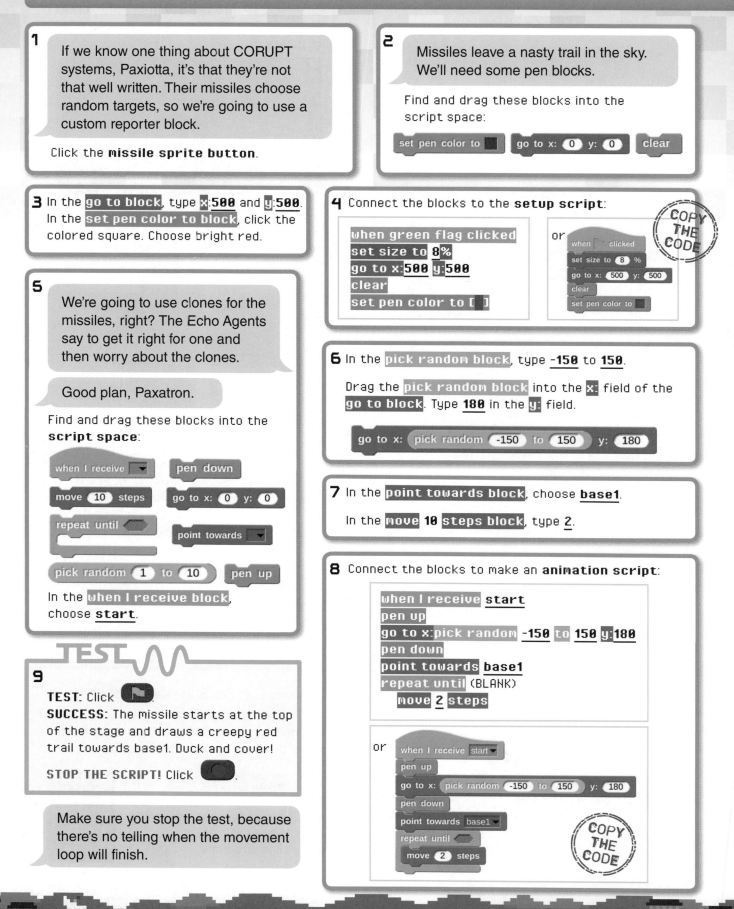

10 Hey, poor base1 gets hit every single time . . .

Dash it, you're right! This calls for a reporter block.

Click **Make a block** to make a new block.

11 We'll write some code to pull out a random base for each missile to target. This could go in operators or variables: it's up to you Paxiote, lil' buddy.

Well, it's random, so let's keep it with the other random block in the **Operators** category.

In the **Make a Block window**, click **Operators** so it's highlighted green. Click the text field. Type **random base**.

12 Now, we haven't used this one before, but it's going to be a **reporter block**. The reporter can tell us almost any bit of information we want. What we want is a base.

Click the **reporter block**. Then click **OK** to open the **Block Editor**.

Find and drag these blocks into the **Block Editor**:

script variables (a) ▶   set ▾ to 0

pick random 1 to 10

if ⬡   ▢ = ▢

13 What's a script variable?

It's a temporary variable. You can use most variables in other scripts or sprites, but not this one! You won't be able to use the **set block** until it's connected under the **script variables block**.

Connect the **set to 0 block** underneath the **script variables a block**.

In the **set to 0 block**, click the drop-down arrow. Choose **a**.

In the **pick random block**, click the text fields. Type **1** to **3**.

14 Click and drag the **a** variable from the **script variables block** into the left field of the **= block**. Type **1** in the right field.

script variables (a) ▶
set a ▾ to 0

▢ = ▢

15 In the **report block**, type **base1**. Connect the blocks:

+ random + base +
script variables (a) ▶
set a ▾ to (pick random 1 to 3)
if (a) = 1
report base1

COPY THE CODE

16 Right-click the **if block**. Choose **duplicate** to make a copy. Click to connect it at the end of the script.

In the second **= block**, type **2** in the right text field.

In the second **report block**, type **base2**.

17 A reporter block MUST return something. If it's not **base1** and it's not **base2**...

It MUST be **base3**!

+ random + base +
script variables (a) ▶
set a ▾ to (pick random 1 to 3)
if (a) = 1
report base1
if (a) = 2
report base2
report base3

Right-click the **report block** Choose **duplicate** to make a copy. Click to connect it at the end of the script.

COPY THE CODE

In the last **report block**, type **base3**.

18

Don't I need the if block and the = block for **base3**?

Nope. This is what the lazy coder calls a default case. It's your leftover: your backup. It's what should happen automatically if nothing else is true.

OK, so if it's not 1 and it's not 2, it's got to be 3?

By default!

Click **OK** to save your new **reporter** block. Go to the **operators** category. Drag the **random base block** into the **point towards block** in the animation script.

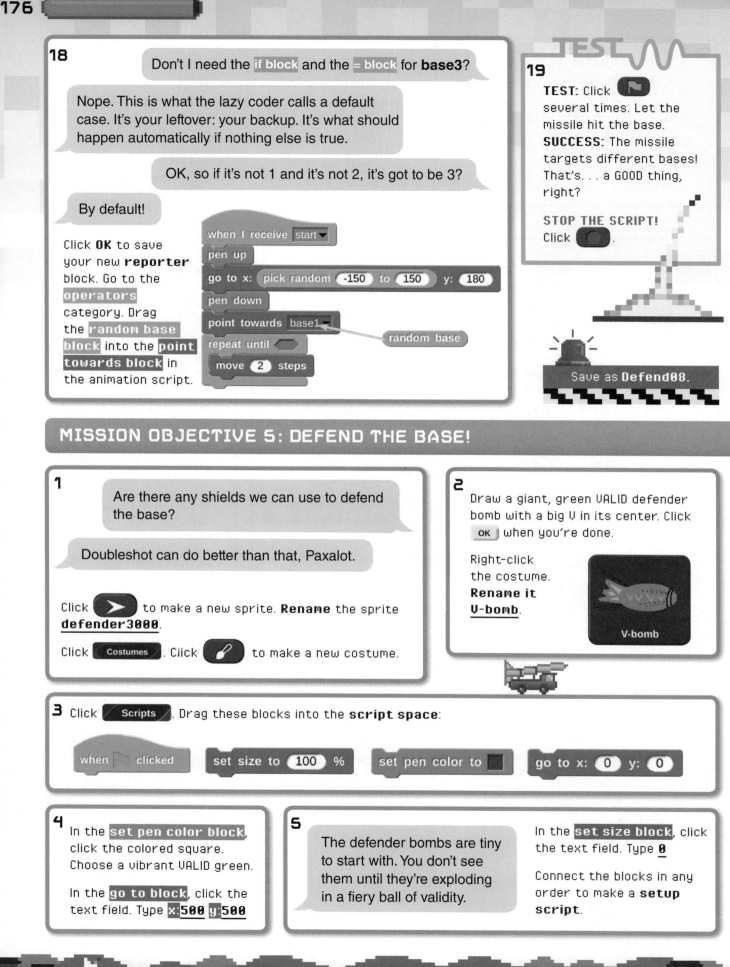

```
when I receive  start ▾
pen up
go to x:  pick random  -150  to  150   y:  180
pen down
point towards  base1 ▾          ← random base
repeat until
    move  2  steps
```

19

TEST 〰

TEST: Click 🏳 several times. Let the missile hit the base.
SUCCESS: The missile targets different bases! That's... a GOOD thing, right?

STOP THE SCRIPT! Click ⬭.

Save as **Defend08**.

MISSION OBJECTIVE 5: DEFEND THE BASE!

1

Are there any shields we can use to defend the base?

Doubleshot can do better than that, Paxalot.

Click ▶ to make a new sprite. **Rename** the sprite **defender3000**.

Click Costumes. Click 🖌 to make a new costume.

2

Draw a giant, green VALID defender bomb with a big V in its center. Click ᴏᴋ when you're done.

Right-click the costume. **Rename it V-bomb**.

V-bomb

3 Click Scripts. Drag these blocks into the **script space**:

```
when ⚑ clicked      set size to  100 %      set pen color to ⬛      go to x:  0  y:  0
```

4 In the **set pen color block**, click the colored square. Choose a vibrant VALID green.

In the **go to block**, click the text field. Type **x:500 y:500**

5 The defender bombs are tiny to start with. You don't see them until they're exploding in a fiery ball of validity.

In the **set size block**, click the text field. Type **0**

Connect the blocks in any order to make a **setup script**.

How much do you know about missile defense systems, Paxable?

Umm. . . I know they exist. To defend. Against. . . missiles? Or maybe WITH missiles?

Hmm, level 2 knowledge. They work like this. We detect an incoming enemy missile here at HQ. We calculate which base is closest and we launch a defender from it to intercept.

And it tracks the enemy missile and destroys it?

Not quite: that's up to the defender control. They carefully calculate the trajectory of the missile and the distance from our base, then hit the button at the exact moment, so it takes out the target.

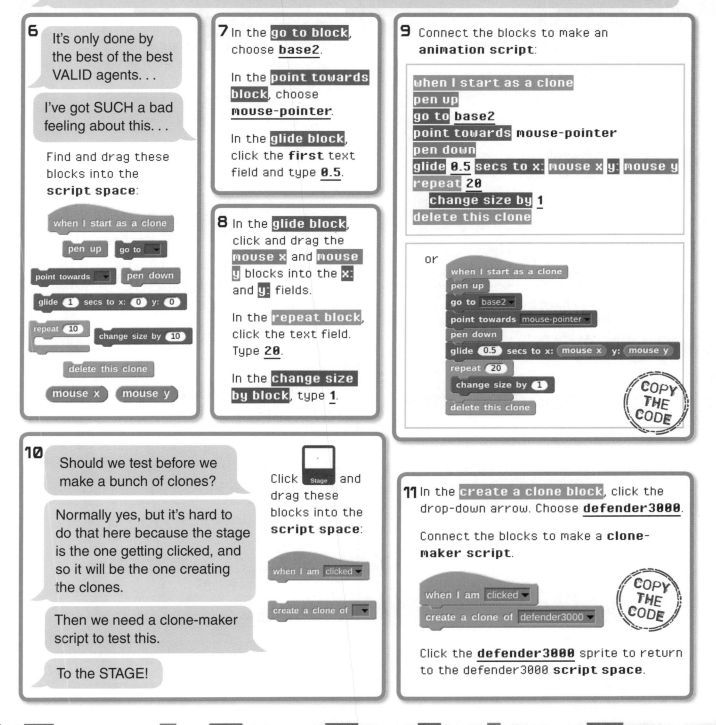

6 It's only done by the best of the best VALID agents. . .

I've got SUCH a bad feeling about this. . .

Find and drag these blocks into the **script space**:

- when I start as a clone
- pen up
- go to
- point towards
- pen down
- glide 1 secs to x: 0 y: 0
- repeat 10
- change size by 10
- delete this clone
- mouse x
- mouse y

7 In the **go to block**, choose **base2**.

In the **point towards block**, choose **mouse-pointer**.

In the **glide block**, click the **first** text field and type **0.5**.

8 In the **glide block**, click and drag the **mouse x** and **mouse y** blocks into the **x:** and **y:** fields.

In the **repeat block**, click the text field. Type **20**.

In the **change size by block**, type **1**.

9 Connect the blocks to make an **animation script**:

```
when I start as a clone
pen up
go to base2
point towards mouse-pointer
pen down
glide 0.5 secs to x: mouse x y: mouse y
repeat 20
    change size by 1
delete this clone
```

or

```
when I start as a clone
pen up
go to base2
point towards mouse-pointer
pen down
glide 0.5 secs to x: mouse x y: mouse y
repeat 20
change size by 1
delete this clone
```

COPY THE CODE

10 Should we test before we make a bunch of clones?

Normally yes, but it's hard to do that here because the stage is the one getting clicked, and so it will be the one creating the clones.

Then we need a clone-maker script to test this.

To the STAGE!

Click **Stage** and drag these blocks into the **script space**:

- when I am clicked
- create a clone of

11 In the **create a clone block**, click the drop-down arrow. Choose **defender3000**.

Connect the blocks to make a **clone-maker script**.

```
when I am clicked
create a clone of defender3000
```

COPY THE CODE

Click the **defender3000** sprite to return to the defender3000 **script space**.

12

TEST: Click 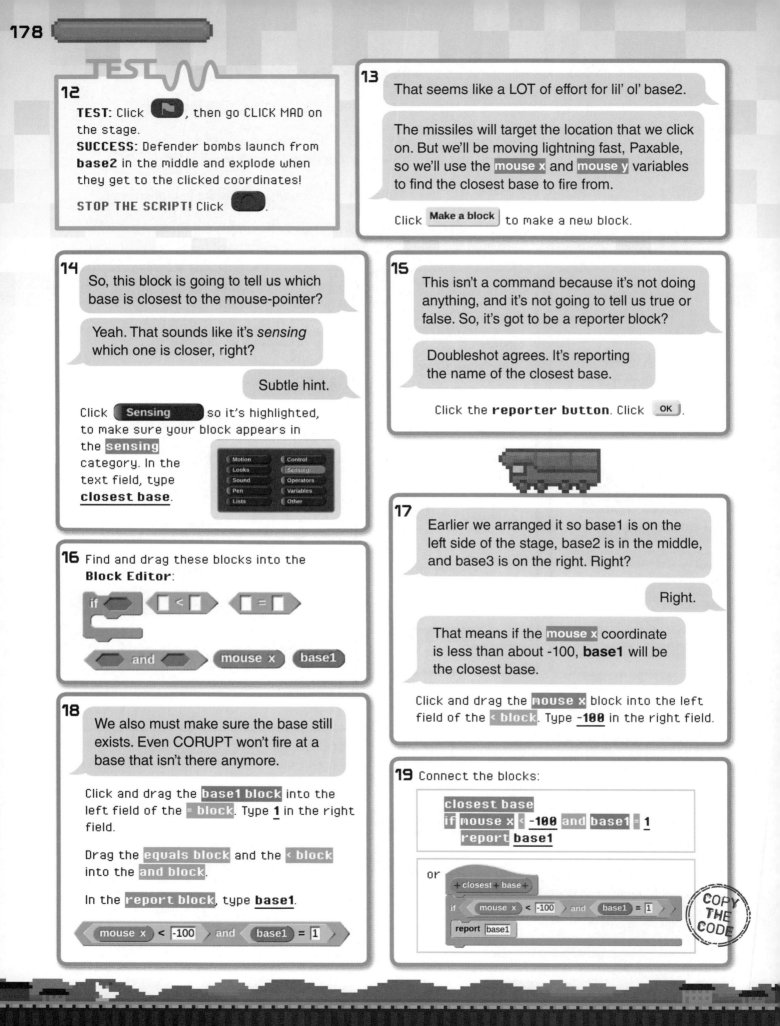, then go CLICK MAD on the stage.

SUCCESS: Defender bombs launch from **base2** in the middle and explode when they get to the clicked coordinates!

STOP THE SCRIPT! Click ⬛.

13

That seems like a LOT of effort for lil' ol' base2.

The missiles will target the location that we click on. But we'll be moving lightning fast, Paxable, so we'll use the mouse x and mouse y variables to find the closest base to fire from.

Click **Make a block** to make a new block.

14

So, this block is going to tell us which base is closest to the mouse-pointer?

Yeah. That sounds like it's *sensing* which one is closer, right?

Subtle hint.

Click **Sensing** so it's highlighted, to make sure your block appears in the **sensing** category. In the text field, type **closest base**.

Motion	Control
Looks	Sensing
Sound	Operators
Pen	Variables
Lists	Other

15

This isn't a command because it's not doing anything, and it's not going to tell us true or false. So, it's got to be a reporter block?

Doubleshot agrees. It's reporting the name of the closest base.

Click the **reporter button**. Click OK.

16 Find and drag these blocks into the **Block Editor**:

if · · · < · · · = ·

· · and · · · mouse x · · base1

17

Earlier we arranged it so base1 is on the left side of the stage, base2 is in the middle, and base3 is on the right. Right?

Right.

That means if the mouse x coordinate is less than about -100, **base1** will be the closest base.

Click and drag the mouse x block into the left field of the < block. Type **-100** in the right field.

18

We also must make sure the base still exists. Even CORUPT won't fire at a base that isn't there anymore.

Click and drag the base1 block into the left field of the = block. Type **1** in the right field.

Drag the equals block and the < block into the and block.

In the report block, type **base1**.

mouse x < -100 and base1 = 1

19 Connect the blocks:

```
closest base
if mouse x < -100 and base1 = 1
    report base1
```

or

```
+ closest + base +
if   mouse x < -100   and   base1 = 1
report base1
```

COPY THE CODE

20

That looks good to Doubleshot! Let's take it for a run and make sure it works before we do the rest.

Click **OK** to save your block.

Click and drag the new block into the **go to block** in the **animation script**.

```
when I start as a clone
pen up
go to base2          ← closest base
point towards mouse-pointer ▾
pen down
glide .5 secs to x: mouse x y: mouse y
repeat 20
    change size by 1
delete this clone
```

22

If I click above the wrong base, I get an error message in the sprite space.

> Inside: Error reporter didn't report
>
> defender:

That's because if the **mouse x** coordinates are over **-100**, our reporter block isn't reporting anything. Let's fix that.

Right-click the **closest base block**. Choose **edit** to reopen the **Block Editor**.

```
+ closest + base +
if   mouse x < -100   and   base1 = 1
    report base1
if   mouse x < 100    and   ☐ = 1
    report base1              ← base2
```

TEST 〜〜

21

TEST: Click 🏴. Click in the sky above **base1**.
SUCCESS: The defenders are launched from **base1**!
ERROR: The defenders don't fire. There's a nasty message from the **sprite button** saying the reporter didn't report.
FIX: Your bases aren't in the right order on the stage. Click above the other bases to see if your defenders fire from a different base. If they do, click and drag those bases on the stage to swap them. If NONE of them fire, right-click and edit your code to open the **Block Editor**. Check your code matches Pax's.

STOP THE SCRIPT! Click ⬤.

Save as **Defend09**.

23 Right-click the **if block** in the script and make a copy.

Click to connect the copied code at the end of the script.

24

I think the code for **base2** should be the same, except with **different** numbers.

Find and drag these blocks into the **Block Editor**:

(base3)   (base2)   ◁ ☐ = ☐ ▷   if▢   report ☐   × 2

25 In the **< block**, click the text field and change it from **-100** to **100**.

Click and drag the **base1 block** into the code menu area to delete it.

```
+ closest + base +
if   mouse x < -100   and   base1 = 1
    report base1
if   mouse y < 100    and   base1 1
    report base1
```

26 Drag the **base2 block** into the empty space in the **= block**.

In the **report block**, click the text field and change it to **base2**.

27 Click and drag the **base3 block** into the left field of the empty **= block**. Type **1** in the right field.

Drag the **base3 equals 1 block** into the hexagon in the **if block**.

In the **report blocks**, click the text field. Type **base3** in one and **NULL** in the other.

28 Connect the blocks at the end of the script:

What does NULL mean?

It's a backup. The reporter must report SOMETHING. If it has nothing to report, it pretends nothing is something and reports that.

```
closest base
if  mouse x < -100  and  base1 = 1
  report base1
if  mouse x < 100  and  base2 = 1
  report base2
if  base3 = 1
  report base3
report NULL
```

COPY THE CODE

29

TEST

TEST: Click 🏳. Click to launch defenders.
SUCCESS: They launch from the nearest base!

STOP THE SCRIPT!
Click ⬡.

Save as **Defend10**.

ACHIEVEMENT UNLOCKED!
BLOCKBUSTER

LEVEL 4

MISSION OBJECTIVE 6: COUNT THE HITS AND MISSES

1

Nothing happens when the missile hits the defender. It just goes straight through.

Let's fix that, so we can blast them out of the sky!

Click the **missile sprite**.

2

Every time, we must check if the missile has hit **base1** OR **base2** OR **base3**. We'll make a predicate to do all that for us.

Click **Make a block**. Click **Sensing** to highlight it blue so your new block will appear in the **sensing** category.

In the text field, type **touching base**.

Click the **predicate button** so it's highlighted. Click **OK**.

3 Find and drag these blocks into the **Block Editor**:

`if` × 3   `touching ▼ ?` × 3
`true ◯` × 4   `report ☐` × 3

4 In the **touching blocks**, choose **base1**, **base2** and **base3**.

Click one of the **true blocks** so that it's **false** (you will need three true and one false)

Connect the blocks:

COPY THE CODE

Click the **OK** button to save your new block.

```
touching base
if  touching base1 ?
  report  true
if  touching base2 ?
  report  true
if  touching base3 ?
  report  true
report  false
```

5 Find and drag these blocks into the **script space**:

`touching base` `touching ▼ ?` `◯ or ◯`

In the **touching block**, choose **defender3000**.

Connect the blocks in the **or block**. Drag it into the empty hexagon of the **repeat until** block in the **animation script**.

```
when I receive start ▼
pen up
go to x: pick random -150 to 150  y: 180
pen down
point towards random base
repeat until  touching base  or  touching defender3000 ▼ ?
  move 2 steps
```

6

TEST

TEST: Click 🏳. Then fire a defender to stop the incoming missile.
SUCCESS: The missile stops in its terrifying tracks when it hits the defender.

STOP THE SCRIPT!
Click ⬡.

Save as **Defend11**.

7 Doubleshot thinks it's time to clone the missiles. We will defend our bases!

Find and drag these blocks into the **script space**:

`delete this clone`   `when I start as a clone`

8 Click and drag the **animation script** and connect it underneath the `when I start as a clone block`.

Drag the `when I receive block` into the code menu area to delete it.

Connect the `delete this clone block` at the end of the **clone animation** script.

```
when I start as a clone
pen up
go to x: pick random -150 to 150  y: 180
pen down
point towards random base
repeat until  touching defender3000 ? or touching base
  move 2 steps
delete this clone
```

9 Click [Stage]. Find and drag these blocks into the **script space**:

`when I receive ▼`   `wait 1 secs`   `gameover`

`create a clone of ▼`   `repeat until`

10 In the `when I receive block`, choose **start**.

In the `create a clone block`, choose **missile**.

Connect the blocks to make a **clone-maker** script:

```
when I receive start ▼
repeat until  gameover
  create a clone of missile ▼
  wait 1 secs
```

COPY THE CODE

TEST

11

TEST: Click 🏁.
SUCCESS: So many missiles incoming! Click to defend!

STOP THE SCRIPT! Click 🔴.

Save as **Defend12**.

CHALLENGE

12 Click 🏁. Defend the bases until air support arrives.

ACHIEVEMENT UNLOCKED!

BLOCKBUSTER

LEVEL 5

We did it? The VALID base is safe?

Yep. The air support team has arrived! Good work Pax. Doubleshot is not easy to impress! The field team has arrived too. We must meet the whole team in debrief.

Whew! That was scary. Wait, there's more?!

Apparently CORUPT has been working on a robot super weapon. ETAMI has called in all the supercoders: Natterninja, Finity, Glitchbane, the Echos, the Introspecter, and Doubleshot . . .

OK . . . just the supercoders? Should I wait here?

You're needed too. Guess ETAMI thinks you're one of us.

NEW MESSAGE ✕

Join ETAMI and the supercoders in the briefing room?

Y/N

THE FINAL MISSION

with the VALID Supercoders

NEW MESSAGE ☒

Would you like to proceed?

Y/N?

The rescued coders are safe but tell a disturbing tale. As ETAMI and the supercoders suspected, the kidnappings were targeted strikes: a security expert, a shield specialist, a robotics engineer, and an artificial-intelligence expert. Gartz, a friend of the supercoders and one of the rescued coders, managed to get a look at CORUPT's terrifying master plan.

This is the eighth moon of Cephalopod 3, a planet on the galaxy's outer rim. Our intelligence indicates this is where CORUPT is building their superweapon.

What kind of weapon we talkin', ETAMI?

A mega-blaster photon cannon?

A computer virus designed to infiltrate our security systems?

An army of clones with laser eyes?

Worse. Gartz believes the only logical explanation is the code they were forced to write is for a planet-sized, quad-shielded, hyper-intelligent killer space robot... named Basil.

Why Basil?

That's why they needed our coders! CORUPT coders could never pull this off!

I agree. They don't have the logic for it.

Basil sounds like someone's friendly uncle...

We need to destroy it, and the entire moon if necessary.

A robot that size could wipe out every planet in the Milky Way!

But—

Agreed! The magnetic interference alone could wipe every hard drive on Earth!

Time for PHOTON BLASTERS!!

STOP IT!!

Potential Agent X?

Basil is just a robot! His operating code was written by GOOD coders! Just like ETAMI's! It's not his fault CORUPT got their nasty tentacles on him! We can't destroy him for something that's not his fault!

Potential Agent X is correct. There is another solution. Basil's code is good, not evil. Gartz says that it's been corrupted by eight spikes that were added by CORUPT's coders. Those spikes control Basil.

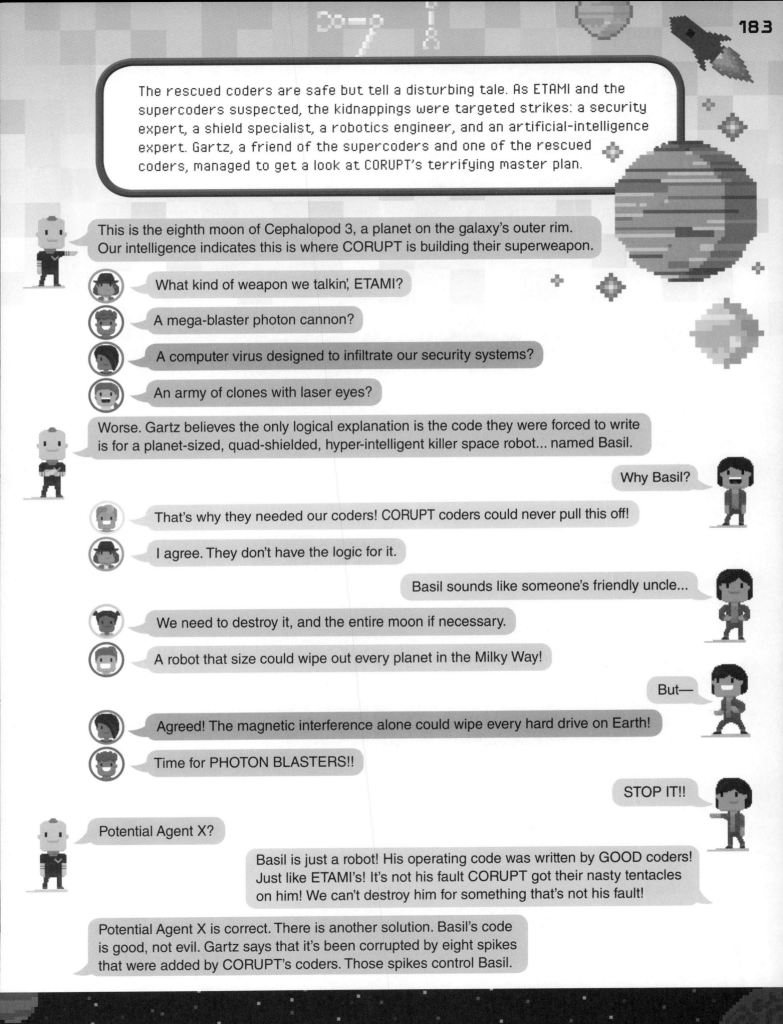

Interesting… I've seen this kind of data corruption before. If we can get rid of those spikes…

A few of Doubleshot's logic bombs might do it…

We could still save the galaxy...

AND Basil!

Can we do it? Long-range torpedoes is one thing. Getting close enough for a precision strike on each of Basil's spikes is a whole different bag of spacecakes.

It will require our best agents in the field and here on supercoding support.

You need me to fly the Adventure-D to Cephalopod-3.

You need me to get through the caves into the facility where they're keeping Basil.

You need Doubleshot's tactical logic skills to fire the logic bombs.

The rest of us will be on code support back here. You'll need clones.

And a security hacker.

And a debugger.

What about me?

Potential Agent X, you are the only coder who has worked on every part of this mission. You should lead the supercoders through this.

I'm a trainee! I can't do that!

You have flown with Natterninja, debugged with Glitchbane, looped with Finity, cloned with the Echo Agents, studied variables with the Introspecter, and made blocks with Doubleshot. Potential Agent X, you know the code better than anyone.

Those were training missions! There's lots I don't know!

Supercoders never stop learning, Pax.

You can do this.

Doubleshot has seen what you're capable of.

You're ready, Newbie…

This is the final test, Potential Agent X.
If you can do this, you have what it takes
to become a full VALID supercoder.

NEW MESSAGE ✕

Lead the team to save Basil,
Earth, and the galaxy?

Y/N

We need a way into the base. Our kidnapped coders say they made five specialized locks and keys.

I could bypass the locks, but if they were designed by our coders, the encryption will take a while to break...

How long?

I could overclock my mega CPU, take over a bunch of supercomputers across the galaxy, then crunch the numbers in… about… 5 years? Give or take a month?

Er, no. Gartz says last month a CORUPT security ship had an accident in an asteroid field over Cephalopod-3. The ship was destroyed, but its cargo was scattered there.

The keys could be in the asteroid field?

It's worth a look.

This sounds like a job for the SPACECLAW! YEEAAAH!

MISSION DOSSIER

>> GET THE KEYS WITH THE SPACECLAW

The only way into the base is with five keys scattered in an asteroid field following a spaceship crash! Use the grabby Spaceclaw to scoop them up.

LEVEL: 8

INSTRUCTOR: Supercoders of VALID

SUPERCODERS

MISSION OBJECTIVE 1: YOU CAN'T TAKE THE SKY FROM ME

PROJECT OUTLINE

NAME: SPACECLAW

GOAL: HELP NATTERNINJA RETRIEVE THE KEYS FROM THE ASTEROID FIELD.

REQUIREMENTS:
1. USE CLONES TO MAKE A SCROLLING SPACE BACKGROUND
2. USE EVENTS TO MANAGE SPACESHIP MOVEMENT
3. DESIGN A SPACECLAW TO PICK UP OBJECTS FLOATING IN SPACE
4. USE CLONES TO MAKE AN ASTEROID FIELD
5. REUSE YOUR CODE TO PLACE THE KEYS IN THE ASTEROID FIELD

1 Open a web browser and go to **snap.berkeley.edu/run**. Start a new project by clicking [ ]. Choose **new**.

2 Click [Stage]. Go to [Backgrounds]. Make a new background by clicking [ ] to open the **paint editor**.

3 Use [ ] to color the background dark blue or black. Click **OK** when you're done.

Right-click and **rename** the background **space**.

Right-click and choose **duplicate** twice to make two extra backgrounds.

space

4 Right-click the **space(2)** background. Choose **edit**.

Write **You win!** in giant letters. Decorate the background.

Click **OK** when you're done. Right-click **space(3)**. Choose **edit**.

Write **You crashed :(** in big red letters. Click **OK**.

Right-click each background. Rename one **win** and one **lose**.

win

lose

Save as **Spaceclaw01**.

5 Click [Scripts] and drag these blocks into the **script space**:

when ⚑ clicked

broadcast ▾

switch to costume ▾

6 In the **switch to costume block**, choose **space**.

In the **broadcast block**, choose **new** to make a new broadcast message. Call it **start**.

Connect the blocks to make a **setup script**:

when ⚑ clicked
switch to costume space ▾
broadcast start ▾

COPY THE CODE

7 Click [Sprite]. Click the sprite **name field**. **Rename** the sprite **background**.

Click [Scripts]. Find these blocks:

when ⚑ clicked   go to x: 0 y: 0

Connect them to make a **setup script**:

when ⚑ clicked
go to x: 0 y: 0

COPY THE CODE

8 Click [Costumes].

Click 🖌 to make a new costume.

Draw a starry background of stars, but don't draw a background color. Click **OK** when you're done.

Untitled

Right-click the costume. **Rename** it **starscape**.

9 Go to the **script space**. Find and drag these blocks into the **script space**:

when I receive ▾

glide 1 secs to x: 0 y: 0
create a clone of ▾

10 In the **when I receive block**, choose **start**.

In the **create a clone of block**, choose **myself**.

In the **glide block**, click the first text field. Type **10**. Type **-480** in the **x:** field.

11 Connect the blocks to make a **clone-maker script** to match:

when I receive start ▾
create a clone of myself ▾
glide 10 secs to x: -480 y: 0

COPY THE CODE

12 Find and drag these blocks into the **script space**:

delete this clone

create a clone of ▾

when I start as a clone   go to x: 0 y: 0

glide 1 secs to x: 0 y: 0   x 2

13 In the **go to block**, type **480** in the **x:** field.

In both **glide blocks**, click the first text field. Type **10**.

In one of the **glide blocks**, type **-480** in the **x:** field.

In the **create a clone block**, choose **myself**.

14 Connect the blocks to make a **clone animation script**:

when I start as a clone
go to x: 480 y: 0
glide 10 secs to x: 0 y: 0
create a clone of myself ▾
glide 10 secs to x: -480 y: 0
delete this clone

COPY THE CODE

TEST

15

TEST: Click 🚩.

SUCCESS: The stars drift past in a continuous loop of delicious starry goodness.

ERROR: The stars don't move, or only some of them move.

FIX: Get your bug-hunting boots and read through your code. What is each block doing? Does it match Pax's code?

STOP THE SCRIPT! Click 🛑.

COPY THE CODE

16 Find and drag these blocks into the **script space**:

`when I receive ▼`   `delete this clone`

17 In the **when I receive block**, choose **new** to make a new broadcast message. Call it **gameover** Click **OK**.

Connect the two blocks to make an **endgame script**.

```
when I receive gameover ▼
delete this clone
```

Save as **Spaceclaw02**.

MISSION OBJECTIVE 2: IN-FLIGHT SPACESHIP MANEUVERS

1 Click ▶ to make a new sprite. Click the sprite **name field**.

Rename it **spaceship**.

Go to `Costumes`.

Click 🖌 to make a new costume.

2 Draw Natterninja's prized spaceship, the Adventure-D, so the nose points to the right of the screen.

Click **OK** when you're done.

Right-click the costume. **Rename** it **Adventure-D**.

3 Find and drag these blocks into the **script space**:

`go to x: 0 y: 0`   `when ▢ clicked`   `show`

`set size to 100 %`   `point in direction 90 ▼`

EXPERIMENT

4 In the **set size block**, type **15** in the text field. Click the block to see how big the spaceship ends up. Change the numbers and test it until it looks the right size.

5 In the **go to block**, click the **x:** field. Type **-200**.

Connect the blocks to make a **setup script**:

```
when ▢ clicked
go to x: -200 y: 0
point in direction 90 ▼
set size to 15 %
show
```

COPY THE CODE

TEST

6

TEST: Click 🚩.

SUCCESS: The spaceship goes to the left of the stage and the stars drift past.

STOP THE SCRIPT! Click 🛑.

Save as **Spaceclaw03**.

7 Click `Make a block` to make a new code block.

Click `Sensing`.

Type **gameover** in the text box.

Click **predicate**. Click **OK** to open the **Block Editor**.

Make a block
- Motion   - Control
- Looks   - Sensing
- Sound   - Operators
- Pen   - Variables
- Lists   - Other

gameover

Command   Reporter   Predicate

● for all sprites   ○ for this sprite only

OK   Cancel

HINT

You can make the **Block Editor** bigger by clicking and dragging the bottom right corner of the window.

OK

8 Find and drag these blocks into the **Block Editor**:

report ☐   message   if ⬡   ☐ = ☐   true ⚪ ×2

9 Click and drag the **message block** into the left field of the **= block**. Type **gameover** in the right field.

Click one of the **true blocks** so you have one **true** and one **false**.

Connect these blocks to make a **predicate block**:

Click **OK** to close the **Block Editor** and save your new block in the **sensing** category.

COPY THE CODE

+ gameover +
if ⟨ message ⟩ = gameover ⟩
report ⟨ true ⚪ ⟩
report ⟨ ⚪ false ⟩

10 Click **Make a block** to make a new command block.

Click **Motion**.

Type **move up** in the text field. Click the **command** button. Click **OK** to open the **Block Editor**.

Make a block

Motion ⟲   Control
Looks   Sensing
Sound   Operators
Pen   Variables
Lists   Other

move up

Command   Reporter   Predicate
◉ for all sprites   ○ for this sprite only

OK   Cancel

11 Drag these blocks into the **Block Editor**:

☐ < ☐   change y by 10   y position   if ⬡

12 Click and drag the **y position block** into the left field of the **< block**. Type **180** in the right field.

Connect these blocks:

Click **OK** to save your new **command** block in the **motion** category.

COPY THE CODE

+ move + up +
if ⟨ y position ⟩ < 180 ⟩
change y by 10

13 Find and drag these blocks into the **script space**:

if ⬡
when I receive ▼
repeat until
move up
gameover
key space ▼ pressed?

14 In the **when I receive block**, choose **start**.

In the **key space pressed block**, choose **w**.

Connect the blocks to make an **event script**:

COPY THE CODE

when I receive start ▼
repeat until ⟨ gameover ⟩
if ⟨ key w ▼ pressed? ⟩
move up

15 TEST ∿

TEST: Click ▶. Press the **w** key.
SUCCESS: The spaceship flies to the top of the screen, then stops!
ERROR: The spaceship has stalled. It stays in the middle of the screen.
FIX: Time to hunt bugs! You can right-click the **move up block** to reopen the Block Editor. Check each line matches Pax's.

STOP THE SCRIPT! Click ⬤.

16 Click **Make a block** to make a new code block.

Click **Motion**.

Type **move down** in the text field.

Click the **command** button.

Click **OK** to open the **Block Editor**.

Make a block

Motion ⟲   Control
Looks   Sensing
Sound   Operators
Pen   Variables
Lists   Other

move down

Command   Reporter   Predicate
◉ for all sprites   ○ for this sprite only

OK   Cancel

17 Drag these blocks into the **Block Editor**:

if ⬡
☐ > ☐   y position
change y by 10

COPY THE CODE

+ move + down +
if ⟨ y position ⟩ > -180 ⟩
change y by -10

18 Click and drag the **y position block** into the left field of the **> block**. Type **-180** in the right field.

In the **change y by block**, type **-10**.

Connect these blocks.

Click **OK** to save the new command block in the **motion** category.

19 Find and drag these blocks into the **script space**:

> key space ▾ pressed?
> move down
> if

20 In the **key space pressed block**, choose **s**.

Connect the blocks and insert them inside the **repeat until gameover** loop underneath the **if block**.

> when I receive start ▾
> repeat until ‹ gameover ›
> if ‹ key w ▾ pressed? ›
> move up
>
> if ‹ key s ▾ pressed? ›
> move down

TEST

21

TEST: Click ▶. Press the **s** key.
SUCCESS: The ship moves down and stops at the edge.

STOP THE SCRIPT!
Click ⬤.

Save as **Spaceclaw04**.

22 Find and drag these blocks into the **script space**:

> when I receive ▾
> hide
>
> when I receive gameover ▾
> hide

In the **when I receive block**, choose **gameover**.
Connect the two blocks to make an **endgame script**.

MISSION OBJECTIVE 3: SPACECLAW ATTACHMENT INCLUDED!

1 Click ❯ to make a new sprite. Click the sprite **name field**. Rename it **claw**.

2 Go to **Costumes**.

Click 🖌 to make a new costume.

Paint a GIANT green spaceclaw with the open claw arms facing to the right.

3 Click ⊕, then drag the circle to the left side of the claw.

Click **OK** when you're done. Right-click the costume. Choose **duplicate** to make a copy.

4 Right-click the duplicate. Choose **edit** to reopen the **paint editor**.

Edit your costume so the claw arms are closer together.

Click **OK** when you're done.

Untitled

Untitled(2)

5 Right-click both costumes. **Rename** them **claw1** and **claw2**.

Click the **don't rotate button** at the top of the screen.

6 Go to the **script space**. Find and drag these blocks into the **script space**:

> when ⚑ clicked
> point in direction 90 ▾
> go to x: 0 y: 0
> set size to 100 %
> clear
> pen up

EXPERIMENT

7 In the **set size block**, type **10%**. Click the block to test the size of the claw. The claw should be about half the size of the Adventure-D. Adjust the numbers until it looks right.

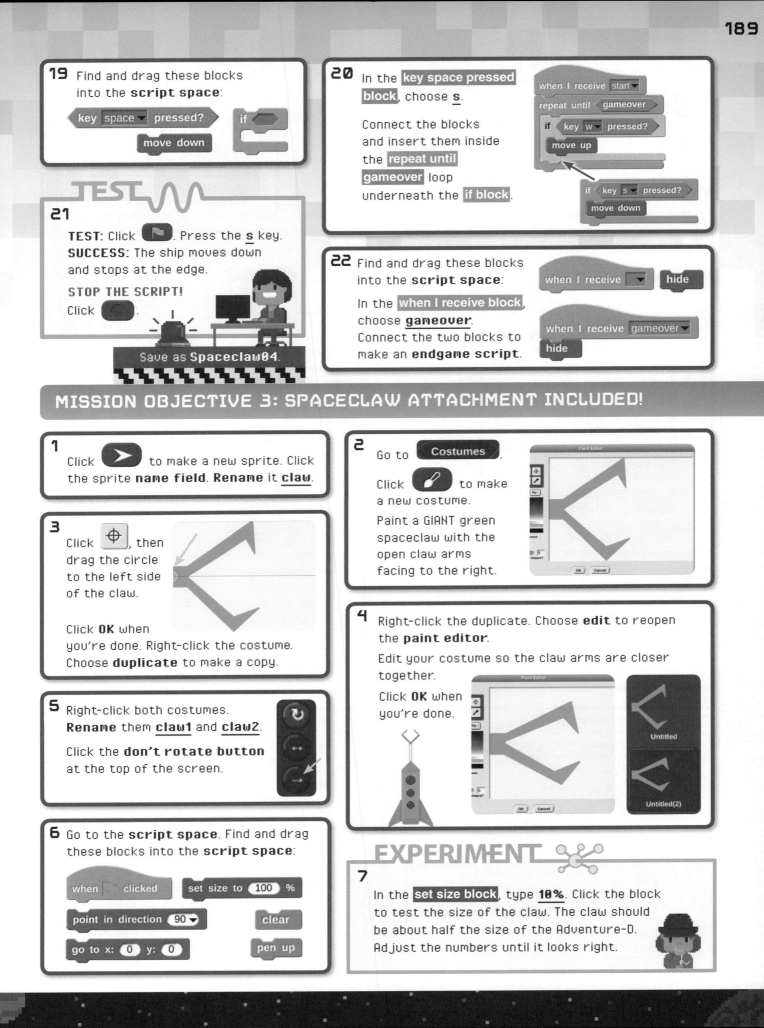

8 In the go to block, click the text fields. Change them to x:500 and y:500.

Connect the blocks to make a **setup script**:

when clicked
set size to 10 %
go to x: 500 y: 500
point in direction 90
clear
pen up

COPY THE CODE

Save as Spaceclaw05.

9 Find and drag these blocks into the **script space**:

when space key pressed

create a clone of ▼

10 In the create a clone block, choose **myself**.

Connect the blocks to make a **clone-maker script**.

when space key pressed
create a clone of myself ▼

COPY THE CODE

11 Click Make a block to make a new code block. Click Motion.

Type **glide to target** in the name field. Click **command**.

Click **OK** to open the **Block Editor**.

12 Find and drag these blocks into the **Block Editor**:

repeat until ◢
next costume
move 10 steps
touching ▼ ?

13 In the touching block, choose **edge**. In the move 10 steps block, type **5**.

Connect the blocks:

+glide + to + target+
repeat until touching edge ▼ ?
next costume
move 5 steps

Click **OK** to save your new **command** block in the **motion** category.

COPY THE CODE

14 Click Make a block to make a new code block.

Click Motion. Type **glide to spaceship** in the name field. Click **command**.

Click **OK** to open the **Block Editor**.

15 Find and drag these blocks into the **Block Editor**:

point towards ▼
move 10 steps
repeat until ◢
touching ▼ ?

16 In the touching block, choose **spaceship**.

In the point towards block, choose **spaceship**.

In the move 10 steps block, type **5**.

Connect the blocks:

+glide + to + spaceship+
repeat until touching spaceship ▼ ?
point towards spaceship ▼
move 5 steps

COPY THE CODE

Click **OK** to save your new **command** block in the **motion** category.

17 Find and drag these blocks into the **script space**:

go to ▼
when I start as a clone
glide to target
delete this clone
glide to spaceship

18 In the go to block, choose **spaceship**.

Connect the blocks to make an **animation script**:

when I start as a clone
go to spaceship ▼
glide to target
glide to spaceship
delete this clone

COPY THE CODE

TEST

19

TEST: Click 🏴. Press space bar to launch the spaceclaw!

SUCCESS: The spaceclaw opens and closes until it gets to the edge of the screen. Then it retracts and disappears when it hits the spaceship.

STOP THE SCRIPT! Click 🛑.

Save as **Spaceclaw06**.

20 Find and drag these blocks into the **script space**:

pen up   pen down   clear

set pen color to ⬛ x 2   set pen size to (1) x 2

21 In the first **set pen color block**, click the colored square. Choose a bright VALID green color.

In the second **set pen color block**, click the colored square. Then click the **space** background on the stage.

In one of the **set pen size blocks**, click the text field. Type **2**.

TEST

23

TEST: Click 🏴. Press **spacebar** to launch the spaceclaw.

SUCCESS: The spaceclaw is attached to the ship with a green rope that erases when the claw retracts.

STOP THE SCRIPT! Click 🛑.

Save as **Spaceclaw07**.

22 Connect the blocks inside the **clone animation script**. Pay careful attention to the order.

COPY THE CODE

when I start as a clone
go to spaceship ▾
set pen size to (1)
set pen color to ⬜
pen down
glide to target
set pen size to (2)
set pen color to ⬛
glide to spaceship
pen up
clear
delete this clone

MISSION OBJECTIVE 4: NEVER TELL ME THE ODDS!

1 Click ▶ to make a new sprite. Click the sprite **name field**.

Rename the new sprite **asteroid**.

2 Go to Costumes. Click 🖌 to make a new costume.

Draw a giant asteroid. Click **OK** when you're done.

Right-click the costume. **Rename** it **spacejunk**.

spacejunk

3 Click Scripts.

Find and drag these blocks into the **script space**:

when 🏴 clicked

go to x: (0) y: (0)

4 In the **go to block**, change the text fields to **x:500** and **y:500**.

Connect the blocks to make a **setup script**:

COPY THE CODE

when 🏴 clicked
go to x: (500) y: (500)

5 Find and drag these blocks into the **script space**:

point in direction (90 ▾)   set size to (100) %   when I receive ▾

go to x: (0) y: (0)   change x by (10)   x position   repeat until ⬡

pick random (1) to (10) x 3   ⬡ < ⬡

6 In the **when I receive block**, choose **start**.

Click and drag the first **pick random block** into the **set size block**. Click the text boxes. Type **5** and **15**.

set size to pick random (5) to (15) %

7 Click and drag the second pick random block into the point in direction block. Click the text boxes. Type **1** and **360**.

In the go to block, type **240** in the x: field. Click and drag the third pick random block into the y: field. Click the text fields. Type **-180** and **180**.

Click and drag the x position block into the left field of the < block. Type **-250** in the right field.

In the change x by block, type **-2**.

8 Connect the blocks to make an **animation script**:

```
when I receive start ▾
point in direction ( pick random ( 1 ) to ( 360 ) )
set size to ( pick random ( 5 ) to ( 15 ) ) %
go to x: ( 240 ) y: ( pick random ( -180 ) to ( 180 ) )
repeat until < x position < -250 >
    change x by ( -2 )
```

COPY THE CODE

TEST

9

TEST: Click 🚩.
SUCCESS: The asteroid moves across the screen from right to left.

STOP THE SCRIPT! Click ⬤.

TEST: Click 🚩, then ⬤ several times.
SUCCESS: Each time you start, the asteroid changes size, y position, and orientation.

STOP THE SCRIPT! Click ⬤.

Save as **Spaceclaw08**.

10 Find and drag these blocks into the **script space**:

```
if ◇
```

glide to spaceship

< touching ▾ ? >

11 In the touching block, choose **claw**. Connect the blocks:

```
if < touching claw ▾ ? >
    glide to spaceship
```

COPY THE CODE

12 Click and drag these blocks to connect them inside the repeat until block after the change x by -2 block.

```
when I receive start ▾
point in direction ( pick random ( 1 ) to ( 360 ) )
set size to ( pick random ( 5 ) to ( 15 ) ) %
go to x: ( 240 ) y: ( pick random ( -180 ) to ( 180 ) )
repeat until < x position < -250 >
    change x by ( -2 )

        if < touching claw ▾ ? >
            glide to spaceship
```

13 Click the **claw sprite button**. Then click the motion category.

Right-click the glide to target block. Choose **edit**.

Drag these blocks into the **Block Editor**:

< touching ▾ ? >   < ◇ or ◇ >

In the touching block, choose **asteroid**.

14 Adjust the repeat until block to match:

```
+ glide + to + target +
repeat until < touching edge ▾ ? > or < touching asteroid ▾ ? >
    next costume
    move ( 5 ) steps
```

Click **OK** to save your changes to the glide to target block.

COPY THE CODE

TEST

15

TEST: Click 🚩. Use the **w** and **s** keys to line up the Adventure-D with the asteroid. Press **space** to launch the spaceclaw.
SUCCESS: The spaceclaw hits the asteroid and pulls it back to the Adventure-D. We have an asteroid! Cool. . . I guess?

STOP THE SCRIPT! Click ⬤.

Save as **Spaceclaw09**.

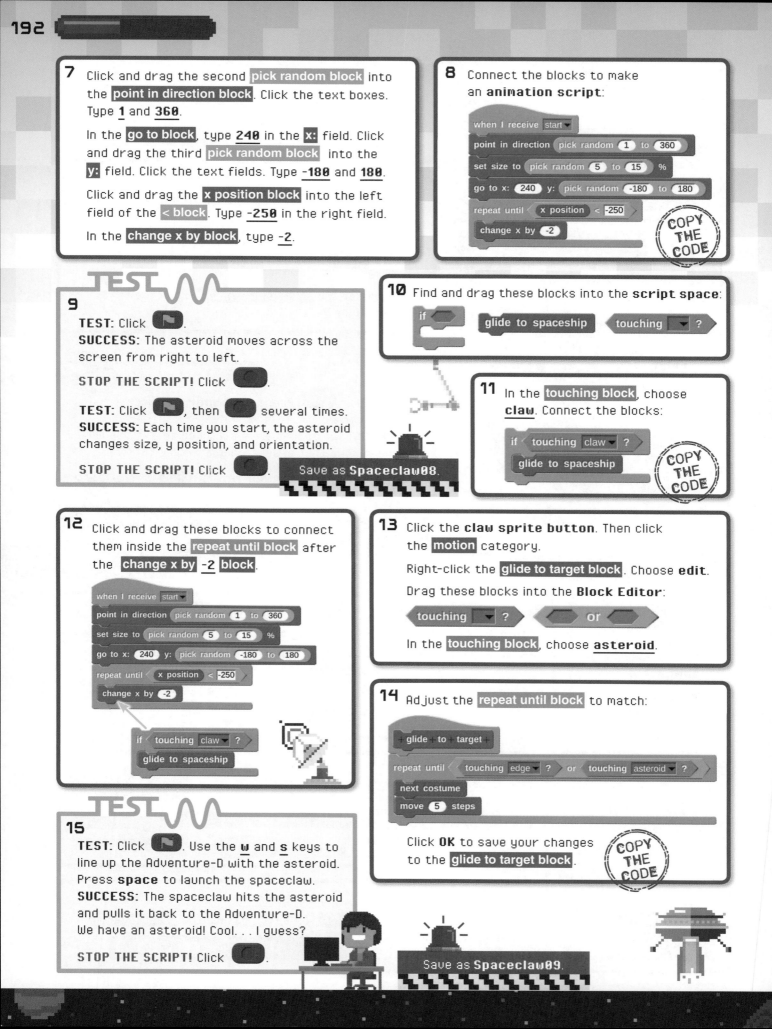

16 Click the asteroid **sprite button**. Find and drag these blocks into the **script space**:

```
when I start as a clone          repeat until <    >

wait 1 secs                      delete this clone    x 2

create a clone of [ ]            < gameover >
```

17 Click and drag the animation script from the `when I receive start block` to the `when I start as a clone block`.

```
when I receive start ▼          when I start as a clone

point in direction (pick random 1 to 360)
set size to (pick random 5 to 15) %
go to x: 240 y: (pick random -180 to 180)
repeat until < x position < -250 >
  change x by -2
  if < touching claw ▼ ? >
    glide to spaceship
```

18 Click and connect a `delete this clone block` after the `glide to spaceship block` inside the `if touching claw ? block`.

```
when I start as a clone
point in direction (pick random 1 to 360)
set size to (pick random 5 to 15) %
go to x: 240 y: (pick random -180 to 180)
repeat until < x position < -250 >
  change x by -2
  if < touching claw ▼ ? >
    glide to spaceship
    delete this clone
```

COPY THE CODE

19 Click and connect the other `delete this clone block` at the very end of the **animation script**.

```
when I start as a clone
point in direction (pick random 1 to 360)
set size to (pick random 5 to 15) %
go to x: 240 y: (pick random -180 to 180)
repeat until < x position < -250 >
  change x by -2
  if < touching claw ▼ ? >
    glide to spaceship
    delete this clone
delete this clone
```

20 In the `create a clone block`, choose **myself**.

Connect the blocks to make a **clone-maker script**:

```
when I receive start ▼
repeat until < gameover >
  create a clone of myself ▼
  wait 1 secs
```

COPY THE CODE

TEST

21
TEST: Click 🏳.
SUCCESS: The stage is full of asteroids of every size and shape!

STOP THE SCRIPT! Click ⬤.

22 Find and drag these blocks into the **script space**:

```
                                 < gameover >

when I start as a clone          < touching [ ▼] ? >

repeat until <    >   delete this clone   if < >

                     broadcast [ ▼]
```

23 In the `touching block`, choose **spaceship**.

In the `broadcast block`, choose **gameover**.

Connect the blocks to make an **endgame script**:

```
when I start as a clone
repeat until < gameover >
  if < touching spaceship ▼ ? >
    broadcast gameover ▼
delete this clone
```

COPY THE CODE

TEST

24
TEST: Click 🏳. Use the claw to pick up an asteroid.
SUCCESS: The game ends! The spaceship and all the asteroids disappear!

STOP THE SCRIPT! Click ⬤.

Save as **Spaceclaw10**.

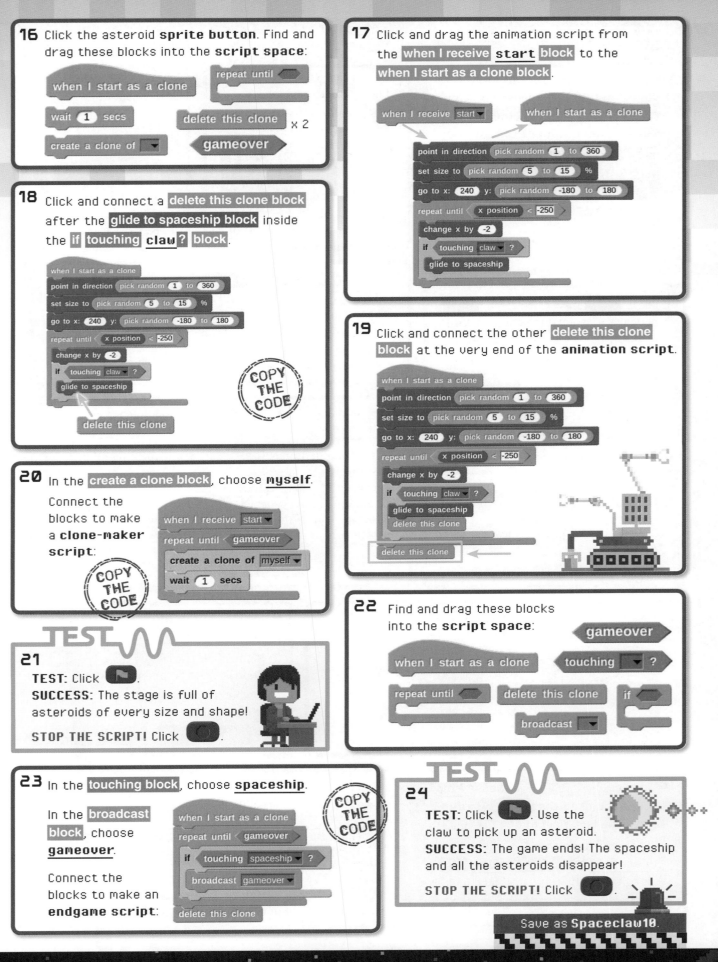

MISSION OBJECTIVE 5: THE KEY TO IT ALL

1 Right-click the **asteroid sprite**. Choose **duplicate** to make a copy.

Click the sprite **name field**. **Rename asteroid(2) to key**.

Click **Costumes**. Drag the **spacejunk costume** into the **code menu area** to delete it.

2 Click ✎ to make a new costume. Paint a giant key to open the CORUPT space base.

C179648
key

Click **OK** when you're done. Right-click and **rename** the costume **key**.

3 Click **Scripts**. In the **wait 1 secs block** of the **clone-maker** script, type **4**.

when I receive start
repeat until gameover
create a clone of myself
wait 4 secs

4 Click **Variables**. Click **Make a variable** to make a new variable. Call it **keys**. Click **OK**.

Find and drag these blocks into the **script space**:

`[ ] = [ ]`
`set [ ] to 0`
`if`
`change [ ] by 1`
`keys`   `delete this clone`

5 In the **set to 0** and **change by 1 blocks**, choose **keys** for both blocks.

Click and drag **set keys to 0**, to connect it at the end of the **setup script**.

when ⚑ clicked
go to x: 500 y: 500
set keys to 0

6 Click and drag the **keys block** into the left field of the **= block**. Type **5** in the right field.

Click and drag the **broadcast gameover** block **out** of the **endgame script**. Connect it **inside** the **if block**.

when I start as a clone
repeat until gameover
if touching spaceship ?

delete this clone

if
broadcast gameover

7 Connect the blocks to match:

change keys by 1
if keys = 5
broadcast gameover
delete this clone

COPY THE CODE

8 Drag the script inside the **if touching spaceship block** of the **endgame script**.

when I start as a clone
repeat until gameover
if touching spaceship ?

delete this clone

change keys by 1
if keys = 5
broadcast gameover
delete this clone

9 Click the **claw sprite button**, then click the **motion** category.

Right-click the **glide to target block**. Choose **edit** to open the **Block Editor**.

Find and drag these blocks into the **Block Editor**:

`touching [ ] ?`   `< > or < >`

10 In the **touching block**, choose **key**. Click and drag the **touching key block** into the left field of the **or block**.

Click and drag the **touching asteroid or touching edge block** into the right field. It should look like:

touching key ? or touching edge ? or touching asteroid ?

Drag the predicate back into the blank hexagon of the **repeat until block**. It should look like:

glide to target
repeat until
touching key ? or touching edge ? or touching asteroid ?
next costume
move 5 steps

Click **OK** to save your changes to the **glide to target block**.

TEST

11

TEST: Click ⚑.
SUCCESS: There are keys in the asteroid field!
TEST: Use the spaceclaw to pick up keys!
SUCCESS: The claw brings a key, and the keys variable increases.
ERROR: The claw goes through the key until it hits an asteroid or the edge.
FIX: Double-check the glide to target block matches Pax's code.

STOP THE SCRIPT! Click ⬡.

Save as **Spaceclaw11**.

12

Click Stage. Find and drag these blocks into the **script space**:

if / else
keys
⬡ = ⬡
when I receive ▾
switch to costume ▾ x 2

13 In the when I receive block, choose **gameover**. Click and drag the keys block into the left field of the = block. Type **5** in the right field.
Click the first switch to costume block. Choose **win**.
Click the second switch to costume block. Choose **lose**.
Connect the blocks to make an **endgame script**:

```
when I receive gameover▾
if   keys = 5
    switch to costume win▾
else
    switch to costume lose▾
```

TEST

14

TEST: Click ⚑. Touch an asteroid with your ship.
SUCCESS: You lose!

TEST: Click ⚑. Avoid the asteroids and collect five keys.
SUCCESS: You win!
STOP THE SCRIPT!
Click ⬡.

Save as **Spaceclaw12**.

ACHIEVEMENT UNLOCKED!
SUPERCODER
LEVEL 1

Basil's hugeness has caused spacetime distortions!

The way through the caves keeps changing!

And there are glowing red bits that turn you inside-out if you touch them!

Finity's our best hope. Once she gets to Basil's hangar, she'll turn on the locating beacon and transfer Doubleshot in.

Stay away from the red zones, Finity!

No sweat, Pax!

MISSION DOSSIER

>> GET THROUGH THE CAVES TO THE BASE

Finity must get through the caves, but Basil is so big, he's warping space AND time. With the risk of seeing your insides on the outside, it won't be easy!

LEVEL: 8
INSTRUCTOR: Supercoders of VALID

MISSION OBJECTIVE 1: KEEP YOUR SKIN ON THE OUTSIDE

PROJECT OUTLINE
NAME: FLUX JUMP
GOAL: HELP FINITY GET THROUGH THE CEPHALOPODIAN CAVE SYSTEM.
REQUIREMENTS:
1. AUTOMATICALLY DETECT ENDGAME BASED ON THE BACKGROUND.
2. SIMULATE GRAVITY USING Y COORDINATES.
3. USE EVENTS TO CONTROL MOVEMENT.
4. AUTOMATICALLY DETECT LEVEL CHANGES.

1 Open a web browser and go to **snap.berkeley.edu/run**. Start a new project by clicking [ ]. Choose **new**.

2 Click [Stage], then [Backgrounds].

Click [🖌] to make a new background. Make a new background to match:

It needs a gray floor, a background color, and a red spacetime distortion.

3 Right click the background. **Rename** it **floor1**.

Right-click **floor1**. Choose **duplicate** to make a copy.

Right-click the copy. **Rename** it **floor2**.

Right-click **floor2**. Choose **edit** to open the paint screen.

Add some extra spacetime distortions in the same red color.

4 Find and drag these blocks into the **script space**:

when [ ] clicked   broadcast [▼]

switch to costume [▼]

5 In the **switch to costume block**, choose **floor1**.

In the **broadcast block**, choose **new** to make a new broadcast message. Call it **start**. Click **OK**.

Connect the blocks to make a **setup script** with **broadcast start** at the end.

Save as **Flux01**.

6 Find and drag these blocks into the **script space**:

when I receive [▼]

next costume

In the **when I receive block**, choose **new** to make a new broadcast message. Call it **nextlevel**. Click **OK**. Connect the two blocks to make an **animation script**.

7 Click [Backgrounds]. Make two new costumes.

Write **You win!** in the paint screen.

Rename the first one **WIN!**.

Write **You lose...** in the paint screen.

Rename the second one **LOSE!**.

Click and drag the costumes so the **LOSE!** costume is at the top of the list of costumes and the **WIN!** costume is the last costume.

8 Click [Scripts]. Click [Make a block] to make a new **predicate** block. Click [Sensing].

Type **last costume** in the name field. Click the **predicate** button.

Click **OK** to open the **Block Editor**.

9 Find and drag these blocks into the **Block Editor**:

costume #   report [ ]   if ⬡ else

my [neighbors ▼]   length of [world]

[ ] = [ ]   true ○ ×2

10 In the **my neighbors block**, choose **costumes**. Click and drag the **my costumes block** into the **length of block**. Click a **true block** to flip it to **false**.

Click **OK** to save your new **predicate** block in the **sensing** category.

+ last + costume +

if ⟨ costume # = length of ⟨ my [costumes ▼] ⟩ ⟩

report ⟨ true ○ ⟩

else

report ⟨ ○ false ⟩

COPY THE CODE

11 Find and drag these blocks into the **script space**:

when I receive [▼]   if ⬡

switch to costume [▼]

last costume   not ⬡

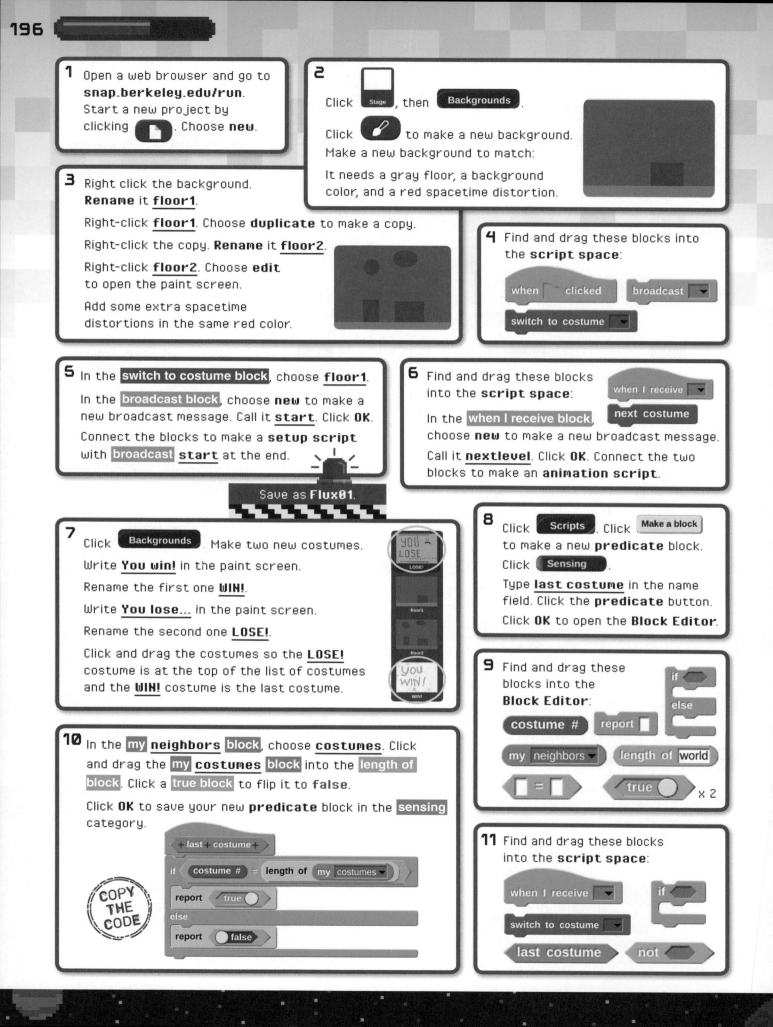

12 In the when I receive block, choose **new** to make a new broadcast message. Call it **gameover**. Click **OK**.

In the switch to costume block, choose **LOSE!**.

Connect the blocks to make an **endgame script**:

when I receive gameover ▾
if not last costume ▸
  switch to costume LOSE! ▾

COPY THE CODE

---

13 Click the control category. Find the broadcast block. Choose **gameover**.

TEST: Click ⚑. Click Backgrounds. Click the **floor1** costume. Then click the broadcast gameover block in the code menu area.
SUCCESS: The screen changes to **LOSE!**

TEST: Click the **WIN!** costume in Backgrounds. Then click the broadcast gameover block in the code menu area.
SUCCESS: The screen doesn't change!
ERROR: Right-click the last costume block. Choose **edit** to reopen the **Block Editor**. Check your code matches Pax's.

TEST

---

14 Click Scripts. Find and drag these blocks into the **script space**:

last costume ▸

broadcast ▾

if ◆

15 In the broadcast block, choose **gameover**.

Connect the blocks to match:

if last costume ▸
  broadcast gameover ▾

COPY THE CODE

16 Drag and connect the blocks at the end of the **animation script** after the next costume block.

when I receive nextlevel ▾
next costume

if last costume ▸
  broadcast gameover ▾

Save as **Flux02**.

MISSION OBJECTIVE 2: CREATE GRAVITATIONAL FORCES

1 Click ▷ Sprite. **Rename** the sprite **Finity**.

Click Costumes.

Make a new costume and draw Finity walking.

Click **OK** when you're done.

2 Right-click the costume and choose **duplicate**. Right-click and edit the copy.

Erase Finity's legs, then draw them in a different position. Click **OK** when you're done.

Rename the costumes **walk1** and **walk2**.

walk1
walk2

Save as **Flux03**.

3 Click Scripts. Drag these blocks into the **script space**:

when ⚑ clicked
go to x: 0 y: 0
set size to 100 %

EXPERIMENT

4 Make Finity about 0.6 in (1.5 cm) tall. In the set size block, type 15. Click the block to check the size. Change the numbers until she is the right height.

5 In the go to block, change the text fields to x:-200 y:200

Make a **setup script**.

when ⚑ clicked
set size to 15 %
go to x: -200 y: 200

COPY THE CODE

6 Click **Make a block** to make a new **predicate** block.

Click **Sensing**.

Type **gameover** in the name field. Click the **predicate** button.

Click **OK** to open the **Block Editor**.

Drag these blocks into the **Block Editor**:

```
report [ ]        message

< [ ] = [ ] >     if < >
                  else

< true ( ) > x 2
```

7 Click and drag the **message block** into the left field of the **= block**. Type **gameover** in the right field. Click a **true block** so it flips to **false**. Connect the blocks:

COPY THE CODE

```
+ gameover +
if < message = gameover >
  report < true ( ) >
else
  report ( false >
```

Click **OK** to save the new **predicate** block in the **sensing** category.

8 Find and drag these blocks into the **script space**:

```
repeat until < >        if < >  x 2

when I receive [▼]

broadcast [▼]           not < >

change y by (10)

touching [ ] ?  x 2

gameover
```

9 In the **when I receive block**, choose **start**.

In one **touching color block**, click the colored square, then the **gray floor** on the stage. In the other **touching color block**, click the colored square, then the **red square** on the stage.

In the **broadcast block**, choose **gameover**.

In the **change y by block**, type **-5**.

Connect the blocks to make a **game-loop script**:

COPY THE CODE

```
when I receive start ▼
repeat until < gameover >
  if < not < touching [ ] ? > >
    change y by (-5)
  if < touching [ ] ? >
    broadcast gameover ▼
```

10
TEST: Click 🏁.
SUCCESS: Finity drops into the stage.
ERROR: Finity falls through the ground or into the red block.
FIX: Get bug hunting. Does Finity start in the right place? Move your red block if needed.

TEST: Drag Finity into the red square.
SUCCESS: The **LOSE!** screen appears.
STOP THE SCRIPT! Click 🔴.

Save as **Flux04**.

MISSION OBJECTIVE 3: MANEUVERABILITY

1 Find and drag these blocks into the **script space**:

```
repeat until < >

when I receive [▼]

if < >       wait (1) secs

next costume

key space ▼ pressed?

gameover
```

2 In the **when I receive block**, choose **start**.
In the **key pressed block**, choose **any key**.
In the **wait 1 secs block**, type **0.2** secs.
Connect the blocks to make an **animation script**:

COPY THE CODE

```
when I receive start ▼
repeat until < gameover >
  if < key any key ▼ pressed? >
    wait (0.2) secs
    next costume
```

3
TEST: Click 🏁. Press any key.
SUCCESS: Tiny Finity's costume changes so she looks like she's walking! To make it faster, slower, or more realistic, adjust the costume or the time in the **wait block**.

STOP THE SCRIPT! Click 🔴.

4 Find and drag these blocks into the **script space**:

repeat until
if x 3

when I receive

key space pressed? x 3

gameover

change y by 10

change x by 10 x 2

5 In the when I receive block, choose **start**.
In the key pressed block, choose **a** in one, **d** in another, and leave one on **space**.
In the change x by blocks, type **5** and **-5**.
Connect the blocks to make a **movement script**:

COPY THE CODE

when I receive start
repeat until gameover
if key d pressed?
change x by 5
if key a pressed?
change x by -5
if key space pressed?
change y by 10

6
TEST: Click ⚑. Use the **a**, **d**, and **space keys**.
Jump the red block to go to the edge of the stage.
SUCCESS: Finity moves right when you press **d**, left when you press **a**, and up when you press **space**.

STOP THE SCRIPT! Click ⬤.

Save as **Flux05**.

MISSION OBJECTIVE 4: LEVEL UP!

1 Find and drag these blocks into the **script space**:

go to x: 0 y: 0

when I receive

2 In the when I receive block, choose **nextlevel**.
In the go to block, type **x:-200 y:200**.
Make an **animation script**:

COPY THE CODE

when I receive nextlevel
go to x: -200 y: 200

3 Find and drag these blocks into the **script space**:

gameover

when I receive

[ ] > [ ]
repeat until
if

x position

broadcast and wait

4 In the when I receive block, choose **start**.
Drag the **x position block** into the left field of the **> block**. Type **230** in the right field.
In the **broadcast and wait block**, choose **nextlevel**.
Make a **game-loop script**:

COPY THE CODE

when I receive start
repeat until gameover
if x position > 230
broadcast nextlevel and wait

5
TEST: Click ⚑. Walk or jump Finity to the right edge of the stage.
SUCCESS: The background changes! Finity drops into the next level!

STOP THE SCRIPT! Click ⬤.

6 Click **stage**, then **backgrounds**. Right-click **floor1** and make a copy. Rename it **floor3**.

Drag the new background so that it's above the **WIN!** costume. If you add any more levels, they must appear after **floor1** and before **WIN!** in the list.

Right-click **floor3** and choose edit. Use 🖊 to copy the colors and paint more gray/red obstacles. Click **OK**.

7
TEST: Click ⚑. Play all levels.
SUCCESS: You complete floor3!
ERROR: Finity can't reach the end.
FIX: Edit your backgrounds, balancing super-fun challenging obstacles with boring impossible ones.

STOP THE SCRIPT! Click ⬤.

ACHIEVEMENT UNLOCKED! SUPERCODER LEVEL 2

Save as **Flux06**.

MISSION DOSSIER

>> SAVE BASIL AND THE GALAXY

Free Basil from CORUPT's evil controlling spikes before he escapes to wreak havoc on VALID, and the whole galaxy! Take down the spikes using mathematically powered logic bombs You have 40 seconds...

LEVEL: 8
INSTRUCTOR: Supercoders of VALID

Finity has transported Doubleshot in!

Doubleshot's logic bombs only last a few minutes, so you can't prep them in advance.

Doubleshot will charge them using mathematical logic. He's done it before.

Not with a giant space-robot breathing down his neck!

That'd make anyone's math skills go bye-bye...

Once Introspecter opens the door, we've got 40 seconds before Basil escapes with CORUPT's spikes still attached.

Doubleshot knows the stakes, Pax! Open the door!

MISSION OBJECTIVE 1: CREATE THE CORUPTED ADD-ONS

PROJECT OUTLINE

NAME: ROBOT OF DOOM
GOAL: USE LOGIC BOMBS TO SAVE BASIL FROM CORUPT!
REQUIREMENTS:
1. ATTACH THE SPIKES TO THE DOOM ROBOT.
2. USE VARIABLES TO CONTROL SPIKE HITS AND MISSES.
3. MAKE A RECHARGEABLE LOGIC BOMB WITH CLONES.
4. USE LOGICAL QUESTIONS TO POWER THE LOGIC BOMBS.
5. USE A VARIABLE TO TIME THE GAME.
6. SAVE THE GALAXY.

1 Open a web browser and go to **snap.berkeley.edu/run**. Start a new project by clicking ⬛. Choose **new**.

2 Click **Stage**.
Make a new background for the battle. It can be as simple or complex as you like. **Rename** it **space**.

3 Create two new backgrounds.
Edit one to say **YOU HAVE DEFEATED THE SPACE ROBOT OF DOOM**.

Edit the second to say **YOU WERE TOO SLOOOW... THE GIANT SPACE ROBOT HAS ESCAPED!**

Rename the costumes **win** and **lose**.

win

lose

4 Click **Scripts**. Drag these blocks into the **script space**:

broadcast ▼

when 🏳 clicked   switch to costume ▼

5 In the **switch to costume block**, choose **space**.
In the **broadcast block**, choose **new** to make a new broadcast message. Call it **start**. Click **OK**.
Connect the three blocks to make a **setup script** with the **broadcast block** last.

6 Click **sprite** and **rename** it **Basil**.
Make a new costume for **Basil**.
Draw his friendly robot face and click **OK**. **Rename** the costume **robotface**.

Robotface

7 Click **Scripts** and drag these blocks into the **script space**.

set size to (100) %   when 🏳 clicked

Make a **setup script**.

EXPERIMENT

8 In the **set size block**, type **20**. Click the block to see how it looks on stage. Basil should be about 0.8 in (2 cm). Change the numbers until it looks right.

Save as **Doom01**.

Save as **Doom02**.

9 Click [Make a block] to make a new **predicate** block. Click [Sensing]. Type **gameover** in the name field. Click the **predicate** button. Click **OK** to open the **Block Editor**. Find and drag these blocks into the **Block Editor**: message / report ☐ / ☐ = ☐ / if / else / true ◯ x2

10 Click and drag the **message block** into the left field of the **= block**. Type **gameover** in the right field. Click a **true block** so it flips to **false**. Connect the blocks: Click **OK** to save your new **predicate** block in the **sensing** category.

+ gameover +
if ⟨ message = gameover ⟩
report ⟨ true ◯ ⟩
else
report ⟨ ◯ false ⟩

COPY THE CODE

11 Drag these blocks into the **script space**:
glide ① secs to x: ⓪ y: ⓪
pick random ① to ⑩ x2
gameover
when I receive ▼
repeat until ⬡

12 In the **when I receive block**, choose **start**. In the first **pick random block**, type **-220** to **220**. In the second **pick random block**, type **-100** to **180**.

Make an **animation script**:
when I receive start ▼
repeat until ⟨ gameover ⟩
glide ① secs to x: ⟨ pick random -220 to 220 ⟩ y: ⟨ pick random -100 to 180 ⟩

COPY THE CODE

TEST

13 **TEST:** Click ⚑. **SUCCESS:** Basil floats randomly around the screen! **STOP THE SCRIPT!** Click 🛑. Save as **Doom03**.

14 Click ▶ to make a new sprite. **Rename** it **C-spike**. Make a new costume for **C-spike**.

15 Paint a CORUPTed spike, with a pointy and a non-pointy end. When you're done, click ⊕. Drag it to the non-pointy end of the spike. Click **OK**. **Rename** it **doomspike**.

16 Click [Scripts]. Drag these blocks into the **script space**:
when I receive ▼
go back ① layers
set size to ⑩⓪ %
show
In the **when I receive block**, choose **start**.

EXPERIMENT

17 In the **set size block**, type **20**. Click it to check the spikes' size. They should be about twice as long as Basil's width.

18 Connect the blocks in any order to make a **setup script**.
when I receive start ▼
show
set size to ⑳ %
go back ① layers

19 On the stage, click and drag the spike so the non-pointy end is in the middle of Basil's face.

TEST

20 **TEST:** Click the setup script. **SUCCESS:** The spike should move behind Basil's face.

21 Click and drag the spike sprite button on to Basil's face on the stage.
C-spike

22

TEST: Click 🏳.

SUCCESS: The spike moves around the stage with Basil!

STOP THE SCRIPT! Click ⬤.

24

TEST: Click 🏳.

SUCCESS: The spike spins around Basil's head as he floats.

STOP THE SCRIPT! Click ⬤.

Save as Doom04.

23

Find and drag these blocks into the **script space**:

when I receive ▾
repeat until ◇
turn ↻ 15 degrees
gameover

In the **when I receive block**, choose **start**.

In the **turn 15 degrees block**, type **5**.

Connect the blocks to make an **animation script**:

```
when I receive start ▾
repeat until < gameover >
  turn ↻ 5 degrees
```

COPY THE CODE

MISSION OBJECTIVE 2: 1 DOWN, 8 TO GO: ADD THE OTHER 7 SPIKES

1

Click **Variables**. Click **Make a variable** to make a new variable. Call it **spikes**. Click **OK**.

Click the **Basil sprite button**. Find and drag these blocks into the **script space**:

when I receive ▾
if ◇
change ▾ by 1
set ▾ to 0
wait 1 secs
broadcast ▾
[ ] = [ ]
spikes

2

In the **set to block**, choose **spikes**. Type **8** in the text field.

Connect the **set spikes block** at the end of the **setup script**.

COPY THE CODE

```
when 🏳 clicked
set size to 18 %
set spikes ▾ to 8
```

3

In the **when I receive block**, choose **new** to make a new broadcast message. Call it **hit**.

Click and drag the **spikes block** into the left field of the **= block**. Type **0** in the right field.

In the **wait block**, type **0**. In the **broadcast block**, choose **new** to make a new broadcast message. Call it **gameover**.

In the **change by block**, choose **spikes**. Type **-1** into the text field. Connect the blocks:

COPY THE CODE

```
when I receive hit ▾
change spikes ▾ by -1
if < spikes = 0 >
  wait 0 secs
  broadcast gameover ▾
```

4

TEST: Click 🏳. Then click the **when I receive hit** script to run it. Click it 8 times.

SUCCESS: The spikes variable goes down. When it hits 0, everything stops.

STOP THE SCRIPT!

Click ⬤.

Save as Doom05.

5

Click the **C-spike sprite**. Drag these blocks into the **script space**:

if ◇
spikes
[ ] = [ ]
hide

6

Drag the **spikes block** into the left field of the **= block**. Type **0** in the right field.

Connect the blocks and insert into the **animation script** after the **turn 5 degrees block**, inside the **repeat until gameover block**.

```
when I receive start ▾
repeat until < gameover >
  turn ↻ 5 degrees
```

```
if < spikes = 0 >
  hide
```

7 Right-click the **C-spike button** and **duplicate** to make a copy.

Click Motion. Click the **turn 15 degrees block** until the new sprite faces the opposite way to the old spike.

On the stage, drag the spike so the non-pointy end is in the middle of Basil's face.

Drag the **C-spike(2) sprite button** on to Basil's face on the stage to link the two sprites.

In the **if spikes = 0 block**, change the **0** to **1**.

HINT

If the spike appears over the top of Basil's face, go to the Looks category. Click the **go back 1 layers block**.

OK

8

TEST: Click 🏳.
SUCCESS: Both the spikes spin around Basil.
ERROR: One spike spins off to the side around the other! Whaaaat??

FIX: You've linked one spike to another. Right-click the new spike. Choose **detach from C-spike**. Relink it with Basil on the stage.

STOP THE SCRIPT! Click 🔘.

9 Follow the directions in Box 7 until there are eight spikes altogether. Turn each one so it faces in a different direction. Link them all to Basil. Always increase the **if spikes = 0 block**, so each spike is numbered from **0** to **7**.

Save as **Doom06**.

MISSION OBJECTIVE 3: WHO NEEDS CLONES ANYWAY?

1 Click ▶ to make a new sprite. **Rename** it **logic**.

Make a new costume for **logic**.

Draw a green circle with a **V** in it. Decorate it with logic and click **OK**. **Rename** the costume **bombsaway**.

2 Click Scripts. Drag these blocks into the **script space**:

```
when [flag] clicked
go to x: 0 y: 0
set size to 100 %
```

3 In the **set size block**, type **10**.
In the **go to block**, type **500** in both text fields.
Make a **setup script**.

```
when [flag] clicked
set size to 10 %
go to x: 500 y: 500
```

COPY THE CODE

4 Drag these blocks into the **script space**:

```
go to [ ]
broadcast [ ]  x 2
repeat until < >
when I receive [ ]
repeat 10
change size by 10
key space pressed?
if < >
touching [ ] ?
else
```

In the **when I receive block**, click the drop-down arrow and make a new broadcast message called **FIRE ZE MISSILES!**.

5 In the **change size by block**, type **5**.

In the **touching block**, choose **Basil**.

In the **go to block**, choose **mouse-pointer**.

In one **broadcast block**, choose **hit**. In the other **broadcast block**, make a new broadcast message called **missed**.

Connect the blocks to make an **animation script**:

```
when I receive FIRE ZE MISSILES!
repeat until < key space pressed? >
  go to mouse-pointer
  repeat 10
    change size by 5
  if < touching Basil ? >
    broadcast hit
  else
    broadcast missed
```

COPY THE CODE

6 Right-click the `set size` and the `go to blocks` in the **setup script**. **Duplicate** them.

Click to connect them at the end of the **animation script**.

```
when I receive FIRE ZE MISSILES! ▼
repeat until   key space ▼ pressed?
  go to mouse-pointer ▼
repeat 10
  change size by 5
if   touching Basil ▼ ?
  broadcast hit ▼
else
  broadcast missed ▼
```

```
set size to 10 %
go to x: 500 y: 500
```

TEST ∿

7

TEST: Click 🏳. Click the animation script. Move the mouse-pointer over the screen. Press space to fire!

SUCCESS: The missile explodes! A spike disappears! The spikes variable goes down!

ERROR: If Basil still has all his spikes, check the spike code from Mission Objective 3 for bugs.

STOP THE SCRIPT! Click 🛑.

Save as **Doom07**.

MISSION OBJECTIVE 4: POWER THE BOMB WITH COLD, HARD LOGIC

1 Click **stage**. Click `Variables`. Make two new variables called **left** and **right**.

Drag these blocks into the **script space**:

```
when I receive ▼        join hello- world ◀▶        set ▼ to 0
repeat until ◀▷         pick random 1 to 10          right   left
                        ask what's-your-name? and wait      gameover
```

2 In the `when I receive block`, choose **start**.

Drag the `pick random block` into the text field of the `set to 0 block`.

Right-click and duplicate the entire block. Click the drop-downs and choose **left** and **right**.

```
set left ▼ to pick random 1 to 10
set right ▼ to pick random 1 to 10
```

3 In the `join block`, click the right arrow until there are 4 text fields.

Type **what is** in the first field.

Drag the `left block` into the second field.

Type **+** into the third field

Drag `right` into the fourth field.

```
join what-is left + right ◀▶
```

4
```
when I receive start ▼
repeat until gameover
  set left ▼ to pick random 1 to 10
  set right ▼ to pick random 1 to 10
  ask join what-is left + right ◀▶ and wait
```
Make a **game-loop script**.

COPY THE CODE

TEST ∿

5

TEST: Click 🏳.
Answer the questions.
SUCCESS: You should get ENDLESS math questions, each one different from the last!

STOP THE SCRIPT! Click 🛑.

Save as **Doom08**.

6 Find and drag these blocks into the **script space**:

```
if ⬡              broadcast ▼          wait until ⬡        ◀ [ ] = [ ] ▶  × 3
                  wait 1 secs          message × 2          ◯ + ◯
right   left   answer                                       ◀ or ▶
```

Click and drag the **left** and **right blocks** into the text fields of the **+ block**.

In the **broadcast block**, choose **FIRE ZE MISSILES!**

In the **wait 1 secs block**, type **0**.

7 Click and drag the message blocks into the left fields of two = blocks. Type **hit** and **missed** in the right fields. Connect the blocks:

COPY THE CODE

```
if  answer  =  left  +  right
broadcast FIRE ZE MISSILES!
wait until  message  = hit  or  message  = missed
wait 0 secs
```

8 Connect it after the ask and wait block, inside the repeat until gameover loop.

```
when I receive start
repeat until  gameover
  set left to pick random 1 to 10
  set right to pick random 1 to 10
  ask join what is left + right  and wait
```

```
if  answer  =  left  +  right
broadcast FIRE ZE MISSILES!
wait until  message  = hit  or  message  = missed
wait 0 secs
```

COPY THE CODE

TEST

9

TEST: Click 🏴. Answer the questions.
SUCCESS: If you are correct, you get a bomb! If not, you get another question.

STOP THE SCRIPT! Click ⏹.   Save as **Doom09**.

MISSION OBJECTIVE 5: THE WINDOW OF OPPORTUNITY

1
Click **Stage**. Click **Variables**. Make a new variable called **timer**. Drag these blocks into the **script space**:

```
gameover          change  by 1
if                when I receive     set  to 0
repeat until       wait 1 secs       timer
                   broadcast         ▢ = ▢
```

2 In the when I receive block, choose **start**.
In the set to **0** and change by **1** blocks, choose **timer**.

Drag the **timer block** into the left field of the = block. Type **40** in the right field.

In the **broadcast block**, choose **gameover**.

Connect the blocks to make a **timer script**:

COPY THE CODE

```
when I receive start
set timer to 0
repeat until  gameover
  wait 1 secs
  change timer by 1
  if  timer = 40
    broadcast gameover
```

TEST

3
TEST: Click 🏴. Wait 40 seconds.
SUCCESS: The timer increases! Basil stops spinning when it hits 40.

STOP THE SCRIPT! Click ⏹.

Save as **Doom10**.

MISSION OBJECTIVE 6: THE END OF THE END: SAVE THE GALAXY!!

1 Drag these blocks into the **script space**:

```
when I receive ▼     switch to costume ▼  x 2
if ◄
else
▢ = ▢
spikes
```

In the when I receive block, choose **gameover**.

Drag the **spikes block** into the left field of the = block. Type **0** in the right field.

In the **switch to costume blocks**, choose **win** for one and **lose** for the other.

2 Connect the blocks to make an **endgame script**:

COPY THE CODE

```
when I receive gameover
if  spikes = 0
  switch to costume win
else
  switch to costume lose
```

TEST

3

TEST: Click 🏁. Answer the questions to destroy all the spikes in time.
SUCCESS: The win background comes up!

TEST: Click 🏁. Let the timer run down.
SUCCESS: The lose background comes up...

STOP THE SCRIPT! Click 🛑.

Save as **Doom11**.

Supercoders, report your status!

Agent Doubleshot reporting mission success. The CORUPT spikes are destroyed. Basil's rampage is over.

Agent Finity reporting. Time/space distortions have halted. Most of their systems are destroyed and I have total access to what's left.

Agent Natterninja reporting. The Adventure-D is in stealth mode behind the moon. There's an escape pod. It's mostly low-level coders and guards evacuating to Cephalopod-3. There's one alien, a Cephalopod, who looks important.

It must be the leader. No way those guards masterminded this by themselves...

They're leaving. Should I move to intercept?

We have their data, their best coders, and their space robot.

And we should get Doubleshot and Finity out of there.

The threat is contained. Stand down Agent Natterninja. That is a fight for another day.

ACHIEVEMENT UNLOCKED! ⭐⭐⭐ **SUPERCODER** LEVEL 3 ⭐⭐⭐

Potential Agent X, you have trained in events and you've mastered predicates, bugs, loops, clones, variables, and blocks. Thanks to you, CORUPT is crippled, the coders are safe, and Basil will use his powers for good. And you have the most important supercoder skill: the courage to make mistakes, learn from them, and try again. Potential Agent X—

She needs a new name! She can't be "Potential" if she's an agent!

He's right. What will your new name be?

Potential Agent X is a bit silly... but can I still be Pax? I kinda like it.

Doubleshot likes it. It's short, easy to remember.

Pax. No nonsense.

Pax means peace. That's what VALID is all about.

A fitting name. Agent Pax, we offer you a permanent place as a VALID agent and supercoder.

NEW MESSAGE ✕

Accept ETAMI's offer and join the elite team of galaxy-saving supercoders?

Y/N

TEAM VALID

Acknowledgements

This book has been an extraordinary collaboration with an army of amazing brainstormers, editors, designers, and proofreaders—so many people have made this book what it is and we are so grateful and impressed with your work. Special thanks to Sheila, Kerri, and Marcus, our amazing proofcoders, who braved the bugs of early drafts with patience and humor.

Endless thanks to Jens Mönig, Brian Harvey, and the entire team of folks who make Snap! and maintain it under an Open Source license so that everyone can benefit from their work. You guys are the real supercoders.

To Stoo, my all-singing, all-skiing co-conspirator in life—thank you for your support, encouragement, and the endless cups of tea. Yer ma wee pal and this would have been a different book without you.

Virginia King, Co-author of The Coding Book*, and Co-founder and Managing Director of Invent the World*